SATYAJIT RAY

Satyajit Ray

by

GASTON ROBERGE

Essays (1970-2005)

MANOHAR
2007

First published 2007

ISBN 81-7304-735-9

Published by
Ajay Kumar Jain for
Manohar Publishers & Distributors
4753/23 Ansari road, Daryaganj
New Delhi 110 002

Typeset by
Ajay Arts
Delhi-110006

Printed by
Lordson Publishers Pvt. Ltd.
Delhi 110 007

In loving memory of

Satyajit Ray

2 May 1921 - 23 April 1992

this book is dedicated to his

wife, Bijaya Ray
son, Sandip Ray
daughter-in-law, Lolita Ray
and grandson, Souradeep Ray

On 23 April 1992, in the city of Calcutta,
a man died.
His mortal remains perished,
but he left behind him a heritage,
which no fire could consume.
It is a heritage of words and music
and poetry,
of ideas and of ideals.
And it has the power
to move us, to inspire us,
today and in the days to come.
We, who owe him so much,
salute his memory.

Satyajit Ray wrote the above lines (except for the date) as an introduction to his film on Rabindranath Tagore. I hope it is not presumptuous of me to have changed the date and used the same words as an introduction to my book on Satyajit Ray. He called his film simply *Rabindranath Tagore*; I call my book simply *Satyajit Ray*, aware that I am unable to encompass in its entirety his rich personality.

GASTON ROBERGE

Contents

PART THREE
Teaching Film with Ray's Films

PART FOUR
The Cinema of Satyajit Ray

PART FIVE
Interview

PART SIX
Satyajit Ray and the Film Societies Movement in India

Conclusion

Production Year of Each Essay included in This Book

Date	*Essay*
1971	*Pratidwandi*
1974	*Pather Panchali* Definition of a film
1974	*Pather Panchali* Editing
1975	The World of *Apu* – The *Apu* Trilogy
1978	Interview: Satyajit Ray on Scriptwriting
1978	Christian Metz' Large Syntagmatic Category
1978	True-to life Image-maker
1979	Humanism in Ray's Cinema
1984	*Ghare Baire*
1992	The Discipline of Art
1992	And Then Came Satyajit
1992	Ray's Faith in Youth
1992	For Love of Satyajit
1994	On Manikda's 1994 Birthday
1998	*Gana Shatru*
1998	*Shakha Proshakha*
1998	*Agantuk*
2002	*Jalsaghar*
2004	What's Wrong with the Indian Film Societies?
2005	*Aranyer Din Ratri*
2005	A Quiet Friendship with Manikda
2005	A Journey to the Cave of the Heart: 'Amar Pather Panchali'
2005	The Film Societies and the New Media
2005	*Jana Aranya*

Acknowledgments

THANKS ARE due to Subhromoni and Subhranda De, Krishna Dutta, Mita Ghosh, Samik Bandopadhyay, and Mark Maclean for their wholehearted encouragement to publish this book; Sarbajit Sarkar (aka Raja) for secretarial assistance; Ujjal Chakraborty for suggesting the Ray Roman typeface designed by Satyajit Ray for the cover; and a photograph by Gust Beeckmans, of *Vivant Univers* and Manoj Kumar for making excellent use of the suggestion in designing the cover; Chitrabani for authorizing the reproduction of four photographs; Joy Sebastian and Claudin Gomes for assistance in preparing the photographs; Sreya Chatterjee for retouching a diagram and formatting photographs; Ramesh Jain, Siddharth Chowdhury, and staff of Manohar Publishers, New Delhi.

GASTON ROBERGE

Introduction

THE ESSAYS offered here were written between1970 and 2005. Teaching assignments, requests for articles, and my own evolving interests prompted them. They were not written with the view to form a book. They are now published together, although they do not constitute a book in the usual sense.

The essays remain fragments that can be integrated in the reader's own mosaic. They have been grouped here, but they can be read in any order. The book is somewhat like a website: you move within it as you please.

These essays on Satyajit Ray deal with Ray as a filmmaker. Important aspects of his multifaceted creativity, like graphic design and literature for children, are not dealt with.

The essays were occasional, and thus there were some repetitions. I have eliminated most of them, keeping a few, when the same idea is expressed in different manners or in different contexts.

I have not tried to homogenize the text. A certain lack of consistency, though not intended, reflects the various times and circumstances that have moulded the essays. For instance, I have been referring to Satyajit Ray, as Mr. Ray, Dr. Ray, Satyajit, Ray, Satyajit Ray, and Manikda, according to different contexts.

The date of each essay is mentioned, in the chronological list of the essays following the table of contents, and in a footnote on the title page of each essay. The date of an essay is important. For example, when, in Essay 7, on *Pratidwandi,* I write that I have not seen *Days and Nights in the Forest,* that means I had not seen the film at the time of publishing Essay 7, in 1971.

Out of the twenty-nine feature films of Ray, only eight, plus the *Apu* Trilogy as a whole, are discussed, making, only eleven films. I am a film scholar, not a film critic. I do not feel compelled to write about all the films as they come out. Moreover, this small collection is not a selection indicating preference, nor a classification rating the films. For instance, as important a film as *Ghare Baire* has only two pages. That was the ideal size for the magazine in which the essay was published. It in no way means that I felt the film did not deserve a longer treatment.

On rare occasions (Essays 13 and 15), I have added a few lines. In Essay 13 (1974), I define film on the basis of the celluloid film. Now, in the digital era, I cannot define the technology of film solely as a succession of still images. Hence, the addition.

The discussion of *Jana Aranya* is the only essay (no. 8) that was added for the purpose of complementing this collection of essays, and more importantly still, of improving my own perception of the evolution that I have sought to describe from the *Apu* Trilogy to the Heart Trilogy.

Generally, I made no attempt to update the essays. Essay 7, for instance, on *Pratidwandi* (1971), written thirty-five years ago, just after the release of the film, reflects the preoccupations of the cinemagoers at the time.

Given Satyajit Ray's deep involvement in film education, especially in the film societies movement in India, I felt it mandatory to include two articles (Essays 22, 23). The first deals with the present state of the Indian film societies, and the other, inspired by Ray, suggests a new type of activity for a new type of film society.

This homage to Satyajit Ray is, I hope, a sincere contribution to film scholarship.

PART ONE

Personal Recollections

CHAPTER 1

A Quiet Friendship with Manikda*

[Satyajit Ray was born on 2 May 1921 and died on 23 April 1992. People close to him called him Manik. The respectful suffix 'da' was added to Manik by persons younger than Ray.]

FIRST MEETING WITH MANIKDA

EVER SINCE I came to India in 1961, people knowing of my interest in cinema used to urge me to 'go and see Satyajit Ray'. I thought the suggestion was preposterous. I would go to see Mr. Ray, but, I thought, I should go only when I had studied cinema further, and seen more of Ray's films. I felt that whenever I did go, it would be the beginning of a dialogue. I therefore waited ... nine years.

The opportunity of meeting with Satyajit Ray was provided by Marie Seton. I knew her already, since she had been one of the lecturers at the film appreciation course I had attended at the Film & Television Institute of India, Pune, in 1967. When I came back from Los Angeles, after completing my Master's Degree, I stopped at London, and visited her. Her flat was a sort of hostel for Indians passing through London. She asked me to take a letter to Satyajit Ray. So, I had a good reason to go to his house. My first visit was to be the beginning of a long dialogue.

There is in Antoine de Saint-Exupery's novel, *Le Petit Prince*, a passage that has impressed me profoundly. Touring the world, the young Prince had met a fox. They became friends. And the little Prince used to visit the fox. The latter once told him,

*These notes were written in the period of time since 1971, and were revised for the present publication.

'you should always come on the same day of the week, at the same time, so that even if it is not sure you will come, I can look forward to your visit.' I decided I would visit Mr. Ray on Sundays, at 9.00 a.m. I did that for quite some time, every two or three weeks; at times more often. What the fox had not told the little Prince, and what I discovered, is that in no time, it was I, the visitor, who looked forward to my next visit to Mr. Ray.

RAY AND FILM CULTURE

When Satyajit Ray died, he was hailed by the media, in India and abroad, as one of the greatest filmmakers of his time. Few knew how deeply involved he was in programmes aiming to spread film culture. For instance, he was one of the initiators of the film society movement in India in the late 1940s. He was the Founder-President of the Federation of the Film Societies of India.

Since 1970, he had taken keen interest in the setting up at St. Xavier's College, Calcutta, of a 'Social Communication Service', and he readily accepted to be a Founder Member when the 'service' was registered as the Chitrabani Society in 1979. He was on the Governing Body of Chitrabani for 2 terms of 3 years each, and then was permanently the Advisor of the Society, thus lending the immense prestige of his name to the organization. In addition, he never failed to help me personally in case of administrative difficulties.

He kindly wrote a preface for my book *Chitra Bani* (1974). He wrote:

> (The) global film scene (has become) one of bewildering complexity. Conflicts and cross currents abound; fashions are rampant; taboos and tenets by the dozen are being daily questioned and demolished; norms and styles and tastes are changing and evolving. Filmmakers, entrepreneurs, critics and educators are floundering in an effort to keep on their feet on a shifting ground.
>
> Making his way through the cinematic maze, Gaston Roberge displays admirable patience, eclecticism and clear-headedness. Wisely, for a book of this nature, he takes nothing for granted. Even basic concepts like art

and language and communication are freshly defined, and related to the cinema in the particular context of India. Talking of drama, Roberge not only brings in Aristotle, but also the *Natya Shastra,* making an illuminating distinction between the Greek and the Indian points of view. . . . The whole book, indeed, is a labour of love, and I sincerely hope it will serve the purpose it is aimed at – *to disseminate film culture and to promote a lively interest in the cinema.* (emphasis added)

RAY'S KINDNESS TO ME

Our relationship remained rather formal till the end. He may have addressed me as 'tumi' (the familiar English 'you' or French 'tu') perhaps only once or twice. But there were so many indications of his appreciation and love for me that our relationship, even though formal, was nonetheless very cordial.

Mr. Ray was very shy and reserved. In the early years, he never asked me if I had seen his latest film. But as I began to tell him more and more about his films, he reciprocated by personally inviting me to attend the private screenings of his latest films. I was moved by the fact that such a busy person could find the time to phone me to extend the invitation. I was glad to give him my reaction to his films, as they came out regularly, almost one a year. I think he appreciated my frankness as well as my own brand of appreciation.

The greatest mark of Manikda's appreciation for me was perhaps that he at times addressed me in Bengali in spite of my lack of elegance in this language, he who knew both English and Bengali so well. On three or four occasions, he described for me in great detail the film he was then about to make. This was an extraordinary experience, because of the force with which he told the story, the precise details he communicated to you. It was as if you saw the film even before it was made, so vividly had Ray's imagination conceived it.

I once was at his flat and he told me that he was to see his latest film, *Pratidwandi,* in a theatre so as to check how it sounded in a hall. He invited me to come along. We were alone in the theatre. At one point, I misinterpreted a gesture made by one of the characters in the film, and I burst out laughing. However, I realized that there was nothing funny in the scene. I had laughed at the wrong place. But one cannot undo one's laughter. Since Ray was a few seats away from me, he surely heard me laugh. I was quite ashamed. But we never talked about that afterwards.

The only time when I was aware of having annoyed Mr. Ray was when I told him that I wondered how he could produce films so well-crafted in such a shabby environment as the Tollygunge studios. He sharply answered that he had all that he needed. That made me think deeply, because he had just told me that at times he had to interrupt shooting because crows were heard cawing through the roof of the studio.

I benefited personally from his kind relationship with me in countless occasions. The most striking manifestation of his benevolent power was the day I was almost accused of 'video piracy'. I had made a video copy of *Charulata* in order to make a shot-by-shot analysis of the film for students of Presidency College. Such a demonstration, if done on a 16 mm projector, would have ruined the print. The students were very happy with my performance, and the matter was mentioned in a newspaper. The next day the police came to Chitrabani to seize the video-cassette. An inquiry was held. First, the producer of the film was approached to find out if he had any objection to a video copy of the film having been made. He did object. Then Satyajit Ray was asked his view. He said to the police that there was nothing wrong in what I had done (of course, it was not wrong morally, although legally it *was* wrong). The matter stopped at that. The word of Ray, who did not own the film and thus had no legal say in the matter, was more important than the word of the owner of the film.

WHO WAS SATYAJIT RAY?

It took me a long time to realize two things with regard to Mr. Ray. The first one was that in filmdom you were nobody in Calcutta, perhaps even in India, unless you knew Ray personally.

When I came back from Hollywood with a very modest documentary film of mine, I requested Mr. Ray to please see the film. At that time, *Chitrabani* did not even have a 16 mm projector. Ray was very gracious in arranging for the two of us to see the film. I do not know what he actually felt about my film. But he did say it was very good. This was like being awarded a second degree, in addition to my university degree. I was so elated that I decided not to show the film to any one else, lest they construed that Ray was being indulgent towards me. Meanwhile, he had already told some people that I had made a very good film. That was enough for me.

The second thing I discovered quite belatedly is that there is in Calcutta a power structure determined by position of prestige. This is a spurious power, but it is very effective. It took me years to realize that most people in Calcutta would not think of doing anything in the realm of film without obtaining the implicit or formal approval — or blessing, as it is called — of Satyajit Ray. For years I did not know about that and just went about doing what I thought should be done. I did keep Mr. Ray informed, but not by way of securing his approval, but by way of sharing information on a subject I knew he loved, and by way of soliciting his guidance.

One day, in the 1970s, I believe, the French film critic Louis Marcorelles, of the journal *Le Monde*, visited Kolkata after he attended a film festival in Delhi. He requested Manikda to show him one of his films. Manikda obliged and arranged a private screening of *Charulata.* I served as an interpreter. Translating what Marcorelles said was not difficult. But there was a thorny difficulty: Marcorelles did not like *Charulata.* What should I convey to Ray?

Surely, Marcorelles, who had occasionally contributed articles to the *Cahiers du Cinéma* and thus belonged to a group of sophisticated film critics, could not fail to notice Ray's brilliant direction and Subrata Mitra's extraordinary camera work. Yet, he positively disliked the film. Not that he found it to be a 'bad' film. But, as I understood later on, Marcorelles was then fascinated by a totally different type of cinema, the so-called 'cinéma direct', and so deep a change in his sensibility had taken place that he could not find *Charulata* an interesting film.

The extraordinary humane quality of Satyajit Ray appeared in the following incident. One day, when I visited him, I found him slightly preoccupied. He told me that about an hour before I arrived, a few persons had come to see him. They were anxious to see some of his screenplays. Ray's screenplays are, indeed, something to see: hand written in Bengali, with notes in English for his set designer, with sketches here and there, and the occasional staff notation of fragments of music. Ray handed a few screenplays to his visitors and allowed them to glance through them for some time, while he himself kept busy with his work. The visitors finally took their leave. And then Ray realized that one screenplay was missing, none other than the *Charulata* screenplay. He told me that he was almost sure he knew who in the group had stolen the screenplay So, I ventured to ask him what action he planned. His reply astonished me: 'Nothing', he said. He briefly explained that he did not want to hurt the reputation of the culprit. I pondered over his humane concern.

RAY'S FILMS AND THE FILM CRITICS

Ray's last films, *Gana Shatru*, *Shakha Proshakha* and *Agantuk* were very badly received by the Calcutta public. I, for one, greatly appreciated what he was trying to do, namely, to convey his personal views about our present society and, especially in his last film (*Agantuk*), about our civilization.

Although we never talked about that, I felt extremely sorry for him, because I could sense how hurt he must have been, especially when these films were so personal. He was too close to his own people, for them, conscious though they were of his greatness, to see what made him great. As the saying goes, 'No one is a prophet in his own country'. That is the case the world over. But this is of little comfort. What may be of some comfort is the fact that often a prophet actually is heard outside his own country.

Several of the best studies of the Ray films have been written abroad by non-Bengalis. One can mention here — not without profound emotion — the article on *Gana Shatru* by Charles Tesson in *Cahiers du Cinéma*.[1] I pointed out that article to Ray, and I translated some passages for him. I did it orally, and did not translate the full text purposely, because it was just too profound and too personal.

While people who do not belong to the Bengali culture may miss the finesse of Ray's art, they may be sensitive precisely to what makes that art so typically Bengali, that is, so deeply different from the culture of these outsiders. In other words, a person from outside the Bengali milieu may be in a good position to notice the characteristics of Bengali culture, characteristics that a Bengali person may take for granted and perhaps fail to appreciate.

If I may paraphrase Satyajit Ray's seminal essay, I would ask: 'What is wrong with Indian critics?' I would submit that they do not take Indian films seriously enough. There is another aspect to the difficulty some local critics experience concerning Ray's cinema. I have discussed it separately in chapter 23. In a word, paradoxically, while outside critics are inclined to deal with Ray's films in the light of whatever they know about the *Natya Sastra,* Indian critics are inclined to deal with the same films in the light of whatever they know about the *Poetics* of Aristotle.

SOME WORK ABROAD ON RAY'S CINEMA

I gave a series of ten lectures on 'The Cinema of Satyajit Ray' at Concordia University (then Loyola College) in Montreal. That was around 1980. Two of my students were from India. They gave great credibility to my lectures. One was Suhasini Mulay, who was then a student at McGill University, and joined my course as a guest student. She is the daughter of the film personality, Vijaya Mulay (also known as 'Akka'), and is herself a noted filmmaker and actress. She acted in Mrinal Sen's film *Bhuvan Shome* (1969). The other Indian who joined my classes on Ray was Ramesh Sharma, of the *New Delhi Times* fame, and now a distinguished video film producer in Delhi.

HOW RAY AND HIS CINEMA INFLUENCED MY RELATIONSHIP WITH INDIA

My relationship with Satyajit Ray is an important aspect of my relationship with India and Bengal. I had come from Canada with a desire to know and love the people of India, and exchange spiritual values with them. However, I had no contact with India, and I was rather ill-prepared to come to India. I hardly knew any Indians.

I was twenty-six, leaving my native Canada for the first time — going to India. My itinerary took me first to New York, where I had to stay one night. That night was my 'nuit bengalie': in an art film theatre I saw the three *Apu* films, one after the other, the entire Trilogy in one night. I already knew about the films through their reputation in Canada, but about Bengal I knew nothing. All I knew was *La Nuit Bengalie* by Mircea Eliade, some Tagore poems and a *Reader's Digest* piece on Mother Teresa. Eliade's novel intrigued me, but I realized it was the work of an adolescent. Still, what sensuality! What intense love! What cruelty even! Who were these Bengalis? Tagore too fascinated me. But the image of Mother Teresa as the 'Saint of the Slums' bothered me. Did such poverty exist? Was helping the poor sufficient? These questions had been following me like phantoms. Seeing the *Apu* Trilogy both reassured me and seduced me. No. Apu, Sarbajaya, even Harihar did not need my help; but how not to love them? I thought it was fortunate that I would be soon among them. I hardly gave a thought to the director; it was his protagonists that were living within me. It was only after nearly ten years, in 1970, that I met Satyajit Ray.

By then, I had seen *The Music Room,* which enchanted me, and *Charulata,* the most perfect film I had ever seen at that time. When I finally presented myself to Mr. Ray, I had the impression of always having known him. His images of Bengal had become mine; all over Calcutta and Bengal I met the heroes so passionately projected in his films. I am always surprised when I hear people criticize *Pather Panchali* for showing too much material poverty. That aspect never touched me, because poverty is relative. But the profound humaneness of Ray's characters has always impressed me. Besides, the spiritual poverty of some rich people is far more deplorable than material poverty.

It is as if all Bengal was in Manikda: the rich and the poor, the powerful and the humble, the peasants and the city persons, children, teenagers, adults and old people, men and women. But of late, in *Gana Shatru* it is Ray himself who is on screen. His films are more and more personal. Having confronted death, he speaks now with the assurance of a man who always sensed the value of life but is now analysing it also. *Gana Shatru* is a hymn of joy, to life, and to creativity. The two films that follow, *Shakha Proshakha* and *Agantuk*, offer reflections on moral integrity and civilization.

MANIKDA'S LAST WORDS TO ME.

Manikda died on 23 April 1992. Some time in March, as he was in the intensive care unit of a nursing home, I was able to see him. He was alone. My visit was of less than one minute. That was the last time I saw him, and I will always cherish the memory of his parting words, in Bengali, *Bhalo laglo*, that is, 'It was nice seeing you, I liked it.'

NOTE

1. Charles Tesson, 'Le bruit du monde', *Cahiers du Cinéma*, no. 422, July/August 1989, pp. 20-5.

CHAPTER 2

For Love of Satyajit*

THE AWARD of an 'Oscar' to Satyajit Ray has triggered off the Indian media, especially the newspapers and magazines, into a paean to the master. It is as if each one of them, not to speak of institutions like the Government of India and the University Grants Commission, feared to be outdone by Hollywood, and to be found silent when everybody else was singing praise. As a result, the media has lost its sense of measure and propriety: the 'tala' has increased to a fast tempo, the ragas rarely suit the circumstance. Mostly, the tributes to Ray lack one of his most endearing qualities, humour. In a word, the well-deserved praise too often smacks of adulation. A foreign institution recognized Mr. Ray's professional achievement: forty years of solid work in film and the production of over 35 films. But our local media have transformed the felicitation into a life assessment. If I may paraphrase the title of a Ray book, *Our Films, Their Films*, here you have '*our* praise, *their* praise'.

Even if the award was given to Mr. Ray at a time when he was ill, it is still much too early to assess his multifaceted career, a difficult task for which a good amount of time is required. Hence, much of what one reads, sees or hears in the media, though surely well intended, should have come much earlier or should come much later. This 'tamasha' endangers Bengali culture by presenting Ray as its main, even its sole, fountainhead. That is not the way Ray himself perceives his role in

*These notes, written shortly before Mr. Ray's death in 1992, later appeared in Santi Das, ed., *Satyajit Ray: An Intimate Master,* 1998, pp. 62-78. The author is indebted to Sunetra Ghatak Chatterjee and Utpal Kumar Basu for valuable comments and suggestions regarding this essay.

West Bengal and India. Surely, he is aware of his own personal stature as an artist, and of his unique role in the cultural life of this country. Yet, he knows very well that the type of culture he has inherited from nineteenth-century Bengal has its limitations. And he has explore these limitations in several of his films. But it is in *Agantuk* that Ray's own assessment of culture, civilization, religion, science, technology, education, is the most wide-ranging and the severest. No art school in the world, says the protagonist, can teach you the art exemplified, twenty thousand years ago by the depiction of a bison in a cave at Altamira. What then is civilized? What is uncivilized? Some cultures are like dried up, contaminated wells, in which man is caught like a frog! To project Ray the way the media has done on the occasion of the Oscar award can only encourage cultural complacency, the one thing we can do without, especially at the beginning of the 1990s, when the Indian Marxists are in disarray, and the country as a whole is experiencing an unprecedented socio-economic crisis.

The Oscar award is indeed an occasion to rejoice with Mr. Ray over the recognition given to his film career by the most prestigious film institution of the world, the Academy of Motion Picture Arts and Sciences. But if Mr. Ray's career as a whole was to be assessed, then should not similar awards have been given to him for achievements in the graphic arts, in fiction writing, and in the writing of literature for children? And there are several other aspects to Manikda's career, which do not concern his films primarily, but have to do with his role in the cultural life of this country. For instance, Manikda discovered, launched and nurtured several new talents and technicians in filmdom. This service to the film industry is intimately associated with his filmmaking, no doubt, and perhaps Ray had to create the actors and technicians he needed for his films. Nonetheless, this contribution is a distinct aspect of his role as a creative artist. It is also an index of his generosity and of his eagerness to help others. For instance, he did compose the music of other directors' films, like Ivory-Merchant's *Shakespearewallah*, for instance, and he accepted to direct

Chiriakhana, someone else's film project that was facing problems.

A second contribution for which we are all thankful to Manikda is his leadership in the creation of the Indian film societies in the late 1940s. He was a member-founder of Chitrabani, a media centre in Calcutta, established in 1970, and he is its adviser. More recently, he played a significant role in the creation of Nandan, the West Bengal Film Centre of which he is the Chairperson. He also helped significantly in the creation of Roopkala Kendro, a development communication centre of the West Bengal Government, set up with the financial support of the Government of Italy. Thus, not only has Ray made films, he has had a life-long commitment towards spreading film culture. For him, this was not just a matter of showing films by foreign directors to rapt audiences. It was, above all, an attempt to locate and articulate the differences between 'our films' and 'their films', in order to lay the foundation of an Indian film culture, with all its diversity, and at the same time, its specific traits.

Third, Ray has successfully advocated the introduction of cinema studies in Indian colleges and universities. Thus, he demonstrated that the development of cine-artists and technicians, the fostering of film culture and film studies go much beyond the making of films. This present essay, however, in line with the Oscar award, deals primarily with Ray's achievement to date in filmmaking. Adoor Gopalakrishnan beautifully expresses that achievement, in very personal terms:

> *Pather Panchali*, for me marks the beginning of the true Indian Cinema (...) an affirmation of the emergence of the first consummate artist on the sub-continent's motion picture scene.
>
> Ray's last films, *Gana Shatru, Shakha Proshakha* and *Agantuk* (here let me take the liberty to group them together as the 'moral trilogy') were reflective of his anxious concern at the erosion of values fast eating into the vitals of the society. The artist who came on the scene saluting life with the sad and sweet saga of *Apu* in a historic trilogy was bidding goodbye to his audience with a pang of pain in his heart.
>
> For me, watching a Ray film is always revealing and rewarding, no matter how many times I have seen it before . . . of how many world masters can one say this?[1]

The impact of Ray's films on the Indian film industry and on the Bengali culture has yet to be felt fully. Young filmmakers, throughout India, acknowledge Ray's unique contribution to cinema. Each of them seeks to emulate him, but with creative freedom, not necessarily by way of imitation. And that is as it should be.

We, in Bengal, have every reason to be proud of Manikda. Yet, too little has been done to have his films shown extensively in Bengal. Now that films can be made available in the form of video cassettes it has become easier, and to that extent more imperative still, to ensure that the people of India, and especially of Bengal, have numerous opportunities to see Ray's films. *Pather Panchali* is well known to persons interested in films, but there are numbers of Bengali youths who have not seen it as yet, and who have seen only a few of the more recent Ray films. We would expect that the praises sung in Ray's honour would also lead to some commitment tc have his films shown more widely, at least in Bengal. In this respect, the film societies of West Bengal have been particularly unimaginative, perhaps even uninterested. They should know that by and large, the people of rural Bengal have not seen many of the films by Ray, not to speak of Utpalendu Chakravarty, Buddhadeb Dasgupta, Ritwik Ghatak, Gautam Ghose, and the Sens — Mrinal and Aparna. Is this not a matter of concern to intellectuals interested in the cinema?

The fact is, our people have too few opportunities to watch the best of 'our films'. It is sad to hear some rural people of Bengal say that thc best film they ever saw was by far *Beder Meye Josna,* a poor West Bengal rendering of a very good Bangladeshi film. The present insignificance of the film societies in general with regard to 'our films' has been more striking still in their inability to assess the later films of Ray, *Gana Shatru*, *Shakha Proshakha*, and *Agantuk*. If they, who, as film society members, are the followers of Ray, do not receive his films properly, then who, in Bengal, will? It is perhaps in these three films, that the greatness of Satyajit Ray appears most. To see this, one must be sensitive to what a film is saying at least as much as to the way in which it says it. In these later films, Ray has made profound socio-political comments. His concern was not just to create film forms. In these comments appear the full implications of Ray's early interest in Italian neo-realist films. And the film envisaged to follow after *Agantuk* questions the relevance to the poor of India of some aspects of science and technology. Ray's fascination for the people inhabiting 'the world of *Apu*' now appears as a loving, questioning concern. Ray has honestly walked along the 'road' until it led him to raise some of the ultimate questions regarding contemporary civilizations.

The greatness of Satyajit Ray as a filmmaker consists in having taken the culture of Bengal — as handed down to him by Bibhutibhushan Bandopadhyay and Rabindranath Tagore in particular — one big step ahead into the realm of cinema. Compare Satyajit Ray and Dadasaheb Phalke. When Phalke saw the life of Christ in a film, he immediately sensed the possibility of projecting images of Hindu deities onto the screen. His reaction was that of a Hindu nationalist.[2] When Ray saw neo-realist films of post-World War II Italy, he discovered a means of expression that greatly appealed to him. His reaction was that of an artist. Phalke contributed to the creation of an Indian film industry. Ray, the humane artist, contributed to world cinema. His films, from *Pather Panchali* to *Agantuk*, portray men, women and children who are fully Indian, and yet are recognized as their brothers and sisters by people the world over.

Because Ray discovered in the cinema a means of expression, he has been able to 'adapt' literary works to the cinema. In fact, adaptation here is a misnomer. For Ray did not translate literary terms into film terms. He took a story, say of Tagore, as in the cases of *Charulata*, *Postmaster* and *Ghare Baire*, and told the story in cinematic terms. He recreated the story in film; he did not translate a novel into a film. That is why his are great 'adaptations'. To use the expression coined by a French film scholar writing about a film by Bresson, you have in a film adaptation by Satyajit Ray 'all that the novel gave you plus its refraction through the film medium'. But Ray created directly for the screen his own stories too: *Nayak*, *Kanchanjungha* and *Agantuk*, for instance. As a young Bengali artist he had been moved by the novel *Pather Panchali*. He felt he could tell that story in film. But at that time, the only medium accessible to him was drawing, and hence he drew the story. As soon as he could, he told it in film. Later on, he felt he could tell his own stories in the same film medium. He had by then made the medium fully his own.

Ray has gained the reputation of being a 'complete' filmmaker. And so he is. He can attend personally to all aspects of the making of a film (and this is reflected in the accuracy of his film scripts): creating the story, writing the script, writing the dialogue, operating the camera, supervising the editing, composing the music, designing sets and costumes, selecting talents, designing advertisements . . . and, of course, directing. One wishes that, like Hitchcock, he too appeared in his films. His voice, at least, can be heard in three films, *Rabindranath Tagore*, *Pratidwandi* and *Agantuk*. However, Manikda is not only a complete filmmaker, he is a complete artist, having several means of expression at his command: music, painting, designing, and writing fiction for both adults and children.

As tributes are being paid to Manikda on the occasion of his receiving an Oscar from Hollywood, it can be hoped that yet some more films will be made by Ray. After *The Return of Feluda,* may we have 'the return of Manikda'.

NOTES

1. Adoor Gopalakrishnan, 'In the beginning, there was *Pather Panchali*', in Santi Das, ed., *Satyajit Ray. An Intimate Master,* Allied Publishers, 1998, pp. 57-8.
2. M. Madhava Prasad, 'The State in/of Cinema' in Partha Chatterjee, ed., *Wages of Freedom: Fifty Years of the Indian Nation-State*, Oxford University Press, 1998, pp. 123.

CHAPTER 3

On Manikda's 1994 Birthday*

BIRTH ANNIVERSARIES are privileged moments to remember beloved lost ones. But I hardly need such occasions to remember Manikda. I think of him daily. I have three pictures of him, on three different walls, in my office, where I spend the major part of my day. Shahjahan had arranged a set of mirrors in a room so that in whichever direction he looked, he could always see the Taj Mahal. Similarly whichever side I turn to, I see an image of Manikda. And in my more pensive moments I hear the last words he had for me when I took leave from him, 'Bhalo laglo', 'I liked it'.

I too say, 'Manikda, bhalo laglo'. I liked to be with him. It isn't that we always talked of profound subjects. But whatever we talked about, he always had a profound impact on me.

For instance, one day I mentioned to him that there was a plan to make a feature film on Mother Teresa. Unfortunately, some persons close to Mother prevailed upon her, and she withdrew the permission she had redily given to have the film made. One argument these persons put forward was, 'How can you make a feature film on Mother even when she is alive?' I told Manikda that so-called documentaries are fictional too. So I felt it was better to make a film on Mother when she was still alive, for after she leaves us, it will be difficult to anchor in actual facts the myths about her, that will very soon mushroom. In that context I mentioned the film *Monsieur Vincent.* And I was surprised to find that the film was well known to Manikda.

Monsieur Vincent is a French film of 1947. It is about Vincent

*G. Roberge, *Communication Cinema Development*, 1998, Chapter 25, pp. 132-5.

de Paul (1581-1660), a pioneer social worker and a famous Catholic saint. When Manikda saw my surprise at his knowing that film, he added to my delight, 'Yes, it was a remarkable film, with an extraordinary performance by Pierre Fresnay. The script was by Jean Anouilh, with a fantastic camera work by Claude Renoir'. I asked Manikda if he had seen the film recently. He told me that he had seen it in the early days of the Indian film societies, around 1950, some forty years before our conversation. I thought that anyone who could remember a 1947 French film in such detail must somehow be a special person. I am French speaking and I had forgotten who the scriptwriter and who the camera person were. But then, I am not a filmmaker and certainly not Satyajit Ray.

There were other such occasions when Manikda showed that he was a special person. Two come to mind. Our Chitrabani team had made an animation film out of some two hundred still photographs of slum children. The film is called *A Portrait of the Pilkhana Child.* I requested Manikda to see the film and he accepted. So, Brian Balen, the film's director, and I showed him the film, in his flat on Bishop Lefroy Road. He had very kind words about the film, but he said that a part of the music, which he liked as music, was not quite appropriate where it was used in the film. He felt that the mood was slightly wrong. We asked him which part of the film he was referring to. He answered, 'I don't remember exactly which part of the film it was, but I can hum the tune for you.' And he did hum the tune accurately. We were dumbfounded and thought, 'How can a person see a twenty-minute film for the first time and then produce the tune of its music?'

The other incident that comes to mind has to do not so much with the culture or talent of Manikda, as it has with his greatness as a person. That incident occurred in the early 1970s. I had to be absent from Calcutta for nearly a year. And although the organization I belonged to, Chitrabani, was then very small, I needed someone to replace me during my absence. I found a young man — let us call him Rajan — to whom I gave the job. When I came back, Rajan had already left for the USA, where he had got admitted into a university. My secretary, who assisted him during my absence, told me that Rajan had sent him to Satyajit Ray. Neither the secretary nor Rajan had ever met Ray. The secretary was to ask him for a recommendation for Rajan. Apparently, it did not occur to Rajan that propriety demanded that he personally go to Satyajit Ray with his request. Upon hearing the secretary, Ray asked him in his deep voice, 'Do I know the gentleman?' The secretary missed the gentle yet obvious irony of the question, and he told Ray that he did not know Rajan but he knew Fr. Roberge whom Rajan was temporarily replacing. On hearing this, Ray immediately wrote a note of recommendation for Rajan. The 'gentleman' was admitted into a university. When I heard about this incident I was absolutely appalled. I felt that only a great person could be unshaken by such an impropriety. At the same time, I loved Manikda for lending Rajan the immense prestige of his name just because he was replacing me.

Towards the end of Manikda's illness, it had become obvious that he would not be with us for much longer. So, his departure was no surprise. Yet, I had not anticipated that the sense of loss I was to experience would be so profound and so pervasive. Manikda was such a towering personality, and he exercised such a unique influence that, when he left, a void was created, which is filled to an extent, by our fond memory of him. But there is yet another way to fill in the void: it is to strive to fulfil the expectations that Manikda nurtured and fostered regarding film culture.

Not so long ago, in 1990, he had written a note for the students enrolled in a Chitrabani Film Studies course. He had these words:

> I find it most heartening that such an event (the film course) has taken place. I have been hoping for a long time that something concrete should be done about the dissemination of film culture among the young people in our country. This course is surely a step in that direction. I hope that the enterprise will continue (29/4/90).

The enterprise continues and, in fact, other organizations and individuals also have taken up the cause of film culture. On Manikda's 1994 birthday, 'I find that most heartening.'

PART TWO

A. Film Discussions

CHAPTER 4

The World of *Apu** 1955–1959

HERE THE 'World of *Apu*' does not refer to the film of that name, but to the entire *Apu* trilogy.

The *Apu* story moved me profoundly the first time I saw it in 1961. Later on, when I was able to read in Bengali the novel by Bibhutibhusan Bandopadhyay, from which the film was adapted, I was amazed to see how much of the book was in the film. No doubt, during my reading of the book the film constantly provided images that influenced my experience of the novel. Still, I found the same lovely characters, the same attention given to detail in both the film and the book. Above all, the book aroused anew those poignant emotions that the film had created in me. More credit should have been given to Bibhutibhusan Bandopadhyay, I thought, for so many of the film's qualities. However, what I had discovered in the book I also found later on all over Bengal. In fact, the book and the film had conveyed to me something of India — at least, of Bengal.

I soon realized, though, how widely different the film is from the book. More credit should be given to Ray, I thought, for his originality. The difference between book and film does not result only from the necessary difference between the literary medium and the film medium. Ray contemplated the same characters, lived the same emotions that were Bibhutibhusan's, although he depicted these in a much more disciplined manner

*Quarterly Journal of the National Centre for the Performing Arts, vol. IV, no. 4, December 1975, pp. 25-30. Appeared in Santi Das, ed., *Satyajit Ray: An Intimate Master,* 1998, pp. 62-78.

than the novelist had done. In the process of making the trilogy, Ray transformed his material into something totally different from the book and, as a result, Ray's film is not 'about the same thing' as the book.

For, what is the novel about? In the manner of Indian music, the novel is an attempt — largely successful — at recreating the impression one can have — especially when one is an Indian — of life in constant flux. *Pather Panchali,* the song of the road, is the song of life. The road here is that of life unfolding. A visual representation of life in the novel is that of the river flowing, flowing, and flowing — the image recurs as a leitmotif throughout the book. For Bibhutibhusan, man is taken by life in its flow, like chaff on the water, whether he wishes it or not. But, mysteriously enough, at the end of his journey, man finds himself at his point of departure. He has not ceased to be carried away; yet, in the end, he has not really moved. The second book of the novel is titled *Aparajito,* the invincible. In Bibhutibhusan's mind, the invincible is not the hero of the novel, but the mystery of life: permanence in change. The last lines of the novel express this clearly: 'The mystery of life, for ever invincible, again appears in all its splendour'. Bibhutibhusan explains that, after twenty-four years, when Apu comes back with his son to his birthplace, the village of Nischindipur, his story starts all over again in his son. Just as Apu had grown up under the care of an old aunt, so also Apu's son is entrusted to an old friend. As for Apu himself, he is made to go on a distant journey to be re-absorbed by nature, to the romance of lush Fiji. Thus, the cycle of life is complete: from Nischindipur to Nischindipur, from boyhood to boyhood. In nearly eight hundred pages, Apu's life is depicted as an endless series of minor events, dreams and recollections.

The narration flows like the Ganga in the Bengal delta, divided into hundreds of rivulets. At times, the direction of the river seems to be lost, yet its movement towards the sea continues, mysterious, unimpeded. In the end, however, nothing actually changes. For all his peregrinations, Apu has not grown much wiser. He comes back to Nischindipur with Kajol, as ignorant of the mystery of life as his 'abodh' son. Concluding his book, *Aparajito,* Bibhutibhusan writes: 'The boy's father was slightly mistaken. For after an absence of twenty-four years, it was the same baffled boy Apu who came back to Nischindipur.'

Bibhutibhusan aims to recreate this impression of a ceaseless flow. This determines his style in two main ways. Firstly, little importance is given to characterization in the novel. The protagonists live their tragedies, they experience human passions, but outside the framework of a personal drama. For the real and unique drama is that of life itself, mysteriously unfolding. The second stylistic characteristic is correlative to the first one: since there is no drama — no action in the sense of Aristotle's *Poetics* — the novel has no linear structure, no beginning, middle or end. Much of it could be suppressed. Much could be added to it. The cyclic structure of the novel taken as a whole (from boyhood to boyhood) is also found in its parts. For instance, the first book of the novel ends with Apu coming back to Nischindipur. Furthermore, several small sections flash back, starting from a point of the story, going back in time and returning to the initial point just to start the same process over again.

Repetition is yet another method through which Bibhutibhusan negates change in movement itself. A striking example of this occurs after Apu's marriage with Aparna, a village girl. Apu returns to Calcutta alone. But he comes back to his wife's village nearly every week. He does this again and again until it becomes inevitable that he should take her along with him to Calcutta. In this way the event is de-dramatized and the necessary change is almost imperceptible.

The importance of these notations is realized when comparing the novel with the film. Satyajit Ray's trilogy rightly bears the name of Apu for it shows Apu's growth through the three main stages of life: boyhood, adolescence, and manhood. The entire trilogy has a beginning, a middle, and an end. In turn, each film has a linear structure. Whereas Bibhutibhusan's novel has the incantatory and repetitive form of most Indian music, Ray's films have a form usually associated with Western music. Because the film is centred on one personage, Apu, the events of the boy's life are organized into a single drama. The *Pather Panchali* film, which contains nearly two-thirds of the book of that name, is more episodic and contains more characters than the next two films. *Aparajito,* which covers the end of the first book and the beginning of the second (*Aparajito*), describes Apu's relationship with his mother until after her death, when he resolutely returns to Calcutta. And in *Apur Sansar* (the last section of the book *Aparajito*), Apu accepts the responsibility of manhood.

Significantly, each film ends with a departure, not a return to an initial point. In *Pather Panchali,* Apu's family leaves Nischindipur, en route to Banaras: Apu leaves his boyhood forever. In *Aparajito* he leaves for Calcutta: adolescence is over. In *Apur Sansar* he again goes to Calcutta, this time a mature man. Thus, in the film, Apu grows out of the mysterious cycle where Bibhutibhusan had thought him trapped. Some critics have pointed out that with the coming of Kajol to Nischindipur the cycle of life begins again. This is true, but what counts at that moment is the final maturing of Apu himself. And Ray does not develop the idea of a cycle starting all over again. If there is a cycle in the trilogy, it is a matter of style, not a vision of life as a circle where nothing happens. On the contrary, the film shows an irreversible process: Apu's growth to manhood. By throwing away his autobiographical and narcissistic novel, Apu drops the shackles that prevented him from receiving his son. As the leaves of the novel blow with the wind, Apu emerges from the womb of romance, ready to literally shoulder his responsibility as Kajol's father.

Bibhutibhusan's *The Song of Life* and *The Invincible* (Mystery of Life) have become under Ray's treatment 'The Song of the Road', 'The Unvanquished' (Apu) and 'The World of Apu'. The point at issue here is not the faithfulness of the film to the novel, a matter for purists to discuss. What is established in the foregoing analysis is the originality of Ray who has injected a new point of view in the very events narrated by Bibhutibhusan. That new point of view has called for a dramatization of the literary material. And because of that new point of view, Apu emerges victorious at the end of the film, instead of disappearing as he does at the end of the book. The main difference between the book and the film is that the former is a contemplation of life as an invincible mystery, while the latter is an apt depiction of the invincible growth of a man to freedom and love.

Life remains profoundly mysterious in Ray's three films. But its mystery is humanized and perceived in technology, like the train or the telegraph, or in events apparently senseless from a human point of view. Furthermore, the mystery is not numbing; it is attractive and challenging. Apu gradually opens up to life. In *Apur Sansar,* where the progressive awakening of Apu is more striking, Apu is seen several times rising from sleep. The news of his wife's death causes him to fall into a sort of torpor. The total sleep of death through suicide is even alluded to. He fully awakes to life only at the end of the film.

From book to film, time, the imaginary duration of the artwork, has been submitted to a new organization. The book proceeds in the manner of a description which itself necessarily evolves in time but is concerned with a static object. The film's time, on the other hand, is the duration of an event, the growth of Apu. Of course, there are two durations in the film: that of the film itself (the time the spectator must sit in order to watch the entire film) and the time of the narration (nearly thirty years of Apu's life, which the spectator must imagine in order to grasp the trilogy's significance). There are two durations in the novel too: the time a reader takes to read through eight hundred pages, and the duration of the situations depicted in those pages. But every effort was made by the novelist to dull the impression of duration. The cyclic form given to the novel creates the impression that time is an illusion. The novel is akin to those multiform Indian sculptures that suggest infinity of movements but participate in the static quality of the rock on which they are carved.

Organization of events in a temporal sequence, dramatic structure, character analysis, teleological narration, all this is typical of Western art and explains why a film like *Apur Sansar* can arouse an enthusiastic response in a Western spectator. The exotic quality of the film and the pleasure of discovering a foreign film so profoundly human, have also contributed towards placing the *Apu* trilogy among the films which are most often shown by film societies abroad.

Is Ray's trilogy, then, a Westernized Indian cinema? Not in the least.

For, there is one thing, which disturbs the foreign spectator: the pace of the trilogy. Not a few Western spectators begin to appreciate the Apu films only at a second or even a third screening. They cannot at first adjust to what they call the 'slow' pace of the film. When one says that a film is too slow-paced, what does one mean if not that one finds it more or less boring? But the perception of a pace as slow or fast is essentially relative. The pace of *Pather Panchali* is certainly not slow for its maker — especially if slow should mean boring — but correct, and not only correct, but probably the only correct pace the film could be given.

The question of pace relates to modes of perception. The pace of a film masterpiece can train the spectator to perceive things as the film's maker does. When foreign spectators begin to enjoy the 'slow' pace of *Pather Panchali*, they begin to look at life the way Satyajit Ray does. To illustrate this point, I would like to mention the series of alternating close-ups at the beginning of the candy-man sequence in *Pather Panchali*. At that point of the film, Apu and Durga are preparing, unknown to their parents, a mixture of pickles that they enjoy with the added gratification of a forbidden pleasure.

There are about ten alternating close-ups of Apu and Durga simply eating, and smiling with joy. The close-ups are not only repetitive; they are kept, each one, for what would be in current film style a 'long' time. Yet, once the spectator has adjusted to that 'slow' pace, he finds this series of images most interesting. For, Ray knows the art of keeping the image in sight beyond the time required for it to convey its information, and generate enjoyment. Before the enjoyment begins to recede, Ray offers a new image. This is more than simply an art of looking; it is an art of living. I have always felt that Indians know, more than Westerners, how to experience life, to enjoy it. From this point of view, the category of time has little importance, and each object, each person, each event, because it is not drawn away by the inexorable onrush of time, becomes an infinite source of pleasure. The Westerner experiences his own existence mainly in his action, whereas, I believe, the Indian experiences existence and life in itself perhaps more than his own personal existence and life. This is reflected in the 'slow' paced trilogy of Ray. I should add, however, that the pace in the Ray films has changed considerably after the trilogy where it was partly determined by the subject matter.

The *Apu* trilogy is still more radically an Indian work of art in yet another way. Generally, the foreign spectator is familiar with the Indian view of life I have described as typical of Bibhutibhusan's, namely, life as a cycle, as the mystery of permanence in change. But there is a complementary Indian view with which the Western spectator may be less familiar: the urge to penetrate the mystery, a dynamism strong enough to break open the cycle. In India, the stronger the cycle of life, and the more impenetrable its mystery, the greater were the men who have attempted to achieve freedom from the cycle, and an insight into the mystery. Only a civilization powerful enough to break the fetters of the cycle can realize how strong that cycle can be. That is what Indian civilization has depicted so emphatically. At the same time, that civilization has produced giants like Buddha, and, closer to us, Tagore and Gandhi. While sensing life as an impenetrable mystery, these men have achieved a realization of its meaning. Does not the invincible Apu at the end of *Apur Sansar* emerge as a victorious Siddhartha or Buddha? Bibhutibhusan leaves him 'abodh' at the end of the novel. Ray, on the contrary, makes of him a modern 'bodhisattva'. Starting from a typically Indian novel, Ray has constructed a film trilogy that may be more easily accessible to the foreign spectator, but is no less typically Indian than its literary counterpart.

DEATH IN THE WORLD OF APU[1]

Some of the most interesting deaths to occur in world cinema are seen in Satyajit Ray's *Apu* Trilogy. Their interest derives from the fact that they are simple, human, natural and credible. In contrast, the Hollywood cinema shows countless dead, but no one seems to actually die in these movies.

At first, one may be surprised to find so many deaths in a trilogy. But, on second thought, these deaths appear necessary. In the 25 to 30 years of his life, Apu has to witness a number of deaths among the people close to him. In fact, the film tells the death of five of Apu's closest relatives: his elderly aunt; Durga, his sister, older than him but still in her teens; Harihar, his father; Sarbajaya, his mother; Aparna, his young wife. Thus, death is established as a normal fact in the course of life. The eventuality of personal death is even contemplated when, after his wife's death, Apu has thoughts of suicide. Death is omnipresent, proximate, and inevitable.

Nowhere in the trilogy is there any allusion to even the mere possibility of survival after death. In that sense there is no transcendence in Ray's deaths. Yet, death is not shown as senseless. It is inevitable, it is painful (but apparently not more so than birth), but it does not seem to affect life. For, life endures. In that sense, there is transcendence: it is life that matters, it is life that continues. Death is part of the life process. Contrary to Bibhutibhushan's view of the world in his novel, life in Ray's trilogy is not cyclical, but linear. For that reason, there is no life-death cycle, there is none of what Mircea Eliade (in *Bengali Night*) called the 'myth of eternal return'. Life continues to evolve and death does not bring about a repetition of the same.

In the *Apu* Trilogy, the dead just cease to be. They have no accounts to render of their lives. Nor could they give any such accounts: for they are no more, in an absolute sense.

Death is immanent in life. Death is transcended by life. So is man himself. He lives in complete unison with nature. He is reabsorbed into life at the time of death. And, thus, for him death is not unexpected — however painful the separation from loved ones may be. It is within life that man finds the source of his own existence. Perhaps because he does not separate himself from the matrix of nature, man in the *Apu* Trilogy does not need a separate, transcendental being, from whom to derive his existence, nor does he need an after life. For, there is no after, there is no beyond. There is only life.

What I seek to emphasize here is the basic monism underlying the Indian theology of God, of moral life, and of death. For a mind rooted in monism, and holding that the individual is but one of the instances belonging to the one, all-encompassing, and only real being, life is not affected by death. Similarly, in that broad context of monism, accountability is not relevant. What counts is to live in unison with the world, mould oneself according to its laws, and identify with the Self. Obviously, this theology has its own risks. But human life itself is a risk.

NOTE

1. This essay was published in 1975, a paragraph from my book, *The Ways of Film Studies*, 1992, pp. 199-200 is added here.

CHAPTER 5

*Jalsaghar**
The Music Room, 1958
or
Bishwambhar's Portrait

A LARGE MULTI-CANDLE chandelier. Seen from some distance against a dark background. Swinging gently, laterally, to the accompaniment of spirited Indian classical music. While the titles appear, superimposed on the chandelier, slow zoom on the chandelier until it is seen in close-up. The music fades out, and the chandelier morphs into a close-up of Bishwambhar. Zoom out from his face. He is pensive, sitting on the terrace of his ruined palace. Ananta, the servant, appears and reverently places a hookah next to Bishwambhar. Chirping of birds. Ananta addresses him, saying 'Master'.

THE WORLD AS A MUSIC ROOM

In hardly three minutes, Satyajit Ray has told you a lot about 'the music room'. First, a strong identification is established between the regal chandelier and the zamindar, Bishwambhar. Second, as Bishwambhar slowly wakes up, as it were — for, he was not sleeping — to the chirping of the birds, and the call of Ananta, there is a sharp contrast between the bird calls and the music heard so far. You realize that the music you just heard was the music Bishwambhar himself was imagining.[1] It was not just 'film music', that is, music added to the image to make

*Based on teaching notes prepared in 2002, this essay was written especially for the present publication.

its mood sonorous. It was the inner music of a protagonist. It was the music of an inner music room. Thus, there are at least two music rooms: the internal and the external — symbolized by the face of Bishwambhar, and by the chandelier, respectively. In addition to symbolizing the music of the concert room, the chandelier, if hit, emits its own sound. Similarly, the silent face of Bishwambhar, when woken up, emits its own sound, the voice of Bishwambhar.

Thus, the chandelier, an object belonging to the real world inhabited by the spectator, draws the latter into the mind of the old man, through a simple, yet efficient, use of the film medium. From the opening of the film, the music was felt to be film music, only for the spectator to enjoy. But then, it is revealed that the music is that imagined by Bishwambhar, and shared with the spectator.

With Satyajit Ray, and generally in India, you hear the world before you see it. And, as Indian scholars put it, the mind sees with the eyes, and the heart hears with the ears. A few moments after Ananta brings him his hookah, Bishwambhar hears the sound of a distant *shehnai.* He asks, 'Where is that sound coming from?' We find similar instances of hearing first and knowing after in several Ray films. In *Pather Panchali,* Apu hears the sound of a train. He is fascinated. Only afterwards does he go with Durga to see the train, as the latter moves across a nearby field. Apu is called on a journey. Again, Apu and Durga hear the call of the candy man, and they go after him. Indeed, the world itself is a sound emitting world. The sound of the world invites you to participate in life. The world is a cosmic music room.

Taking Ray's oeuvre as a whole, it is as if the various protagonists, in their own circumstances, hear the world and respond to it. Apu, called by the train, starts off on his journey, singing his 'pather panchali', his song of the road. Bishwambhar spends his life in a *jalsaghar*, real or imagined. Charu (*Charulata*) and Bimala (*Ghare Baire*) hear the sound of the world, and they look outside through the shutters of their homes. In *Gana Shatru,* the music room enlarges to the dimension of the social environment. Proshanta (*Shakha Proshaka*) so internalizes the sound of the music room as to become unable to relate to reality. Finally, in *Agantuk*, as she enters deeper in her own heart, Anila hears the sound of the Santali dance, the sound of pristine culture, the sound that binds the world together. And she responds to it.

THE FAMILY NOVEL

In Satyajit Ray's cinema can be found what Sigmund Freud called a family novel. That is, an imaginary narrative reminiscent of the actual life situations of the author, and representing an ideal family. Satyajit Ray was the heir of two family traditions: one characterized by dedication to work, the other characterized by the cultivation of art. Both the traditions had their dangers. Too much love for music, for instance, led to a certain distance from reality, in the case of Bishwambhar, and even to madness in the case of Proshanta (*Shakha Proshakha*). As Bishwambhar's wife warns him, 'The love of music is a dangerous passion'. On the other hand, excessive dedication to work led to neglect of social and even familial relations, in the case of Mazumdar, Proshanta's father.

An ancestor of Satyajit Ray in the eighteenth century was a Raja, named Ramkanta Mazumdar. Then Ray's grandfather was Upendrakishore Roy Chowdhury, whose title had been given to him by the British. While in *Jalsaghar*, Bishwambhar has only one son, in *Shakha Proshakha*, Mazumdar has four sons, but their names, each starting with Pro- (as in Proshanta), suggest that the four can be seen as four aspects of the same person, namely, Satyajit. In fact, the claim of 'the blood in my veins' is made in both *Jalsaghar* and *Shakha Proshakha*. As for Satyajit, he was the only son of his father, and he himself had only one son.

BISHWAMBHAR'S CINE-PORTRAIT

Foreign spectators — and even some Indian spectators today — find the *Apu* Trilogy too slow. The same thing can be observed regarding *Jalsaghar*. For instance, Stanley Kauffman wrote in 1963,

> (*The Music Room*) is a deeply felt, extremely tedious film. On the one hand, its Western derivations are patent (the Greek-revival mansion no more than the Chekhovian themes). On the other hand, its chief indigenous element, the Indian music, is simply uncongenial and tiresome to our ears. No doubt, these are excellent musical performances for those who understand them, but they make us start counting the bulbs in the theatre chandelier.[2]

On the other hand, Pauline Kael wrote in 1965,

> *The Music Room* has such grandeur in its best scenes that we must revise customary dramatic standards. By our usual standards it isn't a good movie: it's often crude and it's poorly constructed; but it's a great experience. It's a study of 'noblesse oblige'[3] carried to extremity, to a kind of aesthetic madness. . . . I was exasperated by the defects of *The Music Room* when I saw it; now, a month later, I realize that I will never forget it.[4]

What Does One Think?

Jalsaghar tells a very tragic story, but it is not a dramatic film. For instance, the sinking of the houseboat bringing Bishwambhar's wife and son back to the palace would have normally given occasion for dramatic scenes. Ray has avoided such scenes, because what he was doing was the cine-portrait of a man. There is even a sequence at the beginning of the film, when the zamindar has his portrait done by an artist. Chidananda Dasgupta aptly quotes Auguste Renoir:

> The hero portrayed at the moment when he is defying the enemy, or a woman shown in the hardest pain of labour, is not a suitable subject for a great painting, though men and women who have passed through such ordeals become great subjects when later on the artist can portray them in repose. The artist's task is not to stress this or that instant in a human being's existence, but *to make comprehensible the man in his entirety.*[5] (Emphasis added).

Whether a story is told at great speed or slowly is first of all a matter of sensitivity on the part of the filmmaker. On the other hand, the speed is part of the form. Beyond the style of the artist, there is the form proper to a specific type of narrative. That has to be recognized. That recognition itself is an important aspect of understanding a film. If I find a film slow, I must ask myself if it is a matter of style. If it is a matter of style, then the pace of the film is open to opinion. If that is not a matter of style, and if the film is a recognized masterpiece, then I must accept to be guided by the filmmaker, and begin to look at the film in a different way. That is exactly what Pauline Kael did.

Moreover, in the Indian tradition, the aim of art is to make the spectator experience particular moods giving pleasure or 'ananda'. Observe the obvious pleasure of the audience during the songs and the dance performed for them in the music room. The tediousness and boredom experienced by some spectators of the film often comes from a failure to place themselves in the proper disposition to experience pleasure. When one is solely concerned with plot development and narrative, one is likely to find much of Indian art tedious. There is a word in India to name the proper disposition to appreciate art, 'sahridaya', which means the quality of a heart that is attuned — through training and talent — to art.

In the first *jalsa* of the film, a lot is revealed about Bishwambhar and his guests. But in the second one, nothing much seems to be revealed. The people in the music room are not involved. One more instance of de-dramatization. But in this instance, the de-dramatization occurs at a peak moment of the film, that is, when the dead son of Bishwambhar is brought to him. What matters here is not the dramatic potential of the scene, but the reaction of Bishwambhar, as part of his cine-portrait.

Another point has been made regarding the songs and the dance that affect the pace of *Jalsaghar*. Marie Seton makes the point: these musical items were part of the story, not just entertainment. She explains:

> The concept and presentation of the two long classical songs and Kathak dance which provide the focusing sequences of the film challenged the whole convention of songs and dances in Indian cinema. Audiences in

India, conditioned to the introduction of songs and dances as entertainment interludes and dramatic and romantic stresses, had never before been confronted with a similar presentation to Ray's: classical singing and dancing as integral focal point of realistic sequences integral to the development of the story. Ray had not deviated from the re-creation of the atmosphere of the traditional *jalsa*.[6]

Marie Seton's point is well taken. Yet, more importantly, the songs and dance were part of the emotional pattern of the film.

Add to this that — to his credit — Satyajit Ray purposely sought the best artists available not just to enhance his film, but to preserve the art of these artists.[7]

Back to Bishwambhar's portrait. Long after the painter has finished his work, Bishwambhar looks at himself, at the finished portrait, placed alongside the portraits of his ancestors. He has a toast to the ancestors and then to himself. Once you pay attention to the portraits, you also notice the mirror. Often Bishwambhar looks at himself complacently in the mirror. The image in the mirror is a transitory image that will in time be fixed in a portrait. But not only Bishwambhar, the audience in the music room also is facing the same large mirror. And then, what if the film acts as a mirror in front of the spectator?

However, Bishwambhar's portrait is not just a painting of his appearance. He himself carries a self-image within. And his behaviour is an expression of the self-image. Through a depiction of Bishwambhar's actions, Ray seeks to make the spectator perceive the man's self-portrait.

Bishwambhar wants to be a chandelier, bright, unique, and exclusive in his society. He would like the world to be a lavish performance, with him to preside over it. That is a dream. But there are other sounds coming from close-by. Competing with the sound of the music room. The sound of an uninvited shehnai, the gross sound of trucks reducing to silence the gentle bells attached to Moti, the elephant. The sound of the electric generator feeding harsh light bulbs that make the flickering light of the candles 'passé' and redundant.

A new world arises, the world of Mahim Ganguly. Mahim has travelled a lot, while Bishwambhar can ask his secretary,

'Do I go anywhere?' Indeed, the zamindar has nothing to do with the new world, nor does he want to step out of his imaginary music room. For him, the emerging world is gross, unkempt, without roots, or, as Mahim says ironically, without a 'pedigree'. Like the light of the day — and of reality — electric light is unbearable to Bishwambhar.

In the end, Bishwambhar will give a final touch to his cine-portrait, in a self-destructive prowess, his last ride on his horse, appropriately named Toofan — the hurricane.

SYMBOLISM IN *JALSAGHAR*

Perhaps more than in any of his films, in *Jalsaghar* Ray has used objects and actions as symbols. The most obvious symbol is, of course, that of the chandelier. But there are also the portrait, either of Bishwambhar or of his ancestors; the white horse and the elephant; the contrast black and white or light and darkness, day and night; the mirror; the *jalsa* (concert) and the *jalsaghar* (music room).

Chandelier, portraits, mirror, and concert are all images associated with representation, with display. And the story of *Jalsaghar* is that of the transformation of a man into his own portrait. All his life Bishwambhar has displayed himself. Even his death was a show of prowess. The incident is rich in symbolism. The horse and the rider's garments are white. The horse is called Toofan (hurricane) — a possible allusion to the fatal night, when Bishwambhar's wife and child drowned in the river. The carcass of the boat lying on the riverside is black. It recalls, and may even be, the boat that capsized in the river on that stormy night.

This scene is one of perhaps only two dramatic moments of the film — the other being when Bishwambhar holds the hand of Mahim Ganguly with his cane to prevent him from being the first to give money to the dancer. The zamindar must make that gesture first.

Once the portrait — physically or figuratively — is finished, death takes over. That too is symbolized: when Bishwambhar contemplates his portrait on the wall, he observes a spider on it. He chases the spider with his walking stick, but as he touches the portrait, a strange, lifeless, sound is heard. The portrait is dead. On the contrary, the chandelier responds, as it were, to Bishwambhar's stick, when he touches the chandelier with it.

After four years of neglect, the chandelier is covered with cobwebs. Bishwambhar, pierces through the cobweb of time and touches the crystal of the chandelier. A lively sound is heard, and the music starts again.

Speaking more generally, Henri Micciollo points out three aspects in the symbolism of the chandelier. He wrote:

> The first aspect concerns the opposition between white and black, appearance and reality. Bishwambhar's dream, externalized in the *jalsa*, consists in dazzling, in all the senses of the term, his guests. Sparkling with lights, music, dance movements, drinks, the *jalsa* negates the night, inverses the signs, and creates — precarious yet fascinating — the reign of the appearance. . . . The second aspect is that of the 'mise en scène', the staging, as well as the framed vision in either the mirror or the portrait. Everything except reality.[8]

Micciollo explains the use made by Ray of simple symbols. At the beginning of the storm, when Bishwambhar waits for his wife and son to come back and join the *jalsa*, a small boat placed on a bookshelf is overturned by the wind. The spectator immediately senses that an accident has happened. The spectator might see that symbolism as rather crude. But Bishwambhar does not perceive that symbolism. Since the boat is white, he sees it as a symbol of his dream, and he quietly replaces the boat in its standing position. A few moments later, when a black insect has fallen in his glass of wine, Bishwambhar immediately senses the disaster and goes out to enquire.

The third aspect of symbolism mentioned by Micciollo is seen in the very camera work of the film. Ray's aim is not so much to create the illusion of reality, as to suggest the reality of Bishwambhar's illusion. That is best shown when Bishwambhar enters the music room after a gap of four years without *jalsa*.

> Bishwambhar is seen in a sharp top down shot, between the columns of

crane movement, but he is still seen from a high angle shot while he inspects the room.

At the very end of the film, after Bishwambhar's death on the riverside, the camera comes back in the music room and shows the chandelier:

> But for whom does the chandelier shine in this last appearance along with the word 'end'? No doubt for some Mahim Ganguli . . . but that does not matter! The chandelier comes to close the film, and to remind the spectator that the imaginary world does not die since it constitutes the very essence of cinema.[9]

CONCLUSION

Bishwambhar himself is the symbol of a generation of men whose ambition is to live up to their image. *Noblesse oblige*. He is also the symbol of those who take refuge in art.

Jalsaghar is a period film. It tells a lot about a certain class of people. But we should not be impervious to what it says about us today. Pauline Kael has put it this way:

> (*The Music Room*) recalls the film of *The Magnificent Ambersons* and, of course, *The Cherry Orchard* but, more painfully it calls up hideous memories of our own expansive gestures, our own big-role playing. We are forced to see the recklessness and egomania of our greatest moments — and at the same time we are forced to see the sordid banality of being practical.[10]

As Auguste Renoir (p.49) said, the role of the artist is 'to make comprehensible the man in his entirety'. But since 'the man' is always social, the role of the artist is — if I may paraphrase Renoir — to make comprehensible society in its entirety. That aspect of the role of the artist is symbolized in Ray not so much by the brush of the painter as by the stethoscope of the doctor. Yet, the stethoscope, if I am correct, is seen only twice in Ray's oeuvre. First in *Pather Panchali* — when Durga is fatally ill. Second, it is seen most conspicuously at the beginning of *Gana Shatru*. But it is not used at all during that film. It remains a symbol. The stethoscope permits you to listen to a person's heartbeat or to his breathing. In Ray, the stethoscope is a symbol of the role of the artist in society: to listen to the heartbeat of the world and interpret it, 'to make the society comprehensible in its entirety'.

Chhabi Biswas, one of the greatest actors of the Bengali cinema, the man who played the role of Bishwambhar in *Jalsaghar*, died in a car accident, his car having been run into by a truck. Satyajit Ray received the news in a Kolkata film studio (he was then editing *Abhijan*).

> What a ridiculous thing, muttered Satyajit with indignation — that fate should play such an ironic trick just days after Biswas' performance had been seen by international jurors and critics — he was referring to *Devi* — and just when he had the biggest role of his life! — *Kanchenjungha* was still running in Calcutta after five weeks.[11]

Interestingly, Marie Seton, who wrote about that incident, has entitled her biography of Satyajit Ray, 'portrait' of a director.

About Chhabi Biswas' death, one might add, paraphrasing Ray, 'What an ironic trick of fate! Biswas died in a car accident, after he had enacted the death of Bishwambhar, whose horse took fright while rushing headlong towards the carcass of a boat lying on the riverside.'

NOTES

1. The opening sequence of *Death in Venice* is very similar. While we hear some music, we see a musician sitting on the deck of a ship. And then we realize that the music we heard was the music he was hearing in his mind. Luchino Visconti, who was then 65 years old, made *Death in Venice* in 1971, thus 13 years after *Jalsaghar*. Ray was 37 when he made *Jalsaghar*. Given the popularity of *Jalsaghar* in Europe, one may wonder whether the opening sequence of *Death in Venice* was an homage to Satyajit Roy. However, the Visconti film most often mentioned abroad in connection with *Jalsaghar* is *The Leopard* (1963).
2. Stanley Kauffman, *A World on Film*, criticism and comment. New York, 1966, Harper & Row Publishers, pp. 373. That passage is quoted by Andrew Robinson, at the beginning of his chapter on *The Music Room*, in *Satyajit Ray: The Inner Eye*, p. 113.
3. French expression: one who belongs to the noble class is expected to do certain things, in a certain style.

3. French expression: one who belongs to the noble class is expected to do certain things, in a certain style.
4. Pauline Kael, *I Lost It At The Movies*, Boston/Toronto, Atlantic Monthly Press Book, 1954/1965, p. 251.
5. Chidananda Dasgupta, *The Cinema of Satyajit Ray*, New Delhi, National Book Trust, 2001, p. 61. Auguste Renoir in *Renoir, My Father*, by Jean Renoir.
6. Marie Seton, *Portrait of A Director: Satyajit Ray*, Delhi, Vikas Publications, 1971, p. 149.
7. Charles Tesson, *Satyajit Ray* (Series – *Cahiers du Cinéma*, Collection 'Auteurs') Paris, *Cahiers du cinéma*, 1992, pp. 58-9. I owe more to Tesson than I can acknowledge in this simple reference. In particular, Tesson's writings have helped me to (a) take Ray more seriously, and (b) pay more attention to sound in Ray's cinema.
8. Henri Micciollo, *Satyajit Ray*, Lausanne, Editions l'Age d'Homme, 1981. See pp. 63-5.
9. Ibid., p. 65.
10. Pauline Kael, op. cit. (n. 3), p. 251.
11. Marie Seton, op. cit., p. 281.

CHAPTER 6

*Aranyer Din Ratri**

Days and Nights in the Forest, 1969

The Memory Game and The Dance of Life

INTRODUCTION: *ARANYER DIN RATRI* TODAY

WHY *ARANYER DIN RATRI* today, as we celebrate the fiftieth anniversary of *Pather Panchali*? Simply because *Aranyer Din Ratri* is a Ray film. You could talk with great relevance about any of Satyajit Ray's films on the occasion of the *Pather Panchali* celebration. For, the films of this great master, whatever their diversity, show an astounding unity of themes and of social concerns. What makes *Aranyer Din Ratri* so appealing today is that, as in the case of *Pather Panchali,* one finds that the film still moves one profoundly so many years after it was made. Again, as in the case of *Pather Panchali, Aranyer Din Ratri* takes on an even deeper significance when seen in the light of the later Ray films till the last one, *Agantuk*. Indeed, not only *Agantuk,* but also the other two films that constitute, with *Agantuk* the 'Heart Trilogy',[1] summarize and expand Ray's life message. They thus confirm what might have appeared only as a possible meaning in Ray's previous films. For instance, the references to civilization in *Aranyer Din Ratri* might pass unnoticed or even appear a little far-fetched. But, as I shall show, in the light of *Agantuk* they call for full attention.

*Special issue of *Chitravas* on *Aranyer Din Ratri,* by the North Kolkata Film Society, vol. 40 (nos. 1-4), January 2005-December 2005, published on the occasion of the Book Fair, 2006, Kolkata.

In *Pather Panchali*, the train is of paramount importance as a symbol of the life journey. The train appears in most Ray films, and it comes at least once in *Aranyer Din Ratri*, as one of those pauses that characterize Ray's cinema, giving a moment for reflection. The journey undertaken by Apu in *Pather Panchali* does not end in *Apur Sansar*, with Apu's return to Nischindipur, his natal village. The journey ends in tribal Bengal, and eventually in the cave of the heart, in *Agantuk*. When Asim drives to a rural area of Bihar, is he not somehow Apu on his way to his final destination, Santiniketan? Is not the full significance of the tribal dance in *Aranyer Din Ratri* revealed in *Agantuk*? In *Aranyer Din Ratri*, Asim is fascinated by a tribal dance, but he does not join in as the young woman does in *Agantuk*. He is not even tempted to do so. In fact, he is not ready. And when, somewhat inebriated, he keeps repeating, 'What a life!' is he not being challenged by the unvanquished mystery of life (the Aparajito of Bibhutibhushan's novel) to become the unvanquished man, the Aparajito of Ray's film of that name?

It is not that the mystery of Bibhutibhushan's novel has disappeared in Ray's films. Much to the contrary. Apu and Durga are fascinated by the mystery of modern technology: the train and the telephone. In *Aranyer Din Ratri*, master Tublu is fascinated by the animals around the house and by the circus, very much like the boy, Satyaki and his young friends in *Aguntuk* are fascinated by the mystery of the moon and the sun presented to them by Uncle Manomohan Mitra, the 'Mind Enchanting Friend'. How not to see duplicates of Apu in these two young boys? One more example of the continuity of themes in Ray.

The themes characteristic of Satyajit Ray and his lucid, serene, social concern are found now in Sandip Ray's *Nishi Japon*. Does not one feel at home in the 'English' cottage of *Nishi Japon*, accessible through the bamboo bridge? The same type of situation, the same concern for the human as in *Aranyer Din Ratri*. Though a distinct film, *Nishi Japon* belongs to the same film family.

CULTURED NATURE

Ray once said, 'I find myself trying, through my films, to trace the underlying pattern that binds this life together'.[2] In this film, obviously, the pattern that binds is love. But the protagonists do not know how to love. Love might appear something *natural*, but always the practice of love is *cultural*. This film is indeed about culture. Charles Tesson, has noted that the title sequence of *Aranyer Din Ratri*, with views of the forest through the letters of the title, is a pictorial language, saying, 'in this film we look at nature through culture'.

But while Nature with a capital N is nowhere, nature is now here. As for culture, it is particular and specific. In *Aranyer Din Ratri*, Ray does not deal with Culture but with the culture of Bengal in the early 1970s. In Asim's words, each of the four youths is expected to live up to the ideal of the 'middle class Bengali conventional good boy'.

To Satyajit Ray, a city man, nature is manifest in rural areas. And tribal dances are supreme examples of cultured nature. Their rhythm and simple melodies enrapture a whole community. One's ability to respond to a tribal dance is an expression of one's own cultured nature, dormant in each one's heart. That is what Ray showed in *Agantuk*.

However, city man too often disregards — as in the case of *Aranyer Din Ratri* — his fellow tribal or peasant, unaware that in doing so, he disregards his own nature. The journey to the cave of the heart begins with a return to nature, and, in the same movement, a return to one's heart. In the light of *Agantuk*, this journey is already well delineated in *Aranyer Din Ratri*.

THE MEMORY GAME

For Rabindranath Tagore, memory is the faculty that remembers facts, but also, being a powerful editor, the faculty that forgets some facts, alters others, and enhances yet others. Tagore has emphasized the important role of memory in artistic creation And there is no greater art than the art of living. Thus life is made of our memories as they evolve through our encounters with events and especially with others. A game of sorts. A social game.

In *Aranyer Din Ratri,* you have four friends; in *Shakha Proshakha* you have four brothers. In both the films the four protagonists, friends or brothers, are brought in a special situation where they live together and are forced to commune at a deeper level. One exercise in communion, very 'cultured' indeed, is the memory game that takes place in both the films.

The memory game, as it is called — in English — in *Aranyer Din Ratri,* is interesting as a game. Moreover, it provides an impromptu list of the great men and women that inhabit the collective memory of the group. Consider: Rabindranath, Karl Marx, Cleopatra, Atulya Ghosh, Helen of Troy, Shakespeare, Mao Zedong, Don Bradman, Rani Rashmoni, Robert Kennedy, Tekchand Thakur, Napoleon, Mumtaz Mahal. It might be revealing to study that motley group of icons.

In *Aranyer Din Ratri,* the game eventually turns into an exercise in love: Aparna allows Asim to win so as not to humiliate him. For, Asim has a particularly proud 'nature'. He is aware of it: he feels he is a VIP. But at the same time, he well understands that the higher he rises, the lower he falls. It is known that he has bribed the caretaker; he was seen bathing; he was seen drunk in the night, dancing what he called 'a tribal twist' on the road; he would have lost in the memory game had not Aparna given up so that he could win. Love gradually overcomes Asim's pride and permits him to relate to Aparna who, in the end, gives him her phone number, for a continued relationship.[4]

Aparna too suffers. She is haunted by the remembrance of the suicide of her brother, and the death of her mother in a fire. Her love for Asim helps her to forget herself and care for Asim. In the end, most of the protagonists care for the 'caretaker' whose wife is so ill that he had to accept a bribe for her sake. And in this common concern for the 'caretaker', is expressed a common love, a feeling which transcends nature and yet heals the wounds of nature.

Aparna declares herself defeated in the memory game out

of concern for Asim. On the other hand, Sanjay notices that Jaya might want a pillow, and he gets one for her. Thus, there is a level of the game deeper than the fun of it. Relationships are quietly woven while the game progresses. But once these relationships are established, the memory game continues between the partners: Asim and Aparna 'memorize' their past; so do Sanjay and Jaya. Even Sekhar, who started off the 'game' from the moment the group left the city, develops a friendship — somewhat unexpectedly — with Hari. Towards the end of the film, after Lakha has assaulted Hari, Sekhar helps the wounded athlete back to the guest-house, and at the time of leaving the place, he announces to Hari that his wounds would heal once he is back in the city. Strangely, the outing itself was meant to heal the wounds of each protagonist. The memory game, extended as I have just explained, has revealed other, deeper, wounds that have yet to heal. No doubt, the relationships developed during the outing will contribute to the healing process.

It is not surprising to observe that the memory game, which has such depth, is marvellously crafted. It is indeed a masterpiece of filmmaking. First of all, the game itself binds the group together in a single exercise that is emphasized by the circular photographic work. But once the six protagonists are bundled together, they can be examined in pairs. From that moment, a skillful parallel montage carries on the memory game at a more personal level. The montage is accelerated as the segments showing each pair become shorter and shorter, thus keeping the group tightly knit together while examining each pair. Intercut into the parallel montage are short segments of a tribal dance. While these segments provide short pauses for reflection, they also remind us of the desired outcome of the game: to reach inward to the source of one's humanity. Most of the protagonists seem to evolve towards a more humane life. But, for Sanjay and Jaya, the memory game leads to a painful no-win situation. Sanjay, shows himself incapable of fulfilling the emotional need of Jaya, and thus is a loser as much as the young lady is, deeply wounded as she already is by the mysterious suicide of her husband, the brother of Aparna.

CIVILIZATION

Throughout his career, Satyajit Ray has been concerned with the larger issue of civilization, which he perceived as being in a state of crisis. That concern was affirmed in Ray's film on Rabindranath Tagore (1961). In that film he quoted a passage from Tagore's essay, 'Crisis in Civilization' (1941). At the end of his filmmaking career, Ray again took up the theme in *Agantuk*. World War II had led Tagore to believe that the light of civilization, which the West proved unable to enlighten the world with, might now come from the East. Ray admired Tagore but never felt compelled to follow him. His own view was that the light of civilization would come neither from the West nor from the East, but would be discovered in the cave of the heart of each man and woman. In *Aranyer Din Ratri*, there are a few allusions to civilization. In one of his histrionics, Sekhar dramatically burns up a newspaper in front of his companions, and solemnly announces that he has thereby severed all links with civilization. Later on, he discusses the atom bomb issue. It is difficult not to relate this discussion to the passage in *Agantuk* where, Uncle Mitra describes present-day civilization as a society in which by simply pressing a button one can destroy a whole city, and can even do it without being disturbed.

THE DANCE OF LIFE

Human life, at its best, is a dance. For, dance integrates the human — body and soul — into one graceful movement. As exemplified by the tribal villagers in the film, dance is essentially social, transcending individual associations. In dance is felt, both physically and psychologically, one's belonging to the group.

Dance intoxicates the dancers until their individual egos merge into the personality of the community. One might speak here of the *sadharanikaran*, or generalization, described by Bharat Muni in the *Natya Shastra*. It is no surprise that some Indian traditions see God as the Nataraja, the cosmic dancer, and invoke God, chanting 'Sivanayama'. The invitation, in *Aranyer Din Ratri,* to join the dance of life will be accepted later by Anila in *Agantuk*.

OF SNOBBERY AND OTHER TYPES OF MEANNESS

When they arrived at the guest-house, the four youths felt there was no need to book the house in advance, although the need for prior booking was clearly stipulated on a board in front of the property. They felt that the caretaker could be bribed into cooperation. They felt that the Conservator would make an exception in their favour. To their surprise the latter asked them, 'Can you give me one reason why I should do so?' There are many more instances of their arrogance and lack of concern for others. The priority was, especially in the case of Asim, the leader, not to lose face.

On their arrival at the guest-house, the four men did not have a high opinion of the caretaker. They assumed that he was corrupt. And, when he did take the money offered him, one of the men sighed, 'Thank God for corruption!' That superficial judgement by unscrupulous men is questioned when, later in the film, Aparna tells Asim that she once stayed in that same guest-house and she considered that the caretaker was an honest man. Later on, Aparna even asked Asim if he knew that the caretaker's wife was sick. Ashim knew. The caretaker had told him more than once. But in answer to Aparna's query he replied that he and his companions knew, but they did not have the courage to enquire further. In other words, they did not care. Aparna is sensitive to that lack of concern on their part. She eventually takes Asim to the caretaker's house and makes him see the sick woman.

Hari loses his wallet and immediately thinks that Lakha has stolen it. In fact, Hari himself had lost the wallet while playing badminton. But Lakha proves that, indeed, he could be up to what he was assumed to be. Having spied Hari making love to

Duli, Lakha almost kills Hari and steals the famous wallet. Throughout the film a strong mentality of class distinction inspires the attitudes and actions of the four 'city' men. For instance, on their way to the guest-house, when they ask a group of villagers if there is a guest-house in the vicinity, Lakha tells them there is one close by. Asim asks the man to board the car and guide them to the guest-house. As Lakha is about to get on to the front seat next to Sekhar, the latter directs him to sit behind under the pretext of not crowding the driver's seat, to which Asim, who drives the car, smiles. Asim too, deals contemptuously with Lakha, being over-exacting in claiming the change on small transactions he has entrusted Lakha with. Even, as he receives the change, he remarks, 'Who knows how much you are keeping for yourself.'

CONCLUSION: RAY'S SOCIAL CONCERN

The first image of *Gana Shatru* includes a stethoscope. Charles Tesson[5] sees it as a symbol of Ray's cinema, a cinema that takes the pulse of the world. And that is exactly what *Gana Shatru* does. Here, in *Aranyer Din Ratri*, as the four young men leave the city in a car, Sekhar is told to look out of the window and immediately the blurred image of the forest appears. That image is then covered with a black surface into which the titles are cut out, so that through the titles the image of the forest continues to roll on. This film too is an exercise in awareness. What Ray guides the spectator to is an awareness of his or her society. Some scholars feel that Ray excels in understatement. Agreed, he does not shout, but it would be difficult to say that he is not clear. Indeed, *Aranyer Din Ratri* is quite clear in its depiction of the Bengali society at the time the film was made. The comments offered above show the exquisite sensitivity of Ray to his society.

Pauline Kael has noted regarding *Aranyer Din Ratri,* 'The subtext [of this film] is perhaps the subtlest, most plangent study of the cultural tragedy of imperialism; the young men are self-parodies — clowns who ape the worst snobberies of the British'.[5]

One might ask, Why should Ray, and after him, Pauline Kael, pick on the British? *Aranyer Din Ratri* is a film of 1969, twenty-two years after India won her independence. By the time he made *Agantuk* (1991), his last film, the Bengali youths did not need to clown anybody's snobbery. Their own stance regarding Ray's 'Heart Trilogy' revealed their mindset.

NOTES

1. I have analysed the three films of the 'Heart Trilogy' in my book *Communication Cinema Development: From Morosity to Hope*, New Delhi, Manohar, 1998. These film discussions are included in the present book.
2. From the commentary written and spoken by Satyajit Ray for B. D. Garga's two-reeler, 'Creative Artists of India: Satyajit Ray' (1963). Quoted in *Montage*, nos. 5/6, July 1966. See 'Why I Make Films'.
3. I deliberately do not discuss film language in *Aranyer Din Ratri*, yet I would like to mention here an occasional shot composition reminiscent of television. In the dialogue between Aparna and Asim just commented upon, the two protagonists are often talking together while both are looking, not towards each other, but towards the camera.
4. Charles Tesson, 'Le Bruit du Monde', in *Cahiers du Cinéma*, no. 422, July-August 1989, pp. 20-5.
5. http://www.satyajitray.org/films/Aranyerdinratri.htm 8/17/05.

CHAPTER 7

*Pratidwandi**
The Adversary, 1970

Rebel With A Cause!

INTRODUCTION

PRATIDWANDI, an important film—thematically and aesthetically — makes great demands on the spectator. It is to the credit of Mr. Ray to have dared to make these demands. It is to the credit of the appreciative audience to grant them. In fact, the pleasing aesthetic quality of this film helps the audience to follow it with interest and to understand it. For, apart from the sustained and fine humour that livens it up, this film has none of the so-called compromises: no song, no dance, no star (only masterly-directed, excellent actors!), no romance. The film is short, lasting about one hour and forty minutes. It uses flashbacks, flashforwards, and flashes into present inner-thought — thus, intermingling past, present and future — without any of the conventional transition devices. Moreover, it has no exciting story to tell. Some publicity devices and, more so, the opening sequence of the film itself, concur to give a wrong idea of what this otherwise complex and austere film actually is. I do not know what the full implications of the Bengali term *Pratidwandi* are. I recognize that the expression 'The Adversary' (or 'The Rival', as some have it) is a correct translation. But I feel that, rendered thus into English, the title of the film suggests that *Pratidwandi* is an action-film. As for the image of a young

*G. Roberge, *Mass Communication and Man,* 1971, Lesson 35, pp. 153-73. Original version.

man holding a pistol, which was used — fortunately in a limited way — for publicity, it is a tasteless 'trick' for which the publicity manager may be forgiven. What is more serious still, is the style of the opening sequence. In my view, this style does not fit in with the rest of the picture. The funeral rites in negative,[1] the title *Pratidwandi* alternately flashing on the screen, the long bus ride, all this prepares you to watch a film of action. You feel that things are going to happen in this movie. But none of the things that might happen do occur. Indeed there is an action unfolding. But this action evolves at a much deeper level than that of the events portrayed on the screen. This action is the slow and inner transformation of a young man. The emotional tension created by the opening shots is transmuted, and in fact, sustained. But the passage from one type of tension to a deeper one does not really fulfil the expectation created by the opening sequence. As the opening sequence recedes, the spectator recognizes the style of Mr. Ray at his best. Seeing the film in the context of Mr. Ray's career, *Pratidwandi* stands as 'Aparajito 1970', The Unvainquished 1970. Ever since *Mahanagar* (1963), I have longed for another contemporary city film that would also have the mastery of the *Apu* films. *Pratidwandi* has not disappointed me.

GENRE OF THE FILM

Pratidwandi is not an action film. It is a meditation.[2] In fact, the film can be said to greatly suffer from a lack of plot. But to criticize the film on that ground is to imply that a film ought to have a plot. The extraordinary quality of the *Apu* trilogy should convince anybody that this is false. For a film need not be a drama in the Greek sense — with the necessity of a well-delineated plot. Robert Bresson, for instance, claimed that in films 'theatre destroys cinema'. Furthermore, why should a film made in India be judged by the standards that the Greek Aristotle established in his *Poetics*, on the basis of the famous dramas of his time? Leaving aside set ideas about what a film or a theatrical performance should be, one has to receive a film as it comes to him/her and criticize it by its own standards and terms. *Pratidwandi* is not a story in the usual sense. It is a reflection on a process. To make this fact more apparent, Mr. Ray — was it an after-thought? — makes the film end in the form of a letter. *Pratidwandi* belongs not so much to the dramatic 'genre', but to that of the epistolary novel. For, it can be argued that the whole film is a letter. But this cannot be conclusively demonstrated, because there is no indication within the film itself that it is a letter. Hence, we cannot know from the start that this is so. However, in retrospect, the ending helps us understand the complex structure of the film. In the framework of a letter, the 'flashes' back or forward and the different levels of consciousness are more easily understood. It seems to me that, concluding the film, the Bengali 'iti' ('the end'), the usual ending of a letter is at once brilliant and faulty. It is faulty because we should have known before that the film is a letter. This could have been established at the very beginning — for instance, using some of the shots immediately following the overturning of the table up to the time where Siddhartha reaches his room in the hotel, which could have 'frozen', thus throwing us into the past. At the end of the film, Siddhartha could be seen once more coming to the hotel after the interview and the frame that was frozen in the beginning could now be defrozen. From there the film could have carried on until the ending 'iti'. However, the task of the film critic is not to re-make films according to his/her judgement, but to understand them and point out where they fail as well as where they succeed.

Although it is a possible fault, the ending of the film is nonetheless brilliant. For it is difficult to end a film that has no plot or story. The problem of the filmmaker in *Pratidwandi* was to close a film that had reached a peak of emotional outburst, and to bring about a certain respite. This was done with remarkable economy of means, as I shall show later on. The best moments of Mr. Ray's film are those when an emotion is generated in the viewer as a result of his identifying with a character, and of seeing things as that character sees them.

The lesser moments occur when Mr. Ray makes his actors 'express' or exteriorize their feelings. The emotional tension in *Pratidwandi* is such that when it comes to outward actions, there is a tendency to exaggerate action so as to make it match the inner feelings. This is what happens at the end of the film when, Siddhartha expresses his feelings towards the selection board. This is also what happens when Siddhartha is seen imagining that he is shooting his sister's boss. These two sequences jar (however striking they may be![3]) in a film which is episodic, descriptive and biographical — exactly as *Pather Panchali* was. The film is not concerned with what the people do,[4] but with what they are. *Pratidwandi* is an analysis of characters through a representation of what they do, how they appear, and how they feel in their particular circumstances, and of what happens to them. This approach to the subject seems to be in the tradition of the *Natya Sastra* rather than that of Greek art. Through outward representation, the 'natya' seeks to generate in the spectator very specific emotions. Is it not what *Pratidwandi* beautifully achieves? You do not understand Siddhartha's situation much better, you do not learn of possible solutions to his problems, but you feel an intense sympathy for him, and, what is more important, you feel that in the end, Siddhartha is not crushed by his difficult circumstances.

CHARACTER ANALYSIS

The film is structured around three interviews, with a recurring walk-in-the-street sequence as a sort of punctuation. In the first interview, Siddhartha is rejected. He himself rejects the offer of a job in the second interview. He violently breaks away from the people of the third interview, to finally accept the job offered him in the previous one. Meanwhile, a set of relationships are slowly described. The attitude of Siddhartha is revealed with regard to each person he encounters. In general, each of these — except two of them — suffers from one or another form of alienation, from something Siddhartha sees as some sort of prostitution. This is what he does not want to fall prey to. He does not want to give himself away, to betray what he feels he is. But this is not possible, as is explained later.

His sister Sutapa, his brother Tunu, his friend Adinath, Sutapa's boss, Keya's parents, all have made their choices and have alienated themselves in some way or other: ambition and luxury, politics, prostitution, immorality, selfishness. The two exceptions to this are Keya and the elder Nareshda, whom Siddhartha meets in a restaurant and who first lets him know about the possibility of a job as a medical representative. This man is the only adult Siddhartha can relate to, although the two do not completely agree. Keya is very young in comparison to Siddhartha but she is, precisely, an incarnation of the innocence to which Siddhartha seeks to hang on. While Siddhartha relates rather easily to people of his age, there is a distance between him and the adults, which is emphasized by the physical distance the camera shows between him and Keya's parents or Sutapa's boss. The spectators of *Pratidwandi* are made to observe the interviews. They are introduced to the network of Siddhartha's relationships, and they are led into an analysis of the lad's character. The film flashes Siddhartha back into the past, invades his dreams and reveals even his innermost thoughts. In this way, the spectator gains an insight into the boy's personality. It appears that Siddhartha understands Tunu's present behaviour against the background of past incidents that affected both brothers differently (seeing chickens butchered, for instance). There is an unusual longing in Siddhartha for his lost childhood: his past relationship with his sister when she confidently called him 'Dada' and shared with him the simple joy of a bird's song. But gone are those days. The dream sequences reveal Siddhartha's anxieties: fear of violent death, a negative attitude towards the interviewers, concern for Tunu's life, for his sister's future — even for Keya who might turn out to be a 'bad' girl. While he is awake, Siddhartha's inner thoughts are revealed by his voice heard off-screen. The second interview, in particular, shows his childish attachment to the city of Calcutta, an attachment which keeps him inactive. Calcutta is for him like a maternal womb from which he absolutely refuses to be removed.

Finally, the opening flash-back on the funeral rites (which was perhaps unnecessary) and, more so, the repeated allusions to his father's death, show how Siddhartha, although aged 25, was and remained utterly dependent on his parents for the realization of all his career plans. This situation of dependence is not characteristic of Calcutta youth. It is a contemporary phenomenon in urban and industrialized societies. The protraction of social and psychological adolescence beyond the biological causes acute problems of personality. A few times in the film, Siddhartha is seen observing people in terms of his medical knowledge. Of course, this is very amusing. But at the same time, it is an indication that he is either still incapable of entering into normal relationships with certain persons (an attractive girl, for instance) or simply refuses to do so (Keya's aunt, for instance).

Progressively and in an apparently simple manner, the many facets of Siddhartha's subtle character are revealed in all their complexity[5] and inner tension. The camera keeps watching Dhritiman Chatterjee's meditative face. In his performance, Chatterjee looks energetic, yet hesitant; idealistic, yet helpless; personal in his thinking, yet inactive. The failure to work out these contradictions leads to yet higher emotional tensions. However, what is most striking in Siddhartha's character is his appalling lack of social consciousness. All in him is utterly individualized and self-centred. The only social act he carries out in the whole film is joining other people in beating a driver, who, in effect, has perhaps committed no crime other than working for a wealthier person than himself. Siddhartha's joining in the beating is totally irrational, as he has seen nothing of the incident that led to it. Nor is there much glory in twelve people beating one man. This lack of positive interest in Siddhartha for social matters is so complete that this aspect of his character will have to be discussed separately later on.

THE PLACE OF *PRATIDWANDI* IN RAY'S OEUVRE

In my view, Mr. Ray's career can be divided into two overlapping cycles. The first cycle starts with the Apu trilogy and culminates in *Charulata.* The second cycle starts with *Mahanagar* and is unfinished to this day.[6] The first cycle was a meditation on the Bengali people, seen somewhat romantically, through the remoteness that time and space can create. Whatever the beauty of the films of the first cycle, they did not relate to the heart of contemporary Bengal, Calcutta. *Mahanagar* preluded a new phase in Mr. Ray's meditation. In *Mahanagar*, it was no more the people of the past and of remote places, but the people of the city who were the object of that meditation. But I believe *Mahanagar* had no important sequel (I had not seen *Chiriakhana* and *Aranyer Din Ratri*, and, of course, I made allowance for these films). *Pratidwandi* is indeed a perfect sequel to *Mahanagar.* There is a similarity in the very start of both films: both open with a streetcar and a bus, respectively. This reminds one of the recurring presence of the train in the *Apu* Trilogy.

The formalistic preoccupation of the trilogy found complete expression in *Charulata*, Mr. Ray's most beautiful film. *Mahanagar* marked a change in style, which had been forgotten in *Charulata* but was recaptured in *Pratidwandi. Mahanagar* was not set in a time and place that would give easy occasion for refined beauty. With *Pratidwandi* Mr. Ray appears still more completely free from formalistic preoccupations.

Yet, the style of the film is perfectly appropriate to its subject matter, and the film itself is beautiful. It is not, as in *Charulata*, the beauty of maturity or of a period that has achieved a certain perfection. The beauty of *Pratidwandi* is that of truth, sincerity, and accuracy in the depiction of what we know our society to be, an image that we either love or reject. The figure of Siddhartha also, whose expression is always kept at a low key (except for the two outbursts of anger), is extremely fascinating.

Is it fanciful to perceive a continuity between the *Apu* trilogy and the city films (*Mahanagar* and *Pratidwandi*) ? The detached art of the trilogy with its concern for formal beauty, with its sympathy for the object being depicted in the film is being transferred on to persons and events that are close to us in time and space. But is the personal attitude of the filmmaker altered? I believe it is not. The urgency of the new themes makes the detachment of the artist the more striking. I shall have to discuss this point when I comment on the significance of the film.

The only adult person who shows Siddhartha genuine kindness and understanding is Nareshda. Mr. Ray has lent him his voice. Of course, this may have been an accidental necessity of the production. Nonetheless, one cannot help feeling that Mr. Ray is talking through Nareshda. It will be partly on the content of what is then said that the 'commitment' of the film may be assessed. In his first films Mr. Ray was very Tagorean. Now, retaining the same sensitivity, with perhaps even greater mastery over the film medium, Mr. Ray takes on non-Tagorean themes which he treats in a more personal manner. Up to *Pratidwandi, Charulata* is the last Tagore story, which Mr. Ray put into a film. With *Mahanagar*, and especially with *Pratidwandi*, Ray stands more completely on his own: it is at once a greater freedom and a greater responsibility.

THE EMOTIONAL PATTERN OF *PRATIDWANDI*

Watching a film like *Pratidwandi* is to experience a variety of emotions. These emotions arise and recede in us with a rhythmic continuity. The movie-spectator is like a balloon, which the filmmaker causes to inflate and to deflate. As the film unfolds before us, we are drawned by that movement. Part of our enjoyment in movie watching consists in this experience of emotions. Now, a good film has a definite emotional pattern that can be perceived in isolation. The pattern can be graphically represented. Some theoreticians of film-aesthetics have suggested an explanation of the experience of watching a film in terms of the emotional pattern of the film. However useful this approach may be, it tends to excessive formalism and appears inadequate to account for the overall complexity of the aesthetic experience (for, music, theatre, dance, even the plastic arts too have emotional patterns). Yet, it is possible and even necessary to look at a film as possessing an organic emotional pattern. For, this pattern is like an inner form that makes all the parts of the whole take their places in relation to the other parts. When the film has little plot or story, the emotional pattern is all the more important in order to give the film its unity. If we jot down a line representing the emotional pattern of *Pratidwandi,* we find that this line rises to three major peaks, and lowers to moments of respite. As a graph, the line could take this shape:

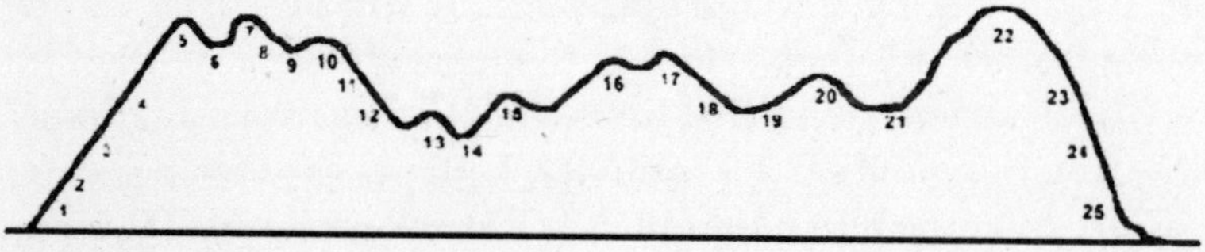

1. Funeral rite, 2. Face of *Pratidwandi,* 3. Titles, 4. Bus ride, 5. Office, 6. Tailor, 7. First interview, 8 Nareshda, 9. Chemist, 10. Bomb, 11. Watch, 12. Hippies, 13. Friend, 14. Swedish film, 15. Home, 16. Keya's boss, 18. Friend, birds, 19. Prostitute, Keya, 20. Skyscraper, 21. Last interview, 22. Posters, paddy fields, 23. Face of *Pratidwandi,* 24. Funeral rite, 25. 'iti'.

EDITING OF *PRATIDWANDI*

The emotional pattern that we have described in the preceding paragraph must be sustained in visual and aural terms. The emotional flow is like the soul of the film, the audio-visual parts, its body. But how are the limbs fastened one to the other? To discuss this question is to discuss the editing of the film. For, finally, the total emotional pattern is carried by the total image (here, by 'image', I mean anything that is perceived by the senses — therefore, sound and image) that the film constitutes.

In a film like *Pratidwandi,* where you have practically no story to link the units of the film together, it was necessary that the filmmaker should find means of joining his pieces of film so as to create a continuous audio-visual flow.

Editing, camera angles, camera movements, and movement in the frame, all of these contribute to creating a continuous movement. Of all the factors, cutting and editing are paramount. The reason why one remains glued to the screen from the beginning to the end is not just the fact that the film shows interesting people and events. The film holds our attention thanks to the continuity of images it weaves together. Along with them is the emotional pattern in which we become engrossed. But first of all, the filmmaker has to make us look and listen in order to make us hear and see as he wishes.

Pratidwandi exemplifies a large number of fine 'cuts'.[7] Here are but a few of them:

(*a*) *Jump-cut*

In this type of cut an action is initiated, and, without any transition, the same action is shown at a later stage, jumping, as it were, over a part of the process. This hastens the pace of the film and eliminates unnecessary descriptions.

Example: Keya: 'Want some tea?' Cut to Siddhartha drinking tea. Again after the last interview, Siddhartha is seen walking in a lane, and the word 'Hotel' can be read. As Siddhartha enters the hotel, there is a cut to him handing some registration papers to the hotel clerk.

(*b*) *Cut to close-up*

An action is depicted, and as it terminates there is a cut to a close-up of an object (usually). This is a strong punctuation that helps you forget what you just saw and nearly hypnotizes you, holding your attention for what follows.

Example: Siddhartha washes his hands after he has changed a fuse at Keya's house. There follows a cut to a glass of fruit juice.

(*c*) *Cut from close-up*

This has an effect similar to that of (b).

Example: during the last interview, twice there is a cut from a rather close shot of buckets in which cigarettes butts have been thrown. The second time the cut is used there are many more cigarette butts than the first time.

(*d*) *Cut through close-up*

This is at once a 'cut to' and a 'cut from' a close-up. It serves as a transition.

Example: at the end of the first interview, as Siddhartha leaves, there is a cut to a close up of a call bell, then another cut to Siddhartha sitting in a restaurant.

(*e*) *Cut on direction*

A movement is initiated in a certain direction, and the cut shows something else moving in that direction.

Example: during the last interview, the applicant wearing a suit is seen walking across the crammed hall. Four other applicants observe him. As he passes in front of them, the young men turn their heads thus directing our attention along the direction of their gaze. Then there is a cut to the man who is seen walking in the direction of the four men.

(*f*) *Cut on movement*

You can combine two movements that are not logically related but that can visually flow one into the other.

Example: After the last interview, a series of posters are seen on a wall in very rapid succession. This is followed without any transition by a panoramic view of paddy fields 'passing', as it were, in less rapid succession but in the same direction. The total sequence transmutes the physical violence (Siddhartha up-ending the desk of the selection board) into a more abstract visual pattern that continues to discharge the pent-up anger. Finally, the movement is shifted to paddy fields 'passing' in front of a train window. This passage from one place to another (office to village), from one mood to another (anger to calm) with the information that Siddhartha has left Calcutta and (we begin to assume), taken up the job as a medical representative, is a remarkable use of cinematic language. The economy of means to achieve this passage makes the sequence the more powerful.

(*g*) *Cut on sound*

A sound can be used to carry a transition from one scene to another.

Example: Sutapa says, 'Dada', and in a flashback, she is seen years earlier calling her brother.

(*h*) *Cut on form or 'form-cut'*

The same graphic form permits smooth transition from one scene to another.

Example: Sutapa is seen in a flashback taking the hand of young Siddhartha and leading him through a doorway (or was it a gate?). There is a cut to the same form of door, and Sutapa is seen leading Siddhartha by the hand through the doorway on to the terrace of their home.

(*i*) *Straight cut*

A cut from one scene to another without any special auditory or visual connection. The connection is supplied by the story, or by the predominant emotion. Often, the audience is not immediately given the clue that permits them to recapture the flow of the film.

Example: During the last interview, Siddhartha thinks of Hippies having a nice time. We see him thinking; then there is a cut straight from him to the Hippies. Yet, the audience does not lose the sense of continuity.

Strikingly enough, there are only two dissolves in the entire film. The dissolve or mix, when two shots are made to fuse one into the other, usually suggests a lapse of time or a change of place. The dissolve can suggest a lapse into thought as when the filmmaker reveals a dream. This type of cutting is associated with a more conventional style of movie making. Older films usually have a large number of cuts in the form of mix, dissolve, fade-in or fade-out.

SIGNIFICANCE OF *PRATIDWANDI*

When earlier in this analysis, I rejected this approach to a film that makes the emotional pattern the main and exclusive aesthetic element, it was because I hold the view that art is primarily a language, a form of communication and not just a form. This discussion of *Pratidwandi*, accordingly, must include an assessment of what the film means.

Hinging on three interviews, and depicting a network of personal relationships, *Pratidwandi* shows Siddhartha hit by the successive blows of his father's death and the difficulties of finding his place in a world that would readily lure him into losing his identity. Overcoming his reluctance to leave Calcutta, and accepting a small job, Siddhartha recaptures the simple joy of his childhood, and he takes a first step towards acceptance of adult responsibility. What *Pratidwandi* is about, therefore, is a process of growth. Siddhartha at first, is solely concerned with finding a job. The attitude of the interviewers thoroughly upsets him as a human person, but he shows no concern for the social system as such. In this regard, the little talk with Nareshda is important. For, the gentleman had at first suggested he should join some political group and help them. This Siddhartha refused. Then, Nareshda told him about a small job in a village. This also Siddhartha did not want.

Finally, however, reacting violently (that is, as violently as his inhibitions permit) he makes an attempt to move outside Calcutta, and he takes the job of a medical representative. One could consider this a surrender, a compromise. Is it? Is it not rather a first step towards some realism? Initially, Siddhartha's determination to get a job is very unrealistic. For how can one hope to obtain a post under the conditions shown in the film, unless one is prepared to lobby for years or use dishonest means? Siddhartha would not use dishonest means. But he finally refused to lobby any more. This is a step towards sound realism. It does not imply a compromise with the unacceptable social set-up. But it does imply Siddhartha's readiness to abandon grandiose plans for a comfortable career. At the same time, the acceptance of Nareshda's idea regarding the job might be a first step towards accepting his advisor's other suggestion to play some actual role in society. Getting out of his own little universe of dreams and self-centred interests, Siddhartha steps into the world. This is still a far cry from exploding crackers, but it is a deep change, all the same, with lasting effects. The permanence of the change is very well conveyed through the final freeze. On seeing that freeze, one is reminded of the ending of *Four Hundred Blows* (1959), one of the most important of the early New Wave films. It seems as if Mr. Ray purposely quoted (as is now often done in cinema) François Truffaut. But the meaning of *Pratidwandi 's* ending does not mean irresolution. It means that a stage in Siddhartha's life has ended and a new start has been made. The traumatic experience of his father's death has been integrated. This could be the meaning of the funeral rite unobtrusively counter-pointing the last word of the film, 'iti'.

It is unfortunate that this positive meaning of the film as a growth towards realism seems to have escaped leftist critics of the film, who were rightly upset by the bourgeois character of Siddhartha. For, Siddhartha is indeed bourgeois to the core. Yet, he has made a step towards social realism. I believe this should be pointed out, for it could help other people to follow this experience to its last implication. While choosing to depict this type of character Mr. Ray could not ignore that this was not the sort of person the majority of the people would like to see. He could not ignore the fact that the change in Siddhartha's personality might escape more than a few viewers. Yet, by refusing to make a film that would have won him immediate and enthusiastic praise, I believe Mr. Ray has been courageous. But this courage does not minimize the serious flaws in the film. It is to these that attention will now be paid.

First of all, the fact that Siddhartha is 25 years old makes him rather incredible. How could he still be so inhibited, sexually and otherwise? How could he still be uncommitted? How could he still look back to his childhood? In the original novel from which the film is adapted, Siddhartha is 21. The problems of Siddhartha in the film are the problems of a 20-year-old person. Siddhartha, with his command of English and his civil manners, could hardly have remained without a job for over two years. Finally, his clothes (especially the expensive Punjabi shirt), his taking Keya to one of the most expensive restaurants in Calcutta make him belong so totally to the wealthiest class of students, that it becomes difficult for many a viewer to identify with him. That is most unfortunate, because what makes Siddhartha characteristic is not primarily the 'class' he belongs to, but his appalling lack of realism and social concern. There are reasons to believe that this lack of realism and social concern is shared by many more people than Siddhartha could ever represent. A proof of this is in the very slowness with which change takes place in Calcutta. Romanticism and self-centredness are not the monopoly of a single group of people. It is, I am afraid, a common human attitude.

We live in a period when people have become aware that our social systems are helplessly corrupt. This is a time when each person's conscience is challenged. To connive with evil is wrong; to overthrow some of its manifestations is to lose one's innocence. Siddhartha would like to live independently of his necessary social context. This is impossible. What happens to Siddhartha — although quite late in his life — is a progress towards maturity. It is a recognition by him that he cannot protract his childhood, that he has to accept responsibility, that commitment is not necessarily alienation, but can also be liberation. What appeared to him, not without some serious reasons, as a form of prostitution now begins to appear as the only way to innocence: the experience of reality as a fact and the determination to re-create it whenever necessary.

There is in *Pratidwandi* a realism that I would call deceptive. I do not mean that it is intended to deceive. But it can be misleading. Several details in the film concur to make you believe Siddhartha is real. For instance, the fact that Siddhartha needs to have his trousers mended before the first interview makes you believe that what you are seeing can happen only to that boy and hence that Siddhartha is true to life. Indeed, at times, the film has an almost documentary quality. To a foreign spectator especially, Siddhartha can appear absolutely true. Other details, however, make him totally incredible to a Bengali audience. First of all, it is difficult for most people in Calcutta to identify with him. His command of English — for which he should, after all, be praised — also makes him incredible as a middle class boy. People in Calcutta know that one may not so easily gain access to the terrace of the Birla Building. It is incredible that Siddhartha who lives on his sister's salary should take his girl friend to a very expensive restaurant. In his financial situation, the fact that Siddhartha does not at least give some tuition to students, to bring in a little money seems incredible. The scene when Keya calls him in the middle of the night is not only incredible, it is rather odd. The role of Siddhartha's mother, surprisingly in a Ray film, is totally unsatisfactory.

Thus, the realism of Siddhartha as a movie character seems highly questionable to a Bengali audience. This does not contribute little to give the impression that the filmmaker of *Pratidwandi* is detached from the persons and events he alludes to in his film.[8] Without going to the extent of saying that he should have made a film on Tunu instead of Siddhartha, one can say that more care could have been given to the depiction of Siddhartha's younger brother. For does he not represent what Siddhartha himself was, not so many years earlier? On the other hand, the change we have analysed in Siddhartha's character is very relevant to present-day situations and problems. *Pratidwandi* does not have the sweeping effect of a film like *Interview,* precisely because it does not aim to explode like a cracker on the screen. What *Pratidwandi* offers is a multi-dimensional analysis of a trait of character: romanticism and lack of social concern. It is left to the audience to be honest enough to recognize themselves or part of themselves, not in Siddhartha as an individual, but in the type of attitude that is his. One can look at that portrait and decipher the meaning of some of the things one lives through, and diagnose the ailments that possibly afflict one. The making of such an analysis is the most valuable contribution an artist can make to his fellowmen.[9]

NOTES

1. In comparison, the negative segment, when the girl lights her cigarette from that of Siddhartha, is much more successful. At that point, a certain level of emotional intensity had been created, and it was easy to identify the action going on.
2. The choice of Dhritiman Chatterjee for Siddhartha's role was very fortunate.
3. This display of violence borders on sensationalism. In fact, the camera, exploring the face, hands and garments of Sanyal, was more effective.
4. Not a single action of any of the characters was shown in its entirety throughout the film. There are perhaps allusions to too many topics. In a way, the film may be said to be overly topical. But that is the atmosphere one lives in: Vietnam war, communism, landing on the moon, bomb, jobless youths, sex, American(?) hippies (one of the rare outsiders in Mr. Ray's films).
5. The complexity of Siddhartha's character is well represented pictorially, by the wrought iron gate against which Siddhartha is seen leaning in Sanyal's house.
6. 1971.
7. Chapter 14 of this book deals with editing from a more theoretical point of view.
8. Some critics have objected to the reference to the French revolution in *Pratidwandi*. They objected to it on ideological grounds. They failed to perceive that Siddhartha is precisely the type of person who can talk beautifully about Vietnam, but has little if anything to say about Calcutta; similarly, he can think about the French Revolution in order the better to avoid thinking about the social revolution he willy-nilly lives in.
9. It would be in order to compare some aspects of *Pratidwandi* with Mrinal Sen's *Interview*. But to do this usefully, the film *Interview* should first be discussed at some length, a discussion that cannot be done within the scope of the present analysis.

CHAPTER 8

*Jana Aranya** The Human Jungle, 1975

The Middleman

'THE MIDDLEMAN'? Yes, this film describes the making of a middleman. And the expression 'middleman' is used with emphasis in the film. We are even told that the Bengali language has a term, 'dalaal', for the middleman. In that sense, the sub-title of the film is correct. But it is not an adequate rendering of the title itself. This film is not about middlemen; it is about corruption, the middleman being just a 'sample' of it. *Jana Aranya,* the title of the book from which the film is made, does not mean the middleman. It means 'the human jungle'.

Does not speaking of a human jungle make of this film a rather bleak one? Yes, it does, and Satyajit Ray has acknowledged the fact:

> The only bleak film I have made [up to 1982, the year of this interview. GR] is *The Middleman.* There's no question about that. I felt corruption, rampant corruption, all around. Everyone talks about it in Calcutta. Everyone knows, for instance, that the cement allotted to the roads and underground railroad is going to the contractors who are building their own homes with it. *The Middleman* is a film about that kind of corruption and I don't think there is any solution.[1]

The entire oeuvre of Ray, however, shows that his vision of our world is not bleak or dispirited. Ray does not despair for the men and women of his time. His faith in the youth (Chapter

*This essay was written for the present book. I am thankful to Samik Bandopadhyay for suggesting that I write it.

20), in particular, remains unshaken till the end. Nonetheless, he calls a spade a spade. If anyone thinks that Ray does not know or does not see the world as it is, let that person have a look at *The Human Jungle*, and generally at the other so-called city films made by Ray. The acuity of Ray's perception of corruption makes his faith in men and women the stronger, and the more challenging.

One is tempted to see a trilogy in the city films, *Pratidwandi, Seemabaddha,* and *Jana Aranya.* According to Ray himself, to these three films should be added *Aranyer Din Ratri.*[2] In this last film, the characters are analysed while they take some time off in the forest, but they are city people. Thus, the city films would constitute a tetralogy. But then, what about *Mahanagar, The Great City* (1963)? The Ray films, are not that easily categorized. The *Apu* trilogy was made over a period of nearly five years, during which time two other feature films, quite disparate, were made (Chapter 17). Even then the *Apu* trilogy stands as a trilogy. The city films form a unit thematically. They may be seen as a continuous narrative of sorts. For instance, the story of Somnath (*Jana Aranya*) can be seen as the continuation of Siddhartha's story (*Pratidwandi*). Both are 25 years old, both are looking for a job, and both are utterly dependent on their fathers. In the same way, the story of Manomohan Mitra (*Agantuk*) can be seen as a continuation of Apu's story. Even then, the Heart Trilogy does not constitute a formal unit like the *Apu* trilogy. The city tetralogy does not either.

It is striking that there should be so many characters in *Jana Aranya.* Penelope Houston is quoted as having said: 'few of Ray's films have offered so wide a range of quick, exact characterizations'.[3]

In my view, she was right, but to some extent only. For, at the end of the film, you know very little about Somnath, the hero who becomes a middleman, a 'dalaal.' And yet, you know exactly the type of person he is. You might speak of 'typage' in Ray's treatment of the characters in this film: each one projects a set of characteristics that make him/her identifiable as belonging to this or that group of people. In most of his films Ray usually goes into greater detail in the depiction of his characters. But then, he usually has fewer of them than he has in *Jana Aranya*. Besides, here he is not concerned with Somnath so much as he is with the middleman.

What 'type' of a person is Somnath? Mr. Mitter, the professional investigator, helps him as well as the film's viewer to find out. Somnath is essentially a weakling. He has been honest during his early youth, but, as Adok, one of his mentors, notes, he had not known the facts of life. When that knowledge came, Somnath found that he had little choice. As his father said at one point, 'If a youth does not find a job, he can only become a revolutionary or go to the dogs.' Somnath would not readily die for a cause; he could only go to the dogs, that is, degenerate. And degenerate, he does.

Unfortunately, Somnath is surrounded by middlemen who (like Mitter) do not consider themselves dishonest, or who take corruption for granted. For instance, Bhombol, Somnath's elder brother, argues that corruption is a tradition. Sanskrit even has a word for 'bribe', he points out.

If Somnath can be seen as a continuation of Siddhartha, his father can be seen as an anticipation of Anand Majumdar (*Shakha Proshakha*). For the ailing Majumdar, his sons can remain honest only to the extent they keep united with him in a commitment to the same ideal. Sharing the same ideal with the same commitment to it is, in Satyajit Ray's view, what binds this life together. Since Somnath's father has made it clear that when his wife died in great suffering, he realized that God meant nothing to him, the question — a question that was put to Somnath by Mitter — is this: would one die for an ideal or a cause? When he implicitly raised a similar question in *Shakha Proshakha*, Ray seemed diffident, and, perhaps he expressed his feeling through having Proshanto listen to the prayer-song 'Lord, have mercy on us.' Speaking of the human jungle — both the film and the world it depicts, Ray explicitly said (in the *Cineaste* interview quoted above): 'I don't think there is any solution.'

Yes, *Jana Aranya* is a bleak film in terms of what it depicts. But it is also a film impregnated with love and hope. Satya Banerjee, Somnath's father, has no thought of anything but of his two sons. He wants their good. And for him 'good' means honesty, freedom and love. He too, perhaps, is a weakling — for instance, during the time of Gandhi, he was afraid he might be called to sacrifice his life. The same can be said of Majumdar (Ray's ancestor was a Majumdar!) and his attitude towards his sons. However, to acknowledge that one is a weakling is indeed to acknowledge the truth of one's existence.

Jana Aranya is a fascinating audio-visual presentation. The decoupage (see chapter 17), that is, the fragments of the total action that are offered to the viewers for them to comprehend the whole, is both intelligent — a Ray characteristic — and arresting. For instance, when Somnath hands in his paper at the end of the examination, the viewer is made to see Somnath's roll number, and especially his overly small handwriting. But when the teacher about to mark the paper looks at it, the handwriting is not shown. Only the roll number '247' is shown. Thus, with a minimum of information, the viewers understand the teacher's problem. How was one to read that paper with defective eyesight and inadequate specs? That was at the beginning of the film. The ending of the film has a similar decoupage. When Somnath leaves Goenka's room at the hotel — named not without a touch of humour 'The Grand Indian' — where he left Juthika with his client, and as he begins to walk away down the corridor, there is a cut, and we see him enter his home. We know that he waited in the lobby of the hotel until he was called by Goenka to receive the note that clinched the contract. That segment, now unnecessary, is skipped over.

At the end of her analysis of *Jalsaghar* (quoted in chapter 5), Pauline Kael admits that *The Music Room* 'calls up hideous memories of our own expansive gestures'. Somewhat similarly, we should not be impervious to what the film *Jana Aranya* says about us today. Every one is confronted with the alternative of becoming a revolutionary or going to the dogs, that is, to play a positive role in society or play the *dalaal*. 'Lord, have mercy on us' . . . 'And yet, I shall not commit the grievous sin of losing faith in man.' (Tagore, 'Crisis in Civilisation', quoted by Ray in his film 'Rabindranath Tagore', 1961)

NOTES

1. Interview in *Cineaste* (1982) reproduced at http://www.satyajitray.org/about_ray/ray_on_ray.htm
2. Ray himself has emphasized the fact during an interview with Samik Bandopadhyay who kindly mentioned it to me.
3. http://www.satyajitray.org/films/jana.htm

CHAPTER 9

*Ghare Baire** The Home and the World, 1984

I SAW *PIKOO,* and loved it. Naturally, I expected Victor Banerjee to play the role of the villain in *Ghare Baire.* However just a few minutes of the film showed me how right Ray had been in his casting. In Nikhilesh, I discovered yet another Victor Banerjee, and in Sandip, a new Soumitra Chatterjee. There was one more surprise: Swatilekha Chatterjee, who gave a superb performance in the difficult role of Bimala. Ray knew what performance this young actress was capable of, and from that point of view his choice could hardly be seen as a risk. He trusted in her capability to live up to the image of Bimala conjured by Tagore: a woman whose charm is not in her physical appearance, but in the strength and subtlety of her emotions. In Tagore's novel, Bimala introduces herself as a person lacking beauty. In the film, Bimala is given no glamour: she does not need any. She rapidly wins over the spectator by the sheer power of her personality.

Ghare Baire made such an impact on me, that in it I felt the emotional intensity of *Pather Panchali,* the refinement of *Charulata,* the subtlety of *Aranyer Din Ratri,* and above all the maturity of Ray combined with that of Tagore. In *Ghare Baire,* Ray displays full command of both his medium and his emotions, as well as a clear vision of personal commitment, in politics or in love. *Ghare Baire* portrays these two forms of commitment at play in the same actions. Nikhilesh is as honest in politics as he is in love. Sandip is a dishonest politician and a selfish lover.

* *Cinewave 6,* April-September 1984, a Seagull publication.

Indeed, *Ghare Baire* reminds you of *Charulata.* But *Ghare Baire* goes much further than *Charulata* in its delineation of characters. For, it shows the attempt of a man to give his wife the freedom which age-old traditions have denied her. The proof of Nikhilesh's love for Bimala is that he takes the risk of losing her in offering her complete freedom. Nikhilesh loves absolutely and demands absolute love. The freedom granted to Bimala is for her the occasion to grow more mature as a human person. In that new freedom she conquers the power to love.

In order to portray his characters and their interaction in a period at once so remote from and so close to us, in order to depict the various aspects of the complex situation where three humans decide what they are or rather what they shall be, Ray needed space and time. The subject is not that of a short piece – written or filmed. And it is to the credit of Ray to have encompassed so much in the length of a single film. The attentive spectator appreciates being given time to 'breathe' and to think as he is taken from emotional heights to higher peaks, and is introduced to new aspects of the characters' tragic evolution.

Ghare Baire, in marvellous colours, is a film one likes to watch, and after the film is over, one is still left pondering. The film makes you feel and think – like all those films that are worth seeing again and again. Scholars may argue as to whether *Ghare Baire* is Ray's best film ever. Meanwhile, cinemagoers will enjoy watching the film, and will derive insight from it because the film deals so poignantly with a human situation the spectator has experienced or witnessed.

PATRIOTISM IN TAGORE AND IN RAY[1]

In his *The Argumentative Indian,* Amartya Sen points out that both Tagore and Ray expressed their view on patriotism in *Ghare Baire,* the novel and film, respectively. Tagore had made Nikhilesh, the protagonist, say – and Sen quotes the passage:

> I am willing to serve my country; but my worship I reserve for Right, which is far greater than my country. To worship my country as a god is to bring a curse upon it.[2]

Tagore needed courage to articulate that view. In no less demanding circumstances, Ray too needed courage. And he had it.

NOTES

1. Paragraph added for the present publication.
2. Amartya Sen, *The Argumentative Indian: Writings on Indian History, Culture and Identity*, Penguin Books, 2005, p. 108.

B. The Heart Trilogy*

The last three films of Satyajit Ray

Gana Shatru, 1989
Shakha Proshakha, 1990
Agantuk, 1991

*Gaston Roberge, *Communication Cinema Development*, 1998, see pp. 174-91.

This book received a National Award (special mention) at the 46th National Film Awards of India in 1999.

CHAPTER 10

*Gana Shatru**
Public Enemy, 1989
Straight from the Heart

I SAW *GANA SHATRU* at a very private show, and I liked it immensely. It's nothing like any other Ray film, but it is a Ray film all right. I would describe it as a gem. It has the compactness of a finely wrought gem. The form is so perfect that the anecdote seems to be a mere pretext for the form itself. Yet, the anecdote is well dealt with. And form here does not mean formalism, that is, form for its own sake. It is as if the form of the story is the form of something else, and that something else is so much more important. One senses that the story is not the main point of the film. The form raises the film to an abstract level where it becomes — not a message, or still less a thesis — but a cry of hope and joy . . . beyond the 'story'.

The film is like music, although I am not familiar enough with musical forms to say which form it is. Music is never the sound of something. It is the form of an emotion. So also this film, as I see it. The extraordinary thing is that the form of the film is also, of course, the form of a story that is told in a very arresting manner. But it is not polemical. It just is.

The acting is, of course, an important element of the form of the film. Each character gives a superb performance. Soumitra is the ever *ganabandhu* (the public friend). Dhritiman is his perfect counterfoil with an amazingly mature interpretation. The film being based on a play, it is normal that it

*G. Roberge, *Communication Cinema Development*, 1998, pp. 174-7.

be an 'actor's film', but this means it is above all a 'director's film', since acting in film, perhaps more than on the stage, has to be 'directed'.

Gana Shatru was certified for exhibition on 4 April 1989. I wrote the above paragraphs on the film in a letter to a friend,[1] dated 19 April 1989. Subsequently, I was appalled at the bad reviews the film elicited in Calcutta. Bad, not because they did not praise the film, but because they were so wrong in their approach. Of course, a film made after a play by Ibsen invites comparison between film and play. But it should soon be evident that such a comparison in this case is a blind alley, simply because Satyajit Ray was not interested in the play as a play. In a word, Ray was not interested in Ibsen. He just took the story of the play as a pre-text for his own film text.

The second misleading avenue explored by critics was whether Ray was taking a stance against Hindu fundamentalism. Ray has never shown any sympathy for religious fundamentalism. In addition, he never was a pamphleteer. However badly disturbed he may have been by the increasing manifestations of religious bigotry and fanaticism at the time of the making of *Gana Shatru,* he had other personal preoccupations. The question of religious fundamentalism is more than just a background to the film, but, on the other hand, the film is not prompted by that question. *Gana Shatru* cannot be said to be a film about religious fundamentalism. Always having his audience in mind, Ray provides good stories. He found a good story in Ibsen's play, and he adapted it for his audience. In the very process, he expressed his own childlike joy at being alive, at being able to make a film, at being supported by his family.

Ray had been very ill and he had been forced to inaction for almost five years. At last, he could again make a film, even though his doctor had set stringent limits on his shooting schedule. Would he then attempt to 'film Ibsen' as others 'stage Ibsen?' Or would he then raise his voice against fundamentalism? Anyone watching the film carefully, without 'a priori' ideas on what the film is supposed to be, would answer no, emphatically, to these two questions.

The film opens with an image of a stethoscope on a table with a telephone in the background. The camera moves slightly in the direction of the telephone, pauses for a moment, just as a hand begins to dial a number. Then, the camera pans further along the cord linking the telephone to its receiver in the hand of Dr. Gupta, the protagonist of the film.

It is not irrelevant to remember that Ray had suffered from heart attacks and that the film was his first 'communication' after a long convalescence. Do I over-stretch the 'line' from stethoscope to telephone if I say that this film is 'straight from the heart'. Indeed the whole film is a personal communication by Ray. What about? Communication, creativity and youth. That takes us far enough from Ibsen and from religious fundamentalism.

Dr. Gupta has something to say. Something vital for the people under his care. He knows for sure that the elixir distributed by the local temple is polluted and poisonous. Vested interests will not let him have his say. He wants to publish this a newspaper. He is not permitted to do so. He attempts to talk in public. His meeting is disrupted, and he is silenced. Stones are thrown at his home. His daughter loses her job. He loses his. He is told to leave the place. But as Dr. Gupta is about to sink in despair, his daughter, her friend, and local students take up the fight. No, all is not lost. One can still live. One can still communicate, one can still be creative. What joy! *Gana Shatru* is Ray's hymn of joy to life, to creativity, and to solidarity.

I had the good fortune of discussing all this with Satyajit Ray himself. As I was talking to him about the form of the film, using my hand to trace in the air a curve going up, then down and up again, he interrupted me, and he said something like, 'yes, it goes up in three steps' and with his hand made a gesture upward in three steps.

This triple ascending movement works well in music. But, as a dramatic denouement, it may be found a little abrupt. Up to that point in the film, the dramatic form and the potential musical form blended harmoniously. Here, perhaps, the musical form — freer than the dramatic form — has escaped, as it were, on its own. Whether the drama ends too abruptly in *Gana Shatru* is open to discussion. But those who are insensitive to the musical form that the drama supports, will not appreciate the graceful exaltation of the film's ending.

I said that the opening image with the stethoscope and phone suggests that the film comes straight from its maker's heart. There is another possible meaning, explored by Charles Tesson. The stethoscope can be seen as an extension of the camera. Through this film Ray listens to the heart of the world, and invites the spectator to both look and listen. In fact, perhaps more than in his previous films, off–screen sounds are heard as part of the imaginary work of the film. That is especially true of the shouting outside Dr. Gupta's home: first the mob shouting and then the students hailing Dr. Gupta as a hero. Indeed, Dr. Gupta's home is a stethoscope. The home is listening to the world — *Ghare Baire!*

In 1989 already, that is, in the year of the release of *Gana Shatru*, Charles Tesson wrote:

> Ray has given us an indoor film entirely turned outward, towards the mad energy of the world. *Gana Shatru* is hard cut and hard cutting, dry and sharp like silex. *Gana Shatru* is a very great political film, the most profound and unbiased look at all that agitates the end of this century: the return of religious fundamentalism (the religious faith belonging to the people and because of that, sacred, out of reach), its collusion with politics (power, the institutions and control of the masses), the economic (its touristic exploitation), and the mediatic (rumour and heretical defamation).[2]

About the final sequence when the students come in support of Dr. Gupta, Tesson says in the same article:

> that collusion of politics and poetics (the students have been mobilized by a students' theatrical troupe. G.R.) in a same voice is really a miracle, and it is beautiful that people whose life is committed to art, to representation, in the end occupy the field of politics. (p. 24)

But Tesson, was not the only one to comment on *Gana Shatru*. In a previous issue of *Cahiers du Cinéma*[3] William Fisher reproduced his interview of Ray during the shooting of the film. Ray said:

I never believed and I still do not believe that a film can change society. In Soviet Russia, for instance, the revolution had already taken place (when Eisenstein made his films. G.R.). (p. 61)

During the major part of my life I was an unbeliever. But there are certain things which I can't explain, and which science too cannot explain. (. . .) As one grows older, when death approaches, I guess one begins to be a believer. But I still do not believe in rituals.

I totally identify with Dr Gupta, an honest man who does not fear the truth. I understand his motivations, his sufferings and his joy at the end. I fully agree with what he says. I believe in the supremacy of science. (p. 60.)

NOTES

1. Mrs. Vijaya Mulay.
2. Charles Tesson, 'Le Bruit du Monde', in *Cahiers du Cinéma,* no. 422, July-August 1989, pp. 20-5, 22.
3. William Fisher, 'Entretien avec Satyajit Ray', in *Cahiers du Cinéma,* no. 417, March 1989.

CHAPTER 11

*Shakha Proshakha**
The Branches and the Twigs, 1990
The Heartbeat of Time

WHO WILL SAVE us? Who will heal our wounded humanity? How shall we regain sanity and, above all, peace? These are the questions *Shakha Proshakha* raises with compassion, and with urgency. Time passes on. Irretrievably. No answer is imposed. However, elements of answers are offered. When the branches are detached from the tree, they can do nothing. Estranged from their father, the Prabirs of the world will gamble life away, and the Prabodhs will cheat. Each of them will consider himself a success. Only those who stay in vital communion with the tree can acknowledge their mediocrity: they are saved by humility.

Since *Gana Shatru*, the films of Satyajit Ray are, more than ever before, direct statements emanating from a man who has undergone deep experiences. Not only are these later films informed by the experience Mr Ray has had of illness, but they vibrate with the thoughts that preoccupy him more forcefully after that illness. *Gana Shatru*, was concerned with environment and fundamentalism of all sorts, but it was first of all a hymn of joy to life and to creativity. Perhaps none of his previous films had been so deeply personal. *Shakha Proshakha* features a seventy year-old man who, at the peak of his fame, has a heart attack and recovers. But he recovers to

*G. Roberge, *Communication Cinema Development*, 1998, pp. 178-81. Appeared in Santi Das, ed., *Satyajit Ray: An Intimate Master*, 1998, pp. 62-78.

what? To the discovery of corruption around him, moral turpitude, a sort of illness from which, it seems, one cannot recover.

All of Satyajit Ray's films are very personal. But previously it was the creative impulse that found its expression in films of relevance. Now, in his seventies, Ray is seized with the urge to express his thoughts. His means of expression or language being 'film', the appropriate film form emerges to convey these thoughts.

One could argue, as indeed Ray himself has done in an interview, that long ago, when he was hardly forty-five, he had imagined the story of Ananda Majumdar. Hence the personal aspect of *Shakha Proshakha* should not be exaggerated. True. On the other hand, it is now that Ray has made that film. And am I wrong in finding in the elderly Ananda (Ajit Bandopadhyay) a facial resemblance to Ray? Be this as it may, the critic has to be clear as to what he wishes to achieve: a biography of the filmmaker through a scrutiny of his films, or a 'reading' of his films against the background of the director's private life, and in the context of contemporary social life. The two, personal experience and films, cannot be separated. But ever since film criticism has taken a semiological orientation, critics have preferred to see the significance of films in themselves rather than in what they can reveal about their makers. They seek to 'read' meaning in films in the context of the social discourse of which films are a part. Whether or not the creator of a film intended a particular meaning is a matter that pertains to his biography, not to film criticism as such. The fact is, a filmmaker is always greater than his film, because no work of art can fully encompass the personality of its creator. On the other hand, the significance of a film is always greater than whatever a filmmaker has wanted it to be, because significance is infinite. The test of the validity of a reading is whether it can be communicated and shared. A viewer may not spontaneously read a film the way a critic or a scholar does, but the viewer can grasp the sense inherent in these experts' reading once he/she comes to know about it. Even filmmaker Jean Renoir said that he learnt about his films from film scholar André Bazin.

Gana Shatru dealt with the external environment. *Shakha Proshakha* deals with the internal environment of the men and women of our time. The film examines the human values that make life worth living, and without which there is no peace, whether in society or in each one's heart. These values are lost or enhanced according to the type of relationships men and women entertain not only with so-called 'nature' but also among themselves, and especially between men and women.

When I said earlier that Ray seems more concerned with saying things than with creating forms, however relevant, I certainly did not mean that the present films are not well crafted. I mean that the primary impulse seems to be different. Form flows as if effortlessly in the service of thought. Once the characters are introduced and their situation established, *Shakha Proshakha* proceeds in marvellous film terms. Ray, at his best, describes the Majumdars' relationships vividly and subtly. There are open conversations at table; there are more intimate conversations in the bedrooms. Each couple's relationship and each person's relationship with the others are directly projected. What immediately appears is the estrangement between all of them. The four sons are estranged from each other, and two of them from their wives, to the extent that they are estranged from their father. Proshanta seems completely alienated, yet he is in deep communion with each and all of them. He is sensitive to the fact that is brothers did not come to celebrate their father's birthday. He is also acutely aware of what is happening to his father: he will be sick, but he will recover, Proshanta feels. And at the end of the film, when Dingo innocently discloses to his grandfather that corruption has crept into the family, Proshanta immediately foresees the devastating effect that disclosure will have on his father, and he comes to comfort him.

I cannot help seeing this film as an illustration of the words of Christ: 'I am the true vine, you are the branches. Whoever remains in me, with me in him, bears fruit in plenty; for cut-off from me you can do nothing.'[1] I am not saying that Satyajit Ray has wanted to make a commentary of this scriptural verse. I merely say that I read the film against the background of that verse, and as a result, the film is the more meaningful for me.

In a corrupt world, one way of maintaining one's integrity is to take refuge in the purity of music. But one cannot hope to take refuge in music and still live in this turbulent world. Such a solution would only lead to complete detachment, and therefore, to a form of madness. Proshanta illustrates this tendency lived to its ultimate consequence. This renders him unfit for work, the highest value in Ananda's Victorian universe. Prabodh feels that Proshanta should be sent to a mental hospital. But Pratap too, in the eyes of both Prabodh and Prabir, has done something 'mad' in giving up his job because he found corruption in the milieu where he was working. Even Ananda is not exempt from failure. If we are to believe Pratap, in years past, Ananda was more preoccupied with 'work' than with love for his sons. In a way, Ananda too was 'mad': work was music to him. He is not the trunk of the tree, but only an important branch.

By the end of the film, it is evident that sanity lies in neither work as worship nor honesty as a rule of life, but in love. Prabodh does not love. At the end of the film, when he takes leave of his father and puts his hand in that of the ailing man, he does not communicate love: so he leaves his father sad as never before. But when Proshanta places his hand in that of his father on the latter's chest, he communicates love and a profound peace. When one loves, one is at peace with the world and with oneself.

Often during the film Proshanta is seen listening to music — that of Bach, we are told. At one point, when Pratap and Dr. De discuss the case of Proshanta, the latter is listening to the Gregorian chant of 'Kyrie Eleison' (Lord have mercy). I am thankful to Ray for having refrained from making of his film a 'musical'. We have just enough music to sense the atmosphere of joy and peace in which Proshanta takes refuge. At the end of the film, the Bach music lingers in our minds until, perhaps, it fades into the 'Kyrie Eleison'. For, indeed, who will save us? Who will heal our wounded humanity?

NOTE

1. The Bible, John 15, verse 5.

CHAPTER 12

*Agantuk**
The Stranger, 1991
The Cave of the Heart

I find myself trying, through my films, to trace the underlying pattern that binds this life together.
SATYAJIT RAY[1]

The pattern that connects.
GREGORY BATESON

SATYAJIT RAY'S last film, *Agantuk*, is one of the six features for which he wrote original stories. It is perhaps the film in which he expresses himself most openly. It is the film that deals with the largest subject, namely, contemporary civilization. Above all, *Agantuk* is a summative film in which Ray has wanted, as it were, to complete a number of projects. I can hope, therefore, to touch upon only some of the aspects of the film, well aware that there are other important aspects that, I trust, other writers will discuss.

AGANTUK AND *THE ALIEN*

In an interview, Andrew Robinson had asked Ray if there were any relationship between *Gana Shatru* and *The Alien*, the film Ray had planned to make in the mid-1960s. Robinson saw some common elements, like the temple, the journalist, the

*G. Roberge, *Communication Cinema Development*, 1998, pp. 182-90. Appeared in Santi Das, ed., *Satyajit Ray: An Intimate Master*, 1998, pp. 62-78.

nexus between religion and money, the Bajoria character. Ray answered: 'It hadn't occurred to me at all.... But now you mention it, I can see the point'.[2] I am sure Ray would see the point if I were to ask him, as Robinson did: 'Would I be right in saying you've put some of *The Alien* in *Agantuk*?' Manomohan Mitra does not come onto earth from a distant planet, but he sees the world from the point of view of an outsider, which is what he has become as a result of living among so-called primitive people. Like the *alien*, Mitra is benevolent. For, Ray has made this his last film character[3] not altogether an *alien*, but a stranger, a newcomer, and even a loving 'uncle'. After all, the name 'Manomohan Mitra' means, the 'lovely friend'. The *agantuk* is closer to people than the *alien*. For although Mitra has left his immediate family thirty-five years earlier, he has always remained with people, in search of what makes them human.

PROBING INTO CONTEMPORARY CIVILIZATION

Like the *alien*, Mitra is able, so it seems, to read other people's thoughts. Above all, like the *alien*, he has eyes to see. To see through, to see into, in other words, to probe into contemporary civilization.

Probing is for Ray the fundamental task of the artist. In 1957, writing about the making of *Pather Panchali* he stated what was and always remained his objective:

> to observe and probe, to catch the revealing details, the telling gestures, the particular turns of speech. . . . The more you probed the more was revealed, and familiarity bred not contempt but love, understanding, tolerance.[4]

All the Ray films have been probes into 'reality', they all lead to understanding, tolerance and love. This is true especially of *Agantuk*. Ray had given the *alien* special eyes to probe into the world around him. He gave Manomohan powers of perception that come from a long experience of observing people of cultures different from one's own, especially simple people, such as children, or tribal people. Coming back to Calcutta after a long absence, Manomohan can share the results of his probing into contemporary civilization. The probing is ruthless: (a) the damaging effect of money (a theme explored in *Kanchenjungha, Nayak, The Alien. . .*), (b) the stupidity of war (*Goopy Gyne Bagha Byne*), (c) the true meaning of civilization, (d) various aspects of Bengali culture, like food, hospitality, music, *adda* (e) the faith in each other which makes love possible and human life worth living, (f) and, above all, the wonderful complexity of the world.

THE UNDERLYING PATTERN THAT BINDS THIS LIFE TOGETHER

In *Agantuk* 'the underlying pattern that binds this life together' (Ray) or 'the pattern that connects' (Gregory Bateson) is shown to be a common experience of life. Anila (the niece) recognizes that Manomohan is her uncle when the latter sings to her a song of her childhood. Conversely, the uncle recognizes Anila as his true niece when she responds to the tribal dance, and joins in. The identity provided by family blood relationships and established by documents like a passport is not at all sufficient. What binds this life together and, finally, what binds people together is the common experience they have of life. There may be a touch of romanticism in Ray's setting the recognition by Mitra of the humanness of his niece in the surroundings of Shantiniketan, among tribal people. Ray, after all, is a city man. And he is well aware of it. This awareness has made *Pather Panchali* possible. The curiosity and wonder of Durga and Apu at the train and the telegraph wires is the counterpart of Ray's own wonder at village life. However, Ray does not suggest that everyone has to actually go to a village. What he does affirm is that a certain 'wanderlust' (to use a German word — used in English, we are told!), a *dépaysement* (to use a French word, *not* used in English, I say[5]) a going out of one's own mental universe, a certain disorientation, a freedom from one's artificial moorings, are required.

RAY'S LIFE PROJECT: TO BE A FILMMAKER

I said earlier, that in *Agantuk* Ray has completed several projects. His main life project was, of course, to be a filmmaker. He enunciated this project lucidly in 1948 in an article entitled, significantly, 'What Is Wrong with Indian Films?' An article that comes six years before François Truffaut's belligerent and generally wrong-headed piece, 'A Certain Tendency of the French Cinema'. When Ray wrote, his seminal article he was hardly 27 years old, he had not yet made any film, he had not yet met Jean Renoir in Calcutta. His article can be seen in retrospect as the 'manifesto' on which is based his entire film work, and which he never betrayed. It was not just one of those youthful statements which greater reflection prompts one to forget and for which one can be forgiven. Ray formulated his programme against the background of Indian films at the time. He wrote:

> (what is needed) is not more gloss, but more imagination, more integrity and a more intelligent appreciation of the limitation of the medium.[6]

Above all, 'a drastic simplification of style and content' will be needed. This will be achieved if the filmmaker 'keeps his eyes open and his ears'. For 'the raw material of the cinema is life itself'.[7]

Ray had also written:

> For a popular medium, the first kind of inspiration should derive from life and have its roots in it. No amount of technical polish can make up for artificiality of theme and dishonesty of treatment. *The Indian filmmaker must turn to life, to reality.*[8] (Emphasis added)

In *Agantuk,* Ray resolutely turned to life, to the reality he could see around him. Earlier on, he had explored the theme of an eventual film, *The Alien.* That film was never made. *Agantuk* is a reflection on the same theme, but at a more profound level. *The Alien* would have been fun with wisdom thrown in as a bonus. *Agantuk* is great fun too, but wisdom is the main ingredient. One might say that in certain respects *Agantuk* is to *The Alien* what *Ghare Baire* is to *Charulata.* But the last two films are Tagore's, the first two were Ray's own conceptions.

THE RETURN OF THE HERO

A thematic approach to the film can be complemented by a morphologic approach on the lines proposed by Vladimir Propp in his *Morphology of the Folktale* (1927). Some critics have noted that *Agantuk* is a tale dealing with 'the return of the hero'. This pattern of story usually implies that the hero has to undergo certain tests. So does Manomohan Mitra in *Agantuk*. Perhaps it was befitting that a film advocating a return to the source of humanness be expressed in a basic story form that is perhaps universal. But a reflection on these lines, however interesting, should not obscure the fact that the *Apu* trilogy too involves a 'return of the hero' after many a test. Apu does come back to Nischindipur, his natal village, with his child, Kajol. Apu surely sees the village in a new way, for he has matured. Mitra comes to Calcutta, but his return is to Shantiniketan. This is Ray's return as well. But strikingly, Mitra does not go to Tagore's school of art. He goes to a tribal village. Ray must have been aware of the numerous implications of Mitra's return to Shantiniketan. From an autobiographical point of view, Ray sides with Mitra. For, in spite of his fine teachers at Shantiniketan, Ray discovered Indian art in contemplating frescoes at Ajanta. Similarly, Mitra who too was an art student discovered the source of what Tagore called 'the human heritage' in the bison of Altamira. Another implication of Mitra's going to Shantiniketan but not to Tagore's school is that, bypassing Tagore as a secondary source, Ray goes to a primary source, the tribal village. Ray had hesitated to join Tagore's school. He felt himself to be too much of a city man. It is as if he said in *Agantuk*, 'if I must go out of Calcutta to Shantiniketan, I may as well go straight to a tribal village'.

WHY A BISON?

Is it not striking that Mitra, the Indian, should be so deeply impressed by a drawing of a bison? Of course, the bison of Altamira is an extraordinary depiction of a living animal. But Ray surely could have used another masterpiece with a similar effect. Why a bison? And what can the bison's connotations be? There are at least two sorts of deities, those in the sky, labelled *ouranian* (from the Greek *ouranos* meaning sky) and those on or in the earth, the *chtonian* (from the Greek *chton,* meaning earth) ones. The bison, is biologically related to the cow. The cow is an earthly animal protected by a *chtonian* god, Shri Krishna. The latter is associated with the aboriginal (Latin *ab origine* means from the origin) people as contrasted with the invaders and colonizers, who worshipped an *ouranian* deity, Indra. The bison, in a word, has pre-Aryan connotations. The return to the sources suggested by Ray is indeed radical.

THE THRESHOLD OF MYSTERY

There is a sequence in *Agantuk* which is as important as it is gratuitous. Gratuitous, because it does not seem to do much to advance the action, perhaps not even to reveal Manomohan Mitra's character. It is the scene when Mitra has gone out on the Maidan with Satyaki and his young friends. The scene is important because it reveals a concern of Ray: mystery, and the wonder mystery evokes.

Sitting on the Maidan, Mitra explains to his captivated audience the phenomenon of eclipses. It takes a good two and a half minutes of film time to lead the children to the point where they realize that they cannot explain a complete lunar eclipse. And they are told emphatically that nobody can explain the occurrence. Mitra calls this 'magic', in a language that children can grasp. But he is himself fascinated. He exclaims:

> I am telling you, of all the wonders of the world, this is the greatest. The sun and the moon, the king of the day and the queen of the night, the shadow of our planet on the moon, and the three heavenly bodies are like three discs of the same size!

Even if you call this magic, I am not sure it will hold the attention of children for a long time. The subject is somewhat austere. It is as if Ray needed an opportunity to express his own sense of wonder. A sense that has grown over the years and led him to the threshold of mystery and of transcendence.

Ray, who might be described as an agnostic, had nonetheless an open mind. He was struck by the complexity of things, like the human body, or of events, like the lunar eclipse. These, it seems, cannot occur by accident. In fact, whether you explain it by positing a transcendental force or by admitting the possibility of an immanent accident, there is room for wonder. For, the chances of such accidents happening are almost nil. And yet they occur. In his interview of November 1988 with Andrew Robinson, while speaking about his coming film *Gana Shatru* and the belief of the masses in the power of 'holy water', he said:

> Doctors generally in my experience believe in God. For instance, they pray. My own doctor, my house physician, says that if you inspect the human body — the incredible complexity of it — you have to believe in a superior force. It can't just happen by accident.[9]

RAY, CONTINUATOR OF TAGORE[10]

At the end of his film *Rabindranath Tagore* (1961), Ray had quoted the concluding lines of Tagore's masterly lecture, 'Crisis in Civilization' (1941).

> I had at one time believed that the springs of civilization would issue out of the heart of Europe. But today, when I am about to leave the world, that faith has deserted me. I look around and see the crumbling ruins of a proud civilization strewn like a vast heap of futility. And yet, I shall not commit the grievous sin of losing faith in man. I shall look forward to a new dawn, to a new chapter of history when the holocaust will end, and the air will be rendered clean by a spirit of service and sacrifice. Perhaps the dawn will come from this horizon, from the East, where the sun rises. On that day, the unvanquished man retraces his past of conquest, surmounting all barriers, to win back his lost human heritage.

These lines read well when you consider they are lines by Tagore. But one cannot imagine Ray uttering as his own the second part of the quotation, from 'Perhaps the dawn will come from this horizon . . .' till the end. There is here a sentimental turn, an eccentric flight into the poetic which, I am sure, Ray could not make his. Yet, in spite of this, *Agantuk* has always been to me Ray's equivalent, or rather his continuation, of

Tagore's *Crisis in Civilization.* When he is 'about to leave the world' faith in civilization issuing from the heart of Europe, if he ever held it, has deserted Ray. Faith in the present civilization itself, as he sees it, with its corruption, with its movement away from the sources of life, has deserted him. Like Tagore, Ray does not lose faith in man. But for him man is not an abstract, universal man, seen in the future. The repositories of Ray's faith are the men, the women and the youths of today. In *Agantuk,* it is a present-day woman who can sway to the rhythm of a tribal dance.

Ray is concerned, above all, with interpersonal relationships and with the response to life of actual, concrete people. He goes much further than Tagore. For Ray, it is not enough to see that light is not forthcoming from the West; it is not enough to turn to the East — which Ray himself has done when he discovered Indian arts in a contemplation of the frescoes of Ajanta. For Ray, it is necessary to ascend to the very source of humanity, of humanness (and humaneness), symbolized by the bison fresco of Altamira. What matters to Ray is the quality of the perception a human person has of life. The Altamira fresco proves that so-called pre-historic man was more sensitive to life than contemporary men and women. Yet, the hero of *Agantuk* and, in him, Satyajit Ray, does not despair. In *Gana Shatru,* Dr. Ashok Gupta discovers that he can have faith in the youth. Manomohan Mitra discovers that he can have faith in his niece. Humanness in her has not completely dried up. There is still hope.

AGANTUK'S QUALITY AS A FILM

In this discussion of *Agantuk,* I have said nothing about the quality of the film as a film. What about the dramaturgy, that is, about the organization of the actions? The crisp dialogue? The music? There is, no doubt, much to say about these. But I am so taken up by the film's significance that I find little interest in commenting about its formal qualities beyond what I said about its narrative structure. Of course, the significance of the film cannot be dissociated from its form. One does not stand without the other. *Gana Shatru* may have had the five-part structure of a drama, yet that film was informed by a musical structure. The dance towards the end of *Agantuk* and the idea of rhythm it conveys suggest that *Agantuk* is informed by a rhythmic impulse rather than a melodic line. The introductory sequence may at first appear literary, with Anila reading a letter. But, in fact, around the immaterial object of a piece of news, Anila and her husband display in a series of alternations, a wide variety of reactions which reveal their characters. Enter the bison, and a whole set of characters in a series of 'pas-de-deux' and 'pas-de-trois' define themselves with regard to it, that is, with regard to Mitra. They perform in the main rooms of a 'civilized' house: the drawing, sleeping and dining rooms. What they are forced to reveal is their reaction to the unknown, to life, to the mystery, to others and to self. Dhritiman Chatterjee, who had played the counterpart of Dr. Gupta (Soumitra Chatterjee) in *Gana Shatru,* again superbly plays the counterpart of Manomohan Mitra (Utpal Dutt).

Since I have related *Agantuk* to Tagore's *Crisis in Civilization*, I may as well relate Ray himself to Tagore. Tagore was eighty at the time of his last lecture, Ray was seventy-one at the time of his last film. Both spoke in their elected medium with the authority given by prestige, with the experience given by a life dedicated to art and communication. Both spoke from the unique position of persons 'about to leave the world', when one puts one's whole being in what one is saying, and one has no time for what is not essential. I have heard a few people claiming that *Agantuk* is not as perfect as some of the earlier Ray films and, as such, it cannot be taken as seriously as these earlier films. Such a response to *Agantuk* appears to me obtuse, nay, incomprehensible. These same people have told me that a film must be judged by film standards. But, precisely, one of the standards that Ray has established for cinema (and in this he was of one mind with his mentor of earlier years, Jean Renoir), is that it should communicate with the audience. And *Agantuk* does communicate. But one must open one's eyes, and ears. *Agantuk* is a statement — shall I say a testament? Ray did not write it as Tagore did. He has painted it on the white canvas of the cinema, wrestling with time and illness to complete the work. Do you not see that Utpal Dutt gives a human face to the bison of Altamira? That Mitra's character has the impetuous strength of the charging bison? That it has its simple lines, its economy? That it results from the 'drastic simplification of style and content' that, as Ray had written in his 1948 manifesto, the Indian cinema needed? In *Agantuk* is revealed a 'pattern that connects', an 'underlying pattern that binds this life together'. The greatest tribute one can pay to Satyajit Ray in front of *Agantuk* is to see the Altamira bison, issuing from the cave of the human heart and vibrant on the screen.

RAY'S FAITH IN HIS SPECTATORS

Ray, like Renoir, had placed his faith in the spectator of his films. In his second article on cinema, in 1949, Ray quotes Renoir who, speaking about the coming of the sound film, had said:

> It was as if someone had opened a secret door of communication between the filmmaker and his audience. It was a great feeling. Everything we did the audience understood. The French cinema could not have made those enormous strides towards maturity without this wonderfully perceptive audience. They helped us all along the way, and I for one feel grateful to them.[11]

NOTES

1. From the commentary written and spoken by Satyajit Ray for B.D. Garga's two-reeler *Creative Artists of India: Satyajit Ray* (1963), quoted in *Montage*, no. 5/6, July 1966. See 'Why I Make Films.'
2. Andrew Robinson, *Satyajit Ray: The Inner Eye*, London: Andre Deutsch Ltd, 1989, p. 344.
3. There is yet another Ray character in screenplay form, made into a film by Sandip Ray.
4. Satyajit Ray, *Our Films, Their Films*, Orient Longman Ltd, 1976, pp. 33-4.

5. I hasten to say, though, that the word is beginning to be used in English in the context of cyberspace. 'Dépaysement' means, literally, 'decountryfy', to take out of one's country materially or/and figuratively.
6. Satyajit Ray, *Our Films, Their Films*, p. 22.
7. Ibid., p. 24.
8. Ibid., p. 127. Emphasis mine.
9. Robinson, ibid., p. 343.
10. This aspect of Ray is discussed in chapter 15.
11. See note 1.

PART THREE

Teaching Film with Ray's Films

CHAPTER 13

Definition of a Film*

AN APPEARANCE OF CONTINUOUS MOTION CREATED BY MOTIONLESS IMAGES . . .

WHAT IS A FILM? A ridiculous question, one might say. Everyone knows what a film is. True. But try to formulate a definition of film. Is it an art? Is it just 'moving pictures' or 'filmed theatre'? To answer this question a discussion of a short excerpt from Satyajit Ray's *Pather Panchali* will be undertaken. Poetry or drama is studied through the works of great poets and dramatists, and whole passages are committed to memory. The same method can be employed in the study of film.

The passage now taken for study is the portion in the film where Durga and Apu, the brother and sister, see a 'candy man' and follow him to a neighbour's house. A part of a film complete in itself is called a 'sequence', and corresponds to a paragraph or, at times, to a chapter in a book. The passage under study will be termed 'the candy man sequence'.

One day, Durga had prepared pickles for Apu and herself, when suddenly she is pleasantly surprised by the familiar sound of a bell — and so on. The first function of cinema is to tell things, cinema being a sort of language.

If the sequence[1] is run, not through a movie projector, but a slide projector, slowly pulling the film along in front of the lens, the viewer will notice that the film is made of small photos, each very similar to the one which precedes it. Each of these photos is called a 'frame'. None of the frames is a 'moving'

*G. Roberge, *Chitra Bani,* a book on film appreciation, 1974, Chapter 10: Definition of a Film, pp. 49-51.

picture. It is only when the images are projected one by one on the screen at a certain speed, that the film, made of still pictures, takes on the life of a movie. One can pull the candy man sequence through a slide projector as fast as one wishes. A moving picture will not be obtained, only a blurred image will appear.

The movie projector shows the frames of the film one by one, but without showing the film when it moves in front of the lens. By means of sprocket holes, the celluloid film is directed in front of an aperture, the size of a frame, through which the light passes. A shutter prevents the light from passing during the fraction of a second it takes for one frame to replace a previous one in front of the aperture. The light is made to pass through that aperture only when the film is static. In effect, 24 frames are flashed successively on the screen in one second, and 24 times the screen is dark, to allow the film's movement. But the eyes retain only the luminous impressions. The successive still images pile up, as it were, and the difference between one and the next is perceived as a movement.

How it is possible for a succession of still images to appear as one continuous moving image has to do with the psychology of human vision. However this may be, it appears that cinema is first of all the experience of a continuous movement, a movement which is artificial, and exists only in the mind. For it is the mind that supplies the 'continuum' required for all the separate pictures to merge into an apparently real movement. Cinema can thus be considered from the point of view of the mechanical, or optical, or photographic elements that constitute the film used in a projector. But cinema can, also, be considered from the point of view of the person watching the film, in terms of that person's experience. In his book, *Film World,* Ivor Montagu has touched upon both aspects when he wrote that cinema is: . . . an appearance of continuous motion created in the mind of the observer by presentation of a series of motionless images in rapid sequence.[2]

In practice, 'rapid sequence' means that 16 or 24 such motionless images are thrown on the screen in one second according to whether the film is a silent movie (16 images) or a talkie, or a talking movie (24 images).[3]

. . . THAT HAVE BEEN ARRANGED IN AN APPROPRIATE SUCCESSION . . .

Now to return to the candy man sequence, one would find that the whole length of this sequence is made up of several clearly identifiable series of images or frames. There are places where two consecutive frames are markedly different: one frame is the last of a series of almost similar images; the following one is the first of the new series. Such series are called shots. Passing the candy man sequence through a slide projector one finds that it contains thirty-nine series, or shots. While the succession of frames generates the appearance of motion, the succession of shots creates meaning and rhythm. Thus one should be able to identify each shot composing the whole sequence, as follows: [1 to 30][4]

1. Durga looking at Apu says: 'you won't tell mother, won't you?'
2. Apu is given some of the pickles, makes a noise, and gets a slap.
3. Durga scolds him.
4. Apu looks at Durga's hands making the mixture.
5. Durga takes some of it.
6. Apu eats, and smiles.
7. Durga eats slowly and smiles.
8. Apu receives some more, smiles. A bell is heard faintly.

9,10. Durga takes some more. She hears the bell, rises, goes towards an opening in the wall, and peeps through the hole.

11. Through the aperture a man is seen walking at some distance.

It is possible to carry on jotting down what each 'shot' reveals. But such an analysis has no literary quality. A book written in a similar way would be dull. Yet, the film with its succession of shots, is most captivating. In fact, the thirty-nine shots flow in a pleasing succession. The film jumps as it were from Durga's face to Apu's, without the spectator experiencing any difficulty to understand. In the case of the frame succession, it is the viewer who provides the continuum or background required for experiencing movement. In the case of the shot succession, the viewer again supplies the background in which the shots complement each other to create meaning. Thus, even when one is most passive while watching a film, one is made to contribute to it much more than one thinks.

The process of arranging the shots in a proper sequence is generally called 'editing', and will be discussed in chapter 14. The following question now arises, 'where does the filmmaker get the suitable shots from?' Very rarely is a whole film photographed in the succession that one observes on the screen. The film is made shot by shot in the order most practical, from the point of view of locations or studio, of actors, and of camera requirements. The filmmaker usually knows at the time of taking a shot how he will use it in combination with preceding and following shots. After the shooting is over, he trims the shots to the correct length and fastens them together. Since editing requires a lot of 'cutting', the process is also called 'cutting', and the filmmaker must 'shoot to cut', that is, photograph the shots, so as to be able to edit them together.

. . . SO AS TO PRODUCE FICTION OUT OF REALITY

The process of making a film demands of the filmmaker the ability to dream his film before or at the time he makes it. Cinema is that particular language whereby the filmmaker shares his 'dreams' with the audience. Cinema has the unique power to lead the audience into a sort of dream, leaving very little freedom with regard to the particulars of that 'dream'. For instance, one who reads the novel *Pather Panchali* by Bibhutibhusan Bandopadhyay, can picture Apu, his features, his manner of talking. But in the film, Apu has definite characteristics, and nothing is left to the imagination, in this respect.

As an example, the first nine shots of the candy-man sequence may be considered. These are photographs of faces looking at each other. The photographs were taken by placing the camera almost at the level of Durga's and Apu's heads. This gives the feeling of being intimately associated with them at their little banquet. Had the camera been higher, one would have had the feeling of observing them from outside, or even of looking down at the children's game. What permits the filmmaker to direct the viewer's 'dream' is that which constantly challenges his skill and creativity: the realism of the photographic image. The filmmaker must wrestle with real-looking images to make them represent *his* 'dream'. The extent to which the filmmaker controls real-looking images determines the extent to which he can create fiction. Thus, the candy-man sequence that looks absolutely real is pure fiction.

To sum up: cinema is an appearance of continuous motion created by motionless images which have been arranged in an appropriate succession, so as to produce fiction out of reality. In fact, the term cinema covers the range of all films taken collectively.

This includes a large number of films that, at times, have little in common. Yet, each is an appearance of continuous movement:

- scientific films (e.g. films taken at high speed, may be up to 4,000,000 frames per second! To slow down such actions as cannot be directly observed by human eye, for instance, the incurvation of a tennis racket when it hits the ball!)
- records of events (e.g. landing on the moon).
- documentary film (where the record of events is arranged with an aim in mind).
- educational, instructional films.
- experimental films (e.g. films made without a camera!)
- fiction films: comedy, drama, suspense, Western, science fiction, detective, 'horror' films . . . .
- animation films (cartoons).

The definition of cinema should now be complemented by

stating that film language can be used, virtually, in an infinity of ways. It is like spoken language: not all speech is poetry or literature. So, also, not all film is 'art'. In other words, film can be filmic without, being artistic.[5]

However,[6] moving picture technology has evolved immensely since the above lines were written in 1974. A question may first be raised. Since films are mostly narratives, was it necessary to include in the definition of a film, the manner in which the imaginary movement is generated in the mind? Yes, it was, for a discussion of narrative, pertains primarily to art. While defining a film, it is necessary to explain how the film exists in the first place. Recent developments of technology have made it possible to generate an impression of movement in the mind of the viewer by projection of images on the monitor's screen. In other words, it is the technique of producing a 'motion picture' and a 'story' that has changed. With the new technology, for instance, you do not manually cut lengths or shots of film. This 'cutting' and 'splicing' (or joining) is done electronically. This results in tremendous possibilities in terms of variety and complexity of cuts. The technology gives unbound freedom to the imagination of the artist.

To start with, the film image (unless it is still done by means of celluloid film) is no more a sort of 'shadow play' created by projection from behind the spectators of luminous images on to a screen placed in front of them. With the new technology, the image is formed on a monitor screen by throwing electrons at light speed from behind the screen facing the viewers. In practice, whole images, as in conventional cinema, are not thrown on the screen. Rather, images are formed continuously on the monitor's screen by shooting electrons that appear as dots on the screen.

In his book, *Understanding Media* (1964), Marshal McLuhan had marvelled at the fact that the TV image offers some three million dots per second to the receiver. From these he accepts only a few dozen each instant, from which to make an image.[7] (p. 273)

What is important to note is that in both instances (celluloid photographic film, or video tape or disc), it is the human mind that provides the basis for a continuous impression of a moving image on the screen, and of the 'story' it conveys.

NOTES

1. Here we have the film in its celluloid form, not on a tape or disc.
2. I. Montagu, *Film World*, Penguin Books, 1964, p. 16.
3. In the case of a talkie 24 frames are used instead of 16, because more space is required to lay the sound-track alongside the pictures.
4. In this chapter and the following chapter on editing, figures within square brackets are both illustration numbers and shot numbers.
5. In this chapter, no discussion has been made of the sound elements that are essential to modern movies. Actually, sound is part of the film image. It is yet another realistic feature of the image itself. Sound in film is discussed in subsequent chapters of *Chitra Bani*.
6. Concluding paragraph added for the present publication.
7. Quoted in *Cyberbani*, p. 45.

SELECT BIBLIOGRAPHY

B. Happé, *Basic Motion Picture Technology*, Focal Press, 1971.
K. Smallman, *Creative Film Making*, London, 1969.

CANDY MAN SEQUENCE

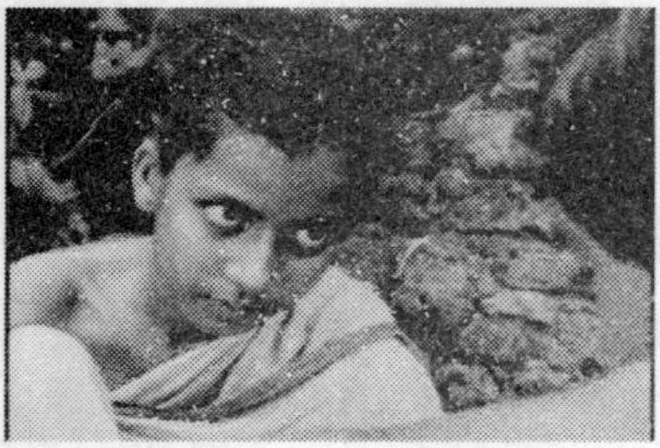

1. Durga: 'You won't tell Mommy?'

2. Apu: 'No'. Sound with mouth. Gets a slap.

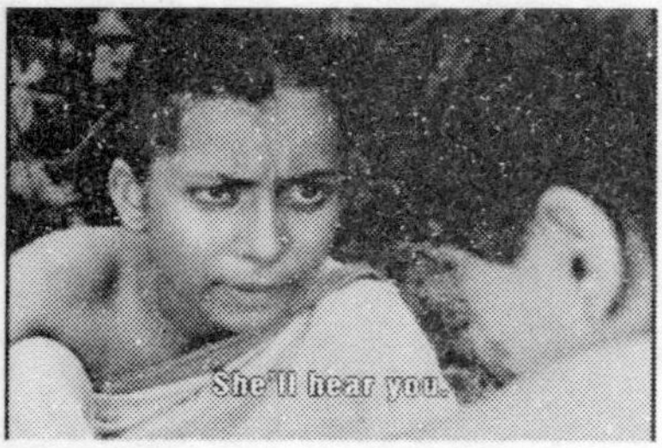

3. Durga scolding

4. Apu wipes his cheek.

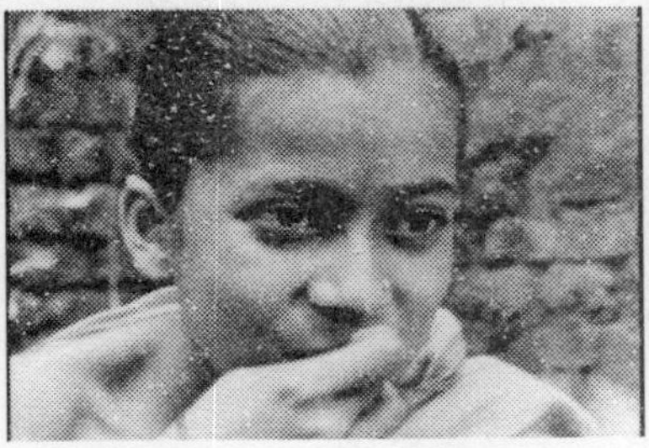

5. Durga eats.

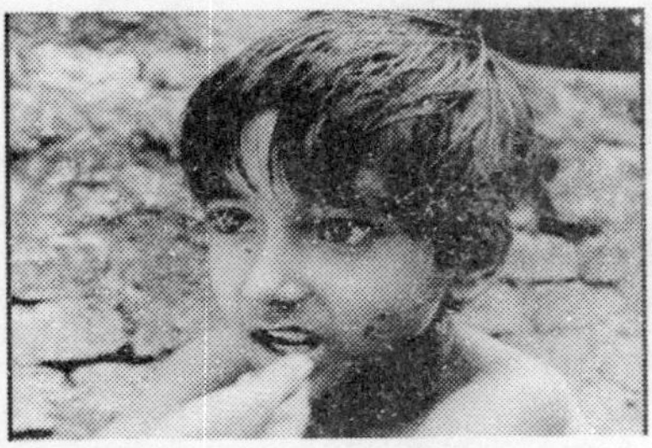

6. Apu eats, smiles.

7. Durga eats, smiles.

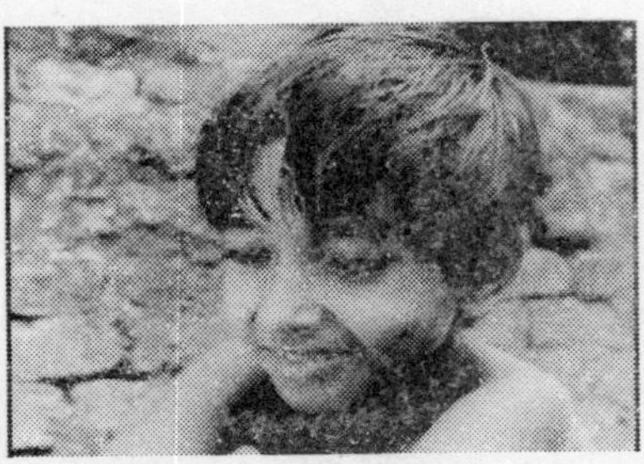

8. Apu eats, smiles.

9. Durga hears sound, goes.

10. Durga looks.

11. Candy man seen.

12. Durga leaves, Apu looks.

13. Durga and Apu look.

14. Durga and Apu standing.

15. Candy man announces sweets.

16. Durga licks her lips, asks Apu to get money from father.

17. Apu. Durga's hand on his shoulder.

18. Durga insists. Apu goes.

19. Apu talks to father. Mother's voice is heard.

20. Candy man: 'You won't take any?'

21. Durga: 'No.'

22. Candy man goes.

23. Durga, Apu, and dog go.

24. Durga and Apu running.

25. Camera pans.

26. Reflection on the pond.

27. Dissolve to pots.

28. Dissolve to tree.

29. Dissolve to ducks.

30. Party arrives at house.

CHAPTER 14

Editing*

IN MOST CASES, editing is the soul of a film: out of the succession of frames comes physical movement; out of the succession of shots comes continuity, meaning or intellectual movement, and fluency. The candy-man sequence will now be examined as to cuts and editing. The analysis of the film *Pratidwandi*, in chapter 7, complements this present chapter by discussing several types of editing methods.

PRACTICE

Editing does not consist only in joining segments of film in the right order. There is a specific place where a shot has to be cut, so that it can be joined satisfactorily to a following or previous piece. Within a few inches of film there may be more than one place where a film can thus be cut. The meaning of the film — or of the cut — may be slightly different according to what decision the filmmaker takes regarding two or more acceptable cuts for the same piece of film. Sometimes the decision of the filmmaker does not affect the meaning of a cut as much as it reveals his own style. Shot 3, for instance, in the candy-man sequence is only about twelve inches long, containing 43 frames (in 16 mm films there are 40 frames to a foot). This means that the shot is seen for less than two seconds, since 24 frames are shown in one second. After Durga slaps Apu in the face, a quick 'cut to' her scolding him, immediately reveals the cause of her anger. And a quick revert to Apu's face creates a brisk rhythm which matches the small manifestation of anger.

*G. Roberge, *Chitra Bani,* 1974, Chapter 13, Editing, pp. 65-8.

Notice also shot 11, lasting three seconds. Through the film's audio-visual language, three seconds are enough to show the cause of Durga's sudden excitement: here comes a confectioner, how great! Shot 17 is also very short (47 frames) in the context of this film. It puts emphasis on Durga's urging Apu to ask for some money from his father. The shot is brief, so as not to interrupt the pace of the events. At the same time, it is a skilful transition from shot 16, where only the face of Durga is seen, to shot 18, where from a greater distance, both Durga and Apu are seen with the house in the background, and even the dog that will become part of the action a moment later.[1] In the opening shots of the sequence the direction of each child's eyes is very important. It would not do to cut the film so that the eyes are raised or lowered indifferently at the very moment of a cut. It may be a matter of only one or two frames to produce a different effect by having, say, Durga's eyes looking up at the end of shot 1. In fact, she looks down at her cooking. As she lowers her eyes, the film cuts to Apu also looking down. In this way, both children look at the same thing, and this makes for a smooth transition from one face to the other. In shots 6 and 7 the eyes of the children looking at each other, create a communion between them. In shot 9, Durga's eyes are raised, and they direct the spectator's attention outside the frame, that is, off-screen, to where the sound of the bell is produced. So far, the children's eyes had kept the viewer's attention riveted to them. But now, with a shift of the eyes, Durga points to a larger space. This, incidentally, can hardly be termed good acting. It is, simply, good direction and good cutting.

The cut between shots 11 and 12 is most interesting. It is a cut on movement, accompanied by a change of camera angle. In shot 12, Durga, having seen through the opening in the crumbling wall, goes towards the left, off frame. One has no time to wonder where she goes, as Apu enters the frame (shot 12) from the right, quickly sees for himself what his sister has seen, and follows her towards the left. As he is about to disappear, the cut takes place, and it is now Durga who enters the frame (shot 13) from the right followed by Apu. The camera itself did not turn towards the left but squarely changed position. There is an illusion of movement from the opening in the wall towards the left thus created. In fact, the wall next to which Durga and Apu are seen standing in shot 14 could be anywhere, in relation to the aperture in the wall. It could even be miles away. But the skilful cut on the movement of the children has created a convincing, real or fictitious, topography.

Moreover, the time is elongated, for Durga should have reached the door by the time Apu leaves the aperture through which he is looking. But caught as one is in the flow of the film one does not think of this, and accepts the time and space created by the filmmaker. In fact, it is much more exciting to see Durga rushing out the better to observe the candy-man, than to see her already standing there. Intensity and excitement distort time psychologically, either protracting it or shortening it.

Cut 18 is interesting: it could have taken place elsewhere. For instance, the filmmaker could have shown Apu crossing the doorway and walking towards his father, after going out of frame in shot 17. The continuity would have been maintained. Instead of this, the filmmaker has Apu go out of frame in shot 18, but then, he shows the courtyard where Harihar is smoking his hookah. This creates a sense of expectation (the shot being static during the time of a few frames reinforces that feeling): what is going to happen? Will Harihar give him any money? Throughout the sequence the viewer is made to identify with Apu and Durga. Now he/she is made to feel what Apu must be feeling as he walks towards his father. It is then that Apu steps inside the frame and makes the viewer sort of accompany him inside, towards his father. Most filmmakers would cut here to a closer shot of Harihar and Apu talking together. This would certainly be a 'nice' shot. But here, rather unexpectedly, the filmmaker has the viewer stay at the door, thus heightening the sense of expectation. This time, with Durga, who watches the results of Apu's mission, the viewer observes and waits. From far, the viewer understands with Durga that thanks to Sarbajaya (voice off-screen) Apu's request is being turned down.

It is, then, logical that when in shot 20 the candy man asks: 'Aren't you taking anything?' (42 frames), there is a cut straight to shot 21, showing Durga sadly answering with a shake of the head.

The succession of shots 23 to 30, where Durga, Apu, and the dog follow the candy-man, creates a moment of respite in the sequence. It does little to advance the story, yet, it conveys deep feelings. Indeed, this segment of the film functions like a dance in other Indian films. It is delightful to watch. But, whereas, the dances in Indian films are usually brought in for their own sake, and impede the development of the story, here shots 23 to 30 do show the environment in which Durga and Apu live. Moreover, they associate that environment with their simple joy and sense of wonder. The bamboo grove quivers with joy, as it were. The pond in which the little group are reflected, seems to take on a new life. Observe carefully how these shots are joined one to the other. When a film describes events unfolding, as in the opening shots, the 'story' serves as a means of holding the shots together meaningfully. But in a succession like that of shots 23 to 30, there is no story to fall back on. That is why the filmmaker emphasizes the graphic continuity of one shot to the other. The form of one image is made to merge with the next one. For instance, in shot 22, the candy-man turns and leaves, thus initiating a movement. Shot 23 reveals Durga just about to follow him. She has almost started to go when shot 23 shows her. If the filmmaker had left a few more frames at the beginning of shot 23, the whole movement would have been slowed down, perhaps to the point of creating a slight malaise in the viewer — the first sign of boredom. Correct cutting makes for rhythm and liveliness.

Next, the candy-man leaves, Durga follows him, Apu joins her, and finally even the dog, so far immobile, suddenly starts running.[2] All of them go one after the other out of the frame. The viewer does not see immediately where they go, but this causes no difficulty, as the frame of the screen does not limit the space in which they move. It is an imaginary space. As they run, the three protagonists determine a sweeping movement from left to right. The next shot carries on the same movement from left to right. Visually, the two shots are so well-linked that the camera can change position to show a new, larger area. The spectator hardly notices the change of viewpoint. Again, as the three protagonists go out of frame the camera tilts to reveal the candy man walking ahead a distance away. Then as one is led to expect another shot showing the children catching up with the candy man, instead there is shown a rather close shot of the pots containing the coveted sweets (shot 27). This is done through a 'mix', that is, by making the end of one shot fuse with the beginning of the next one. This usually suggests a leap in time or in space. In this case, the mix allows skipping over a segment of movement (the children catching up with the candy man) without producing a jerk in the continuity of the sequence. The close shot, also, has an almost hypnotic effect and grips the viewer's attention. Besides, too many shots of people seen from far (long shots as these are called) might wear out the attention of the spectator. In this case, the mix has a pleasing and unexpected effect; it recaptures close attention to the film.

The next shot is another mix where the pots merge into trees. This allows a change in the direction of the people walking. Finally, the trees merge into ducks which introduce into the frame the pots, the man, and the children. Thanks to these few mixes the distance from the children's house to that of their neighbours is covered. The reader may like to examine and discuss for him/herself the manner in which the subsequent shots have been joined together. When this is done, the film can be run once more in a projector at normal speed. The sequence is much more enjoyable to one who can appreciate the delightful manner in which it is put together. The joy of appreciating films is next only to that of creating them.

But a film is so complex a means of communication, that one cannot fully appreciate a film in a single screening, even if one is well trained.

THEORY

The practice of editing rests on the principle that 'shots rightly selected and viewed from the correct angle, in a right order, cut to the right length, beginning and ending at the right moment are apprehended as a single whole'.[3]

While this principle is true and has been applied in the creation of most masterpieces of the cinema, its application is not absolutely necessary. In other words, one can make films in which the continuity is not created by editing, as has been discussed in the candy-man sequence. There is indeed some sort of cutting or editing in all films (barring oddities like Hitchcock's *The Rope,* 1948, made in one shot!). But the idea that editing is an essential part of film language, and hence of film art, has been successfully challenged by recent filmmakers, notably by J.L. Godard. In those films where editing is considered not as an essential but as an optional device, the continuity required for understanding the film is established at a different level than that of the story line or that of the graphic line. Then, the segments of the film are projected on the screen in the manner of a mosaic, and perhaps this may require a greater effort to grasp the overall meaning of the fragments.

Under the influence of the early Russian filmmakers, like S.M. Eisenstein (1898-1948) and Vsevolod Pudovkin (1893-1953), a theory of editing was developed, and *montage,* a French word, was used to denote the process. Meanwhile, the American David Wark Griffith (1875-1948) made hundreds of films in which he instinctively discovered and used most of the types of editing. Griffith lacked the leisure, and, perhaps, the inclination to develop theories about his work.

One of the main tenets of the Russian theory is that when one shot is made to follow another, a meaning is created which was in neither of the shots. If one shot is represented by 'a', and another shot by 'b', then a+b = c, that is, a third film image. The theoreticians of montage were simply — and rightly

— taken up by this idea. They studied its implications and even made experiments to assess the power of the editing process. The most famous of these experiments consisted in cutting into three segments a lengthy shot of the face of an actor. Between these segments were placed three different shots: a bowl of soup, a dead woman, and a girl playing. When the six shots were projected in this order:

soup + actor + woman + actor + girl + actor,

the viewer had the impression that the face of the actor took on various expressions according to the shot that was next to it. In fact, the facial expression was the same throughout. This experiment is known as the 'Kuleshov effect', after the name of the great theoretician who conducted it.

Another phenomenon created by editing or montage is that shots at times may proceed like a train or like a layer of bricks, where each brick adds to the preceding one. Pudovkin who was fond of this type of montage used it very successfully in his *Storm over Asia* (1929). One has a fine example of this type of montage towards the end of *Pratidwandi*. After Siddhartha leaves the interviewers and walks on the street, a series of posters are seen on the wall. Suddenly the posters give way to a series of paddy fields shown in succession in the same direction.

NOTES

1. In terms of 'continuity', however, there is a small fault between shots 17 and 18. For, shot 17 shows Durga with her hand on Apu's shoulder; and in shot 18 Durga's hand is resting by her side. But this is hardly noticeable — and hardly significant.
2. Ray has commented on this scene in his interview on scriptwriting. Chapter 21.
3. I. Montagu, *Film World*, Pelican Books, 1964, p. 109.

SELECT BIBLIOGRAPHY

K. Reisz, et al., *The Technique of Film Editing*, The Focal Press, 1968.
E. Walter, *The Technique of the Film Cutting Room*, The Focal Press, 1969.

CHAPTER 15

Metz' Large Syntagmatic Category Applied to Three Ray Films*

Apur Sansar (The World of Apu), 1959 *Charulata*, 1964 (The Lonely Wife), *Aranyer Din Ratri* (Days and Nights in the Forest), 1969

IN HIS BOOK *Film Language*, Metz has given a 'General Table of the Large Syntagmatic Category of the Image Track' in which he has listed eight types of sequences. Metz himself has re-worked that table several times, and I have taken the liberty to also re-work it a little more. Metz calls syntagmas those segments of films which are usually called sequences and which have a degree of autonomy within a film, as they constitute definite parts of the story. Some of the syntagmas are chronological; others are a-chronological, according to whether or not they imply a reference to time. The a-chronological syntagmas are of two sorts: the *parallel syntagmas*, when a few shots are put in parallel to establish a comparison, e.g. the house of a rich boy and that of a poor boy, and the *bracket syntagmas*, when a number of shots which are not necessarily connected from the points of view of place and time, suggest an idea, like shots of bombs thrown from aircrafts suggest the idea of war. The chronological syntagmas are by far the most numerous in ordinary narrative films.

*G. Roberge, *Films for an Ecology of Mind: Essays on Realism in the Cinema.* 1978, pp. 89-93.

They can be *descriptive syntagmas*, or narrative ones. For, a narration often includes descriptions that seem to suspend the course of its story but are nonetheless necessary to it. For instance, shots that establish the place where an event happens belong to the narrative's time, although they seem to interrupt it momentarily. Another sort of descriptive syntagma is the *sequence in the potential mode*, although there are relatively few examples of such a sequence. In a story, it may happen that various courses of action are open to a protagonist. The filmmaker may show these various courses of action, leaving it to the spectator to speculate — should he care to — what course the protagonist actually took. The narrative syntagmas are linear or alternate. The *alternate syntagmas*, show chronologically and alternately the unfolding of two or more actions. The linear syntagmas are firstly those in which the time of the action and the time of the film coincide: these are *the scenes.* When the time of the film and that of the action do not coincide, then, one has a sequence. Sequences are of two types: *the episodic* sequence, is made up of shots showing parts of a total process which are too short to be autonomous. For instance, in *Citizen Kane,* the 'breakfast sequence' shows Kane becoming progressively estranged from his wife, is an episodic sequence.[1] Finally the *ordinary sequences*, are autonomous narrative segments that do not include the small and incomplete scenes characterizing the episodic sequences. In an ordinary sequence the time of the film is either longer or shorter than that of the story. The eight large syntagmas or autonomous segments of a narrative film can be listed as in Table 1.

Bearing in mind that Metz's large syntagmatic category pertains only to the image track of the sole narrative film, we can now attempt to utilize its concepts in order to analyse a few sound films, and see if we can uncover in these films correlates to the responses we experience while watching them. The films I have chosen are Satyajit Ray's *The World of Apu* (*WA*), *Charulata* (*CH*) and *Days and Nights in the Forest*

TABLE 1: *General Table of the Large Syntagmatic Category of the Image Track in Narrative Films after Christian Metz*

- autonomous segments or syntagmas
  - a-chronological
    - 1. *parallel syntagmas*
    - 2. *bracket syntagmas*
  - chronological
    - descriptive
      - 3. *descriptive syntagmas*
      - 4. *syntagmas in the potential mode*
    - narrative
      - 5. *alternative syntagmas*
      - linear
        - 6. *scenes*
        - sequences
          - 7. *episodic sequences*
          - 8. *ordinary sequences*

(*DN*). One can easily perceive a stylistic evolution from the first of these three films (1959) to the third (1969). The narration in *DN* is much freer than that in *WA*. One has the definite impression that the latter film is tighter and less 'slow'. This impression rests on the specific way in which these films are made. For instance, the number of shots is obviously greater in *DN* than in *WA*, and this can be perceived at a first screening of these films. A shot by shot study of the films reveals that, in fact, the number of shots in *WA* is only 435, while it is almost double, namely 858, in *DN*. On the other hand, the number of large syntagmas is much greater in *WA* than in *DN*. Even though the identification of the large syntagmas might vary to an extent from one student to another, since in the present case the same method has been applied by the same person, it is significant that the number of syntagmas in *WA* is 34 and only 20 in *DN*. Thus, in these two films the number of shots and the number of large syntagmas are inversely proportional. As for *CH*, in almost every respect, this film stands between *WA* and *DN*. The various points mentioned so far can be summarized thus:

TABLE 2: *Syntagmas and Shots in Satyajit Ray's The World of Apu* (*WA*), *Charulata* (*CH*) and *Days and Nights in the Forest* (*DN*).

		WA	*CH*	*DN*
1.	date of the film	1959	1964	1969
2.	screen time in minutes	117	112	115
3.	film time (time of the story)	5 years	5 months	3 days
4.	number of shots	435	500	858
5.	number of large syntagmas	34	24	20
6.	dissolves	40	15	few

The number of shots mentioned in Table 2 does not include the inserts. However, while there are very few inserts in *WA*, there are many of them in *DN*. The diminution of large syntagmas in *DN* is predictable, given the short duration of the story time. But on the other hand, the increase in the number of shots is the more significant from the point of view of style. It is largely because there are a greater number of shots that one feels the style is freer, swifter and as such, more exciting in *DN* than in *WA*. In *DN* the unity of space and time does not need to be preserved, as in *WA*, within the shot itself. It transcends the succession of shots. Again, the interpersonal relationships are established by straight cuts from one person to the other, from one point of view to another. Nor can one observe in *DN* these shots lasting for a long time as in *WA*. On the other hand, the story time and the film time coincide in *DN* for quite a few moments in several occasions. Then, the intensity of the emotion replaces the rapid succession of shots. One notices also a great diminution in the number of mixes (or dissolves). There are but few of these in *DN* while there are some fifteen in *CH* and as many as forty in *WA*. Again, the stereotyped sequence opener of *WA*, namely, a close up widening into a middle or long shot, is almost absent from *DN*.

What these differences between *WA* and *DN* point to, and what one feels while watching these films, is a greater freedom in the use of the film medium, as if Ray had broken the spell the image seems to have had on him in his early films. In *DN*, Ray totally masters the image he creates. Perhaps one could compare *WA* to a painting and *DN* to music. Again, one might argue that *WA* is somewhat like traditional, conventional, theatre while *DN* is more similar to a novel. In a way, whatever the qualities (mainly beauty, strength, and truth in the depiction of emotions) of *WA*, *DN* is much better cinematically than *WA*. The foregoing discussion has provided correlates to this response to the films, a response which was expressed with great perceptivity by Penelope Houston in her review of *DN*:

> In terms of the subject, *Days and Nights in the Forest* risks being classified as small-scale Ray. In fact, one would rate this lucid, ironic and superlatively graceful film among the very best of his work, not least for the evidence of how much a director actually learns about his craft. It's no insult to the *Apu* Trilogy to say that the Ray of those days lacked the sheer confidence, the ability, to turn around and manoeuvre within a film and a scene, that enables him to achieve that exact pitch and balance of *Days and Nights*.[2]

Thanks to the contribution of linguistics to film study, it has become possible, as the above examples show, to uncover and state with a degree of accuracy those elements in a film that cause a critic and even a simple cinema-goer to give a specific response to a film.

The comparison between *WA* and *DN* was discussed within the same film aesthetics. What if we now compare these two films with *The Battleship Potemkin*? Eisenstein's film is of about 70 minutes (according to the print used) and has 1472 shots.[3] The Average Shot Length (ASL) is 2.85 seconds and 8.04 seconds in *Potemkin* and *DN*, respectively. *Potemkin* shows over 21 shots a minute, *DN* over 7 shots a minute. But then, Ray and Eisenstein created their films in the framework of two different aesthetics, one committed to preserve the realism of appearance to make things radiate their 'universal' meaning, the other committed to manipulate the appearance of things to make them convey a particular meaning. The screen: a transparent window open onto the world/an opaque surface on which to interpret the world.

NOTES

1. The sequence is made of fragments of breakfast scenes. Each fragment shows Kane and his wife at table. But the breakfast table is longer and more lonely from one fragment to the next.
2. Penelope Houston, in *Monthly Film Bulletin,* December 1971.
3. I am thankful to Yuri Tsivian for this information. See http://www.cinemetrics.lv/cintsi.php

Photo: Bimal Samaddar, 22 January1988 © Chitrabani

Gaston Roberge escorts Satyajit Ray to a meeting of the heads of the production centres of the educational television programmes, 'the Countrywide Classroom.' Ray had kindly accepted to inaugurate the meeting. The meeting was hosted by the Educational Media Research Centre of St. Xavier's College, Kolkata.

Photo: Bimal Samaddar, 22 January 1988 © Chitrabani

From right to left: Satyajit Ray, Gaston Roberge,
Prof. E.V. Chitnis, Dr S.S. Swani

Photo: Brian Balen, 13 February 1976 © Chitrabani

Ray and Roberge in the Rita Ray Memorial Library, Chitrabani.

Photo: Brian Balen, April 1976 © Chitrabani

Subrato Mitra, cinematographer of the Ray films from *Pather Panchali* to *Charulata*, and of *Nayak*.

PART FOUR

The Cinema of Satyajit Ray

CHAPTER 16

And Then Came Satyajit*

THE EMERGENCE of a cinéaste like Satyajit Ray in a city like Calcutta is not surprising, if one bears in mind that in the last two centuries Bengal has produced remarkable personalities in nearly every aspect of life: social, cultural, religious, scientific, political or intellectual. Ramakrishnadeb (1836-86), Shri Aurobindo (1872-1950), Swami Vivekananda (1863-1902), and, of course, Rabindranath Tagore (1861-1941) are perhaps the best known Bengalis outside India. But there are several others who would deserve to be better known, like S.N. Bose (1894-1941), for instance, who was in communication with Einstein, and who gave his name to the atomic particle, the 'boson'.

SATYAJIT RAY, INHERITOR OF TAGORE

Rabindranath Tagore was well acquainted with the family of Satyajit Ray. Both Satyajit's grandfather and father were renowned artists. The grandfather was also a printer, and one notices the printing presses in Ray's films. He had created a children's magazine, and he used to write for that magazine and to illustrate it. Satyajit's father too was a well-known writer of children's literature and nonsense verse. Shortly before his death, when he was very ill, Tagore had come to see him and, at the request of the sick man, Tagore had interpreted a few of his songs. Satyajit was about two years old. Can it be that he remembered the scene? Did he hear about it? Whatever that may be, the incident shows that there was a very deep emotional link between the Rays and Tagore. As for Satyajit's

*December 1992.

mother, she used to sing Tagore's songs very well, an aptitude that had won her the favour of her future husband, the father of Satyajit. She had one day visited Tagore with Satyajit, still a child, when the poet gave the boy a poem in his own handwriting.

Satyajit has, therefore, lived in a Tagorean atmosphere from his early childhood. Tagore had founded a University, called Shantiniketan, with the money from his Nobel Prize. He was experimenting with methods of education adapted to Indian cultures. When, at the urgent suggestion of his mother and of Tagore himself, Satyajit was persuaded to join Shantiniketan, he was nineteen. Tagore was nearly eighty years old and somewhat inaccessible, so venerable had he become. Satyajit was there to learn painting, and so he did. At the same time, he read Tagore's novels, though not much of his poetry; he heard the songs, watched the plays interpreted by the students of Shantiniketan. Shortly after Tagore's death in 1941, Ray left Shantiniketan, perhaps in search of his roots. On a journey across India, he discovered Indian art and culture, especially in the mural frescoes of Ajanta.

Around 1945, when Ray was hardly twenty-four, he wrote a film scenario of Tagore's novel, *Ghare Baire.* The film could not be made at the time. But Ray finally made it— needless to say with a fresh scenario—some forty years later. That shows how lasting the influence of Tagore has been on Ray. Then, in 1961, on the occasion of Tagore's birth centenary, Ray selected three short stories by Tagore and made them into a film trilogy, *Teen Kanya* (Three Daughters). In the same year, Ray made an exceptional documentary on Tagore, called, with Ray's typical directness and simplicity, *Rabindranath Tagore.* In 1964, Ray made the film *Charulata*, from a novella by Tagore. However, Ray has remained totally free while handling Tagore's material. He even transformed the material whenever he felt that he could not follow Tagore without betraying his own sensibility. As he once said, 'I too am an artist, I too have my way of seeing things.' But each time he departed from the master, Ray encountered disapproval in Calcutta. It could be said that

Ray was so close to Tagore that he was entitled to some freedom with regard to the work of Tagore. In 1961, when he had made his documentary on Tagore, Ray had opened his film with these words, as if he was talking about himself some thirty years ahead of time:

> On 7th August 1941, in the city of Calcutta, a man died. His mortal remains perished, but he left behind him a heritage, which no fire could consume. It is a heritage of words and music and poetry, of ideas and of ideals. And it has the power to move us, to inspire us, today and in the days to come. We, who owe him so much, salute his memory.

We are concerned here with the cinema of Satyajit Ray. But we cannot altogether forget the fascinating personality of the filmmaker himself. For Ray was not just a filmmaker, he belonged to a specific society, and, in fact, he played a significant role in that society, even though it was not always the role expected of him. As time went on, and with increasing recognition abroad, Ray became more independent from the Calcutta public, but he nonetheless remained deeply rooted in the Bengali culture.

Bengali society confers a great power on its great sons and daughters. Because of this power Ray was able to play an important role in Bengal as well as in India. Most matters pertaining to the production of films and to the spread of film education were brought to him for his opinion, or as we say in Bengal, for his 'blessing'. Throughout, though, Ray avoided the pitfalls, even the traps, of second-rate politics.

RAY DID FOR THE BENGALI CINEMA, WHAT TAGORE HAD DONE FOR THE BENGALI LITERATURE

Like Tagore, Ray mastered various means of expression. But, if Tagore came to painting when he was seventy years old, Ray was young a painter, a musician, and a film expert. Until the end of his life, he edited the magazine *Sandesh* started by his grandfather, and he would also write a novel almost every year for publication in a popular magazine, on the occasion of Durga Puja. He designed several book covers. He even created two type faces which won an international award in 1971, Ray Roman (see the cover design of the present volume) and Ray Bizarre.

Satyajit Ray is often mentioned as a filmmaker who became a master without ever going to a film school. But this does not mean that he did not learn his craft. Few young men, I suppose, study on their own, as Ray did, the films they see, and imagine alternative scenarios for those films. As the years passed, Ray himself performed most of the tasks involved in filmmaking: screenplay, camera, editing, music, decor, and direction. Few filmmakers have mastered, as he did, all aspects of film production. Abel Gance used to complain that between his conception of a film and its realization, there was a drop of voltage, as it were, of some 20 per cent. That is due to the fact that a film is a collaborative creation. And it is difficult to enthuse each of the persons working on a film with the original inspiration. Ray, with a small and permanent team, limited means and, of course, a multifaceted talent, saw to all the details of his films.

There has been a profound evolution in the films of Ray ever since the *Apu* trilogy. Penelope Houston, for instance, has noted this fact after the first few films made by Ray. There was, first of all, a greater mastery of film language: the films are less and less dependent on theatre conventions as the work progresses; from *Teen Kanya* (1961) already, Ray had started composing the music for all his films. After *Charulata* (1964) Ray himself often handles the camera, especially if a shot involves a camera movement that must adjust to an actor's performance. He writes all his scripts, and has even created several original screenplays, including six feature films, five documentaries, and two short films.

But there is also a thematic evolution, in particular, in the images Ray offers of women. Of course, he is not a staunch feminist. Yet, he has shown on the screen women that are responsible and independent, in sharp contrast to the image of the woman submissive to the point of slavery in a popular film like *Mother India*, for instance. But Nargis the heroine of

Mother India, accused Ray of showing the poverty of India in his masterpiece *Pather Panchali.* Her own reactionary and socially harmful depiction of a woman did not bother her.

Ray's film career was exceptional in every way, from the start till the end. Cannes felt compelled to give him a special prize for his first film, and Hollywood gave him a special Oscar for his career as a whole. But it was too late, Ray was already very ill. Meanwhile, France, always a little avant-garde, at least in matters of cinema, had given Ray her *Légion d'Honneur.* Since Cannes in 1952 to Hollywood in 1992, the prizes and honors bestowed on Ray are countless.

RAY, LIKE TAGORE, WAS A GREAT MORALIST

What is the major impact of Ray's cinema? How should it be characterized? Integrity — aesthetic and ethical — is the theme that inspires and informs the whole work of Ray with an astonishing perseverance. I fully concur with Henri Micciolli who could write in 1981, and the years following the publication of his book have confirmed his view:

> His (Ray) films show by their very language that for him, strictly, cinema is a 'matter of ethics'. They speak (. . .) of the nostalgia for lost purity, which art alone can recover in the very moment when it expresses it. How not to see that the Calcutta master is first of all a great moralist?[1]

Satyajit Ray was confronted by political action. He showed, like Tagore before him, that the specific action of an artist is artistic. When Gandhi asked Tagore why he was not joining him in his political movement, Tagore had answered, 'You spin cotton, I spin words. Each to his vocation.' Tagore needed a lot of courage to pursue his personal vocation. Ray needed no less to do the same in circumstances that were perhaps even more constraining by their dogmatism and doctrinaire rigidity.

The integrity which was of concern to Ray was that of life, and of truth to self. Look at the characters created by Ray. Apu becomes himself very progressively. He must abandon his romantic dreams: his life is not a novel. He has to become an adult man, the husband of his wife, and the father of his child. Charulata finds her truth in self-expression, but also in her confrontation with her husband. But the integrity Ray sees constantly denied is professional (*Pratidwandi*), economic (*Seemabaddha*), and political (*The Chess Players*). In this respect, Ray's last but one film, *Shakha Proshakha,* is perhaps his final word on the subject. In this film, the elderly man who had lived according to ideals of integrity all his life, and who had been eminently successful, is struck by illness. As he recovers, he awakes to the fact that the world, including his sons, is rotten to the core. The moral values that had inspired him have vanished. And there seems to be no one left to even care for them. Only a certain madness can keep one sensitive to these values.

Moralist, yes. But Ray is no judge. He damns no one. He does not condemn. He does not admonish. Nor is he moralizing. He does not try to change society (chapter 11, last lines). He takes note, he wonders, he probes, always with compassion. And, like Tagore, he affirms his faith in man and woman.

At this point, I wish to comment on two characteristics for which Ray has been praised. He has often been hailed as a humanist and as a master of understatement.

BUT WAS RAY A HUMANIST AND A MASTER OF UNDERSTATEMENT?[2]

Ray was not committed to a system of thought, however sublime. He was himself. And before being a humanist — if he was — he was profoundly humane. His humaneness — not just humanness — was marked by sympathy, compassion, mercy, and love. This attitude is marvellously manifested in a particular gesture of Apu. Towards the end of *Pather Panchali*, and after the death of Durga, Apu accidentally discovers the necklace Durga had been accused of stealing. Apu just throws the necklace in the nearby pond — the silent witness of his family's life. The pond is covered with plant seeds. As the necklace falls into the pond, the seeds recede, the clear water is seen, and slowly the seeds close the circle. The pond has received Apu's secret. The sequence opens with a shot of Apu reaching up on a shelf to take a coconut shell. That shot is reminiscent of a similar shot earlier in the film: from the same shelf, Apu gives Durga an object. Then, Apu and Durga secretly enjoy some pickles cooked by Durga. That moment of shared happiness remained unknown to the children's mother. A childhood secret. So, when Apu discovers the stolen necklace, he is now in possession of another secret, which he shares with Durga. Instead of making a fuss, of spreading the news, in a profoundly humane gesture, he throws the necklace into the pond. In that simple gesture is expressed loyalty, forgiveness, and love, which is, to use Ray's phrase, what 'binds this life together'. Would you call that humanism? I would not. That is humaneness. And, to introduce my next point, would you call that scene an 'understatement'?

The scene of Apu disposing of the stolen necklace cannot be seen as an understatement. It is clear and emotionally laden. Similarly, the magnificent scene when Harihar comes to know that Durga is dead is extremely powerful in its theme and filmic rendering. Consider: Harihar has just come back after a long absence. He does not know Durga is dead. He has brought gifts for the whole family. When he gives Sarbajaya the sari he has brought for Durga, we see her biting the sari to contain her wailing, and immediately the music takes over, and the spectator hears, as it were, the silent cry of Sarbajaya. But Harihar does not know of Durga's death, he does not see Sarbajaya biting the sari, he does not hear her silent cry. But the spectator knows, sees and hears. The poignancy of the scene is maximized. Would anyone call this scene an example of understatement? And, to cut the story short, when in *Agantuk*, Ray speaks out his mind through his bison — Utpal Dutt — about present-day civilization, is he making an understatement?

CONCLUSION

In 1990, almost at the same time, two films were made in Calcutta. One with enormous means, the other with a very limited budget. One seeking to be a film on the city of joy within Calcutta, namely Pilkhana, in Howrah. The other modestly speaking of nothing less than contemporary civilization. It is difficult not to ponder over this coincidence. Coincidence in time, first of all. But, coincidence as well in the manner in which the two films were received in Calcutta, that is, in complete misunderstanding. Roland Joffe's film, is simply a bad film. It has hardly anything to do with Dominique Lapierre's book, and still less with the reality of Calcutta. *City of Joy* is, in fact, a poor fantasy on American interventionism. Ray, in *Agantuk*, needs no exotic locale. From within his own culture, he looks with great lucidity at the world. He takes up Tagore's reflection on civilization where Tagore had left off, and he takes it one step ahead: neither West nor East, but a return to the sources of the human person, to what makes the human person human. Shall I dare say the word which Ray evokes so strongly but never utters? Love is the source.

NOTES

1. Henri Micciollo, *Satyajit Ray*, Lausanne: *L'Âge d'Homme*, 1981, p. 22.
2. This paragraph has been added to the original article for the present book. I have discussed at length, but from an ideological point of view, the question of humanism in Ray's cinema, in an article of 1979. See Chapter 19.

CHAPTER 17

The Discipline of Art*

SATYAJIT RAY has the reputation of working with great discipline. The shooting of his films is minutely planned. His direction is firm and precise. Takes are few, and the shooting ratio is extremely low. The budget is moderate. Ray himself performs several major tasks in the making of his films: scriptwriter, music composer, director and, at times, cameraperson. In addition, he closely supervises all other aspects of the production, especially art direction and editing. He has a stable and well-knit production team. The same actors appear in several of his films. All this, of course, makes for efficiency, and the Ray films follow each other in rapid succession.

Such a discipline is almost surprising in an Indian industry that is notoriously wasteful and, indeed, undisciplined. Filmmaking is so expensive a proposition that restraint and discipline would seem to be absolutely required for its commercial success. But that is not the case: extravaganzas of all types are an ingredient of the present Indian commercial formula. Satyajit Ray is as concerned as any other filmmaker with the commercial success of his films, but he does not rely on, and, indeed, does not need, the *tamasha* characteristic of part of the 'commercial' cinema. The formative principles of Ray's cinema are not commercial; they are aesthetic and moral.

Ray himself has demonstrated that the Indian film industry is quite capable of discipline, and can even enjoy working in a disciplined manner. Some time in the mid-1970s, I happened to meet Mr. Ray just as he came back from Mumbai. He had gone there to prepare the production of his next film, in Hindi,

*1992.

The Chess Players. He was worried. After he had signed contracts with a few artists, some members of the local film industry warned him that he should be prepared for disappointment. Most stars, he was told, never turn up on time for the shooting, and occasionally come inebriated. Mr. Ray told me he would not tolerate any such indiscipline, and would cancel contracts if need be. Several months later, he came back to Kolkata, having completed the shooting and editing of the film. He was elated. He told me that the film stars, without any exception, had been exemplary, punctual, fit for shooting, and had memorized their lines. It was obvious that they too were happy with their own performance under the masterly direction of Satyajit Ray.

TWO FORMS OF DISCIPLINE IN FILMMAKING: PROSPECTIVE AND PROJECTIVE

There is no art without discipline. For art itself is a discipline: the discipline of form. Artists create order and harmony, not quite out of chaos, but out of what Pushkin has called 'the indifferent nature'. Every element of an artwork is 'in-formed', set in order, by the creative impulse. There generally is no room in an artwork for stray, undisciplined, elements. That is why, art, like life itself, is improbable and always something of a surprise.

In filmmaking, the discipline of form is practised in two different ways. Some filmmakers' approach is prospective: they look for their film, as it were. Theirs is a search, patient, though at times reckless, prompted by a shape, an event, or a rhythm, and by the conviction that a film is out 'there' as a latent being, and that it is the filmmaker's task to bring it into existence. This approach always seems to lack discipline.

Yet, it has its own demands, namely, that the filmmaker be unconditionally sensitive to the inner impulse possessing him, and to the messages emanating outside him from a location, for instance, or a text, or an actor's performance, or a sound. One can yield to these impulses and messages — inside and outside — only if one is capable of an attention and a docility that together constitute a manner of discipline. That discipline is, of course, a nightmare for the film's producer who, naturally, has to obey other impulses and messages from other quarters.

The other form of discipline in filmmaking is projective. The film is in 'here', in the cinéaste's imagination. His task is to project it out, to cause it to materialize. This approach is consonant with the two chief characteristics of film, namely, to be an expensive commodity and to be a collaborative production. As an expensive product, film can accommodate but few deviations from a pre-established budget of time and money. As a collaborative endeavour, a film requires that each member of the creative team know exactly what has to be done. Satyajit Ray's method is an example of the projective approach to filmmaking.

However, a filmmaker is not free to adopt the projective or the prospective method. This is not left to his choice. He is predetermined by his particular talent to follow one or the other method. A filmmaker cannot use the projective method, for instance, unless he is endowed with a vivid creative imagination. Since this precious gift is unequally distributed among filmmakers, in practice you have a wide range of variations and combinations between the projective and prospective methods. Even in the case of Ray, an artist for whom the projective method is almost natural, the prospective method is not excluded.

THE QUALITIES OF SATYAJIT RAY FROM WHICH DERIVES HIS ART DISCIPLINE

Satyajit Ray has a unique set of qualities and attitudes that make the projective discipline most suitable to him. First, he has the required basic quality, namely, a precise visual and aural imagination. This permits him to see and hear in his mind his characters in great detail. His power to imagine, that is, to form images, is served and enhanced by his mastery of film language, his firm aesthetic judgement, and his versatile story telling ability. With that set of qualities one knows what one wants, and one can set out to do just that systematically. Above all, one can communicate to others what one wants. It is most fascinating, for instance, to hear Ray telling the story of a film he is working on. One remains haunted by the intense narration and the vivid images it evokes. One does not get a vague idea of what the film will be; to an extent, one gets the film itself. Ray does not share his 'dream' only in words, he does it through drawings also. One is reminded of Eisenstein who too could describe and even draw the details of the film he envisaged. When teaching film direction at the film institute of Moscow, he helped his students develop this ability.[1] One is struck by the accuracy of both Eisenstein and Ray's drawings of their intended characters, locations, costumes, and sets. In addition to words and drawings, Ray has yet another means of expression: music. As he goes along creating a film in his mind or on paper, fragments of music emerge with enough clarity for Ray to jot down their staff notation. He can hum the tune or play it on the piano or synthesizer. It is on this sort of creative imagination that rests the ability to plan the shooting of a film meticulously and to direct actors clearly.

The qualities just mentioned, however, would not be operative to the extent they are in Ray if he had not also developed two more attitudes. The first one is the will to leave nothing out of control. Often in less accomplished artists a certain laziness leads to sloppy results. The determination to attend to details and to plan out everything is an artist's manner of commitment. The aim is not simply to have the correct detail but to make each detail a meaningful element, a bearer of sense, a sign. Again, this is not just commitment to 'art for art's sake', but a commitment to self — to the standards one has set for oneself — and to others, that is, to the standards one must maintain out of respect and concern for the audience.

Commitment to self, to others, to standards, the quasi-inability to do otherwise, all these illustrate yet another aspect of discipline.[2] To be disciplined is to make oneself a 'disciple'. The master here is self, on the one hand, and form, on the other. The self accepts to be possessed by a form. And at the same time, the self takes form, that is, comes to be. For instance, the ending of *Gana Shatru*, where the musical form prevails over the dramatic form of the film. This shows that, in *Gana Shatru*, Ray was committed to the musical form, that of a hymn to joy, not to the form of the drama.

The concern for others noted above derives from the other moral attitude Ray has developed: love. When you care for others, you take pains not to cause them hardship or inconvenience. Thus, a well-thought out shooting script, for instance, spares last minute pressure and disappointments over loss of time and effort to all the people involved in the production of a film, from the stars down to the last helper. A production that is planned and executed with discipline saves a lot of unnecessary expense to the party paying for making the film. Ray has always had consideration for his producers,[3] his collaborators, and his public. So, you have a creative imagination that 'foresees' the film with great precision, a courage to work out details at all stages of production, and a concern for others. And the result is Ray's personal discipline of film art.

SOME EXAMPLES

Examples of Ray's discipline are countless. They are documented in the abundant literature about him. Only a few examples will be given here. Marie Seton has written that when Kanu Bannerjee (Harihar) first appeared with a fresh haircut for the shooting of *Pather Panchali,* Ray postponed the shooting and waited for Bannerjee to grow his hair anew. 'Harihar' should not have a fresh haircut. And Bannerjee should not wear a wig.

An example of flexibility within the discipline of a minutely-planned shooting script is provided by *Kanchenjungha.* According to Marie Seton, in her *Portrait of a Director*, while Ray was shooting an outdoor scene, a convoy of donkeys just happened to pass by. Instead of waiting for it to move away, Ray restructured the scene he was about to shoot, and he included the train of donkeys in it to very good effect. Again, in the same film, while on location, Ray noticed a young Nepali boy whom he found interesting, and he created a role for him in the film. Let these few examples suffice. I would like now to offer two comments concerning Ray's discipline. One comment regards the incredible tenacity of Ray, the other regards the relationship his own film discipline entertains with Western music, a musical from being itself a discipline.

It is in the overall conception of a film that the filmmaker's discipline can best be perceived. By 'conception' here is meant what the French call 'découpage'. This notion has not yet been explored in English film literature, although it has at least been noted by Noel Burch, and it is known in English as *decoupage* when dealing in graphic arts. The decoupage of a film — its conception — is the selection of the film's images and sounds. Each filmmaker has his own particular way of selecting fragments of images and sounds, choosing the angle from which the visuals will be shown or the place from which the sounds will be heard, the order of the fragments, the length of time they will be held. Of course, the filmmaker does all this intuitively and holistically. And the *decoupage* can be observed only in the finished film. In the finished film, you can see what fragments of the whole imagined by the filmmaker have been projected on the screen for the viewers to imagine — recreate in imagination — the same whole on the basis of these fragments.

I would like to illustrate this notion with the sequence of *Charulata*, where Charu comes to know that Amal has written an article that has been accepted for publication by a magazine. Charu had made a copybook for Amal, with the understanding that whatever he would write in that copybook would be for her alone. But Amal has written an article in the precious copybook, and he has given his article for publication without even telling Charu. That pains her deeply. Both Amal and Bhupati are totally unaware of Charu's anguish. Amal offers her some *kulfi*. Bhupati speaks to her of politics and of the smell of printed paper. Manda, the sister-in-law, is alone aware of the drama.

This is the story Satyajit Ray has filmed in one of his purest film sequences. When the spectator sees the sequence he imagines the entire space where the action takes place, that is, a verandah running along the four sides of the building above the inner courtyard. In fact, only fragments of that space are shown in the film. For instance, the verandah cannot be seen when Charu is in her room with her door closed. But the spectators hold the whole place, room and verandah, in their minds at any one time. The fragments offered them by the film's maker constitute the *decoupage.* The word *decoupage* means making cut outs from a whole. So, when the filmmaker imagines a whole scene, the *decoupage* is the cutting out of pieces from the intended scene, offering the viewers these cut out pieces for them to imagine the whole scene. However, the *decoupage*, or selection of cut outs, is arrived at by the viewers of the film on the basis of the finished film. As for the filmmaker, he proceeds intuitively.

In this scene, Ray uses only one of the four sides of the verandah. In one corner is a swinging door closing the verandah, and in the opposite corner is the door of Charu's room and, diagonally, the place where Manda is standing.

The evolution of the extremely complex set of relationships between Amal, Bhupati, Manda, and Charulata is filmed in 37 shots, lasting 3 minutes and 47 seconds or a total of 227 seconds, from the moment when Charu, picking up Amal's slippers, leaves the room, and the old servant gives Amal his letter, to the moment Amal is about to throw the unwanted *kulfi* down the verandah for the cat to eat it. The shots alone do not define the fragments that constitute the *decoupage.* Movements in frame, movements of the camera, and sound on or off-screen are as many fragments. Given the complexity of the relationships to be established, Ray has used physical space to great advantage, at times showing the characters spaced out, or separated by a door, or walking in opposite directions, at other times in the same space, but without actual links; the newsprint and the *kulfi* are offered as mediating objects. Moreover, the voice off-screen of Amal and afterwards of Bhupati permits full attention on the face of Charu. The music adds to the intensity of the scene.

What is happening in Charu's mind and heart is not said; it is projected by her composure, her gestures, and the music. She does not say, for instance, 'Oh God, what shall I do now?' or some such thing. Yet, the spectator knows what she thinks and feels. The sequence is made the more fascinating by its tempo. Within the 227 seconds of the sequence, two of the 37 shots last 113 seconds. The first one lasts 32 seconds (when Charu fetches the new slippers and hears Amal say his article will be published) and the other 81 seconds (when Bhupati talks with Charu in their room — a shot which is divided into two, 35 and 46 seconds each, by a shift of camera some 45 degrees). Thus, if you remove these two relatively long shots, you remain with 112 seconds for 34 shots, an average of about 3½ seconds per shot.[4] This alternation of shots of long and short duration creates tempo and excitement.

Here, everything seems to happen on its own, yet everything, even the smallest detail, is marshalled to create the impact of the film. As can be seen, the discipline is mental before it is directorial and pragmatic.

TENACITY

The fact that the *Apu* trilogy was made over a period of over five years is well known. What perhaps needs emphasis is that between the second and third films of the trilogy, two other films were made, *Parash Pathar*, and *Jalsaghar*. These two films are quite different from the Trilogy. But making them did not affect the coherence of the Trilogy itself, a trilogy which was not even intended originally. *Aparajito* was made as a sequel to *Pather Panchali* with no thought of a further sequel that would complete an eventual trilogy. And yet, the three films form a single, complete structure. It must have taken a singular continuity of perception, matched by an equal determination, to create that overall structure in three different, at initially unrelated, films.

This is the more astonishing in view of the fact that the structure of the *Apu* Trilogy is entirely different, in whole and in parts, from that given by Bibhutibhushan Bannerjee to his two-part novel, *Pather Panchali* and *Aparajito*.

Film projects like *Ghare Baire* and *Shakha Proshakha* have been nurtured over long periods of time, 25 years in the case of the latter film. And *The Alien*, a project of 1964, was never totally abandoned as a film idea. These also are examples of tenacity, an aspect of discipline.

WESTERN MUSIC

Ray's life-long interest in Western music too is well known. What actual influence or role has Western music played in Ray's career? One can say that Ray is as comfortable with Western music as he is with the English language. The question one might ask is whether English influenced Ray's Bengali prose and the dialogue of his Bengali films. The answer is that it is most likely that there has been a profound influence. Yet, Ray's Bengali prose is not found to suffer from Anglicism. There cannot but have been an influence, but the end product is Bengali. An artist is not closed to influences; he transmutes them. This creative act cannot be explained by the causality of influences. Indeed, to explain the creative act would mean to explain it away. Similarly, has Western music prepared him to give his films a form — a discipline — which as such is more akin to Western music than it is to Indian music generally? After all, not every one of his contemporaries enjoyed Western music. There surely was an influence of Western music on Ray. But what is the result? Westerners readily tune in to Ray's films, but few, I think, would find that Ray's films are 'Western'. Through his creative imagination Western musical form along with Western film form blended with the Indian arts to give a definitely Indian product.

On the other hand, Ray inherited from India a wide range of emotions with their subtle nuances. He has also inherited from Indian arts a vitality that gives his film form the strength to support the details that make for realism, without the form itself being weakened or thwarted. But all these presumed influences have been transmuted. Andrew Robinson wrote that speaking of the songs in his film *Goopy Gyne Bagha Byne*, Ray has said, 'I have definitely set a style of singing which doesn't come from Tagore, doesn't come from Western music, but which is essentially me.' Possibly, something similar could be said of his film form, it doesn't come from Western music or Western film, it doesn't come from Indian arts, it is essentially Ray.

CONCLUSION

It is Ray. But then who is Ray? His is the discipline of classicism, in form and in moral value, a classicism that is derived from Tagore? Chidananda Dasgupta has discussed this aspect of Ray in an article of 1980. Dasgupta wrote:

> The characters of the post-Tagore era are observed from a Tagorean moral point of view. In *Jana Aranya*, the focal point of the moral judgment is in the retired father with a memory of the uprightness of his time.[5]

We find a similar situation in the last films of Ray. Uprightness with all its values is on the wane. It is embodied still by lone characters; the doctor in *Gana Shatru*, the ailing father with his mentally disturbed son in *Shakha Proshakha*, and the 'alien' in *Agantuk*. Tagorean classicism is fading, perhaps forever. If anyone is saddened by this departure, let him be brave, and, like little Ratan in *The Postmaster*, let him not show a tear. And in this very stance, classicism, at least of the Ray type, will endure for yet a while.

NOTES

1. For instance, if a student wrote in a script that there was a table, Eisenstein would argue that 'a table' does not exist; you only have a square, a round, an oval table. That would help the student to be more precise in his imagination.
2. When Ray had to depart from Tagore and alter the end of his senior's story in *The Postmaster,* he could not help it. If he had to be true to

himself, to the type of emotions he felt at ease with, he had to make the girl refrain from showing her tears to the postmaster who was leaving her.

3. Ray himself has commented on his concern for his producers in his interview on script writing. See Chapter 21.
4. In comparison, the average duration of the shots in the entire *The Battleship Potemkin* is of 2.85 seconds.
5. 'Classicism', in the *Satyajit Ray Issue*, 1980, Kakinada Film Circle, Andhra Pradesh.

CHAPTER 18

True-to-life Image-maker*

WITH A THIRD honorary doctorate conferred upon him (this time by Oxford University),[1] Satyajit Ray is now established still more unquestionably than ever as one of the most highly rated contemporary filmmakers in international academic circles — a fact which can only deepen the sense of inadequacy one experiences when seeking to formulate a response to Ray's voluminous body of films.

This new token of recognition, no doubt to be followed by others, will further isolate Ray at home. There are not very many persons in local filmdom with whom he can have a dialogue about his art. Film criticism generally is of very little help to filmmakers. While filmmaking is one of the most difficult professions, one which very few exceptionally talented persons master, nearly everyone feels quite competent to criticize the work of filmmakers. But from the criticisms, often hostile, rarely constructive, which are addressed to him, Ray can gain very little. His most outspoken critics are rarely known for having themselves contributed to the art of making films or to the more delicate art of thinking and talking about them. Like S.M. Eisenstein, who once complained that the students of his films were not cultured enough, Ray may feel at times that his critics often seem to lack basic film culture.

Ray borrows most of his film ideas from existing novels, but when it comes to transferring these into films he is left to

*Part of this essay appeared in Santi Das, ed., *Satyajit Ray: An Intimate Master,* 1998, pp. 62-78. Originally published in *Sunday*, an Ananda Bazar Publication, 20 August 1978, pp. 15-19. The original version was slightly revised for the present book.

himself. This isolation is a consequence of his being what the French have called an *auteur* (author), that is, a filmmaker who is mainly responsible for his films. A film *auteur* creates private imaginary worlds, absolutely needed for the collective life of society. Ours being a cinema of scarcity, we have too few *auteurs*, and this means again, too few opportunities for Ray to exchange at his own level. An *auteur* needs to be in constant dialogue with the widest possible range of people, otherwise he runs the risk of losing touch with the ever-changing sensibility of his milieu. This is not happening to Ray, fortunately. Few persons are as well-informed and as sensitive to contemporary life as Ray is.

However, over the years a certain radicalization has taken place among film audiences and filmmakers, in India as elsewhere in the world. At home, Ray's audience is increasingly polarized. While some reject all Ray films, others praise them all, in either case not always for very profound reasons. At the basis of this polarization is a shift in sensibility that is growing ever more accentuated, and may well be irreversible. A dialogue should take place about this phenomenon among film people, artists, intellectuals and persons concerned with the cultural life. But there is no forum that I know of for such a dialogue.

It is in this context that I wish to ponder over some of the options that, I feel, may be open to Ray. I do not doubt that he has already considered them and has even made his choice. But as we felicitate Ray on the honour bestowed on him by Oxford University, a reflection on the Indian film scene may help the better to appreciate Ray's achievement. First, however, I must discuss the question of sensibility to films.

Ray himself provided an excellent example of difference in sensibility when, in the course of an interview he gave me in 1970 (reproduced below, Chapter 21), he explained his attitude towards some of Tagore's writings:

> Certain stories of Tagore are quite Victorian in their feeling. Take the *Postmaster*. At the end of the original story, the postmaster is supposed to leave, and the little servant girl falls at his feet and says, 'Please, don't

leave me alone, please take me with you.' This struck me as being sentimental. I could not express that because it was an emotion I don't feel, being a man of the twentieth century, being brought up in certain surroundings, being exposed to certain influences. So I made the ending of the story drier, yet moving in its own way. I made it into the opposite of what it was. The girl in the film hides her grief instead of displaying it. She ignores the postmaster. She is so hurt that she does not even want to tell this man that she is unhappy. You see her weeping by the well from which she is drawing water. But the moment he calls her, she wipes her tears. She walks past him carrying the bucket of water and ignores the tip that he was about to offer her. That was my interpretation as a twentieth-century artist working in 1960. The purists object to these changes. Well, I made them because I also am an artist with my own feelings. I was using Tagore's rendering of a story as a basis, and this was my interpretation of it.

Tarkovsky illustrated this sort of difference in sensibility recently. In his film *Andrei Rublev,* Tarkovsky has two contemporary image-makers have a dialogue on their art : Theophanes the Greek and Andrei Rublev. The iconographers of old were the precursors of modern filmmakers and, of course, through their dialogue, Tarkovsky discusses his own social function as a filmmaker. Theophanes argued that there was so much evil in the world, causing people to experience so much suffering, that he felt impelled to paint icons of the Last Judgment to remind people of the impending wrath of God. That would make them mend their ways, he hoped. Rublev, on the other hand, said that he also witnessed his people's suffering, but he could not paint the image of the Last Judgment any more; he could only paint a figure of Christ, as the 'Compassionate Lord'. He felt that people did not need to be reminded of their sins and of the terrible judgment of God. What they needed was to experience the compassion of the Saviour, and regain faith in life and in themselves.

Rublev loved Theophanes who was senior to him and was then at the peak of his career. Yet, however pained he was at this necessary parting of the ways, he had to paint in a different manner than Theophanes did. In retrospect, it is possible to argue that both the images by Theophanes and those by Andrei, had their role to play in the life of the iconographers' society. One type of picture was not exclusive of the other, and it was best that the image-makers be true, each one to his spontaneous response to contemporary life. Had they not been so, the collective life of their people would have been impoverished.

I can well imagine, in some distant future, an Indian Tarkovsky making a film on image-maker Satyajit Ray, and staging a dialogue between Ray and another image-maker — a veteran like Ritwik Ghatak or Mrinal Sen, or a younger cinéastes like Shyam Benegal, Adoor Gopalakrishnan, Mani Kaul, Kumar Sahani, or Anup Kurian. Historical situations never quite duplicate themselves! Hence, I'd rather not be too specific as to the counterpart chosen for the dialogue. Ray would in all truth say that he sees his people's suffering, and that he feels impelled to describe them all. Is there any other Indian filmmaker who has dealt with as many aspects of Indian life — social, cultural, political and economic — as Ray did? According to his sensibility, Ray makes true-to-life images that he offers to the onlookers for them to reflect on, and to react to if they so want. Evidently, this is not the only type of image one can create starting from the same life situations. Another filmmaker will shout his distress. Another will teach some way out of a social impasse. Correspondingly, a particular onlooker will resent as a lack of commitment the reserve with which Ray depicts unbearable situations. Yet another will hold that the time to 'do something about it' has long come, and he will question the usefulness of making 'statements' about sordid aspects of our lives. Good. But to declare that this or that approach is wrong and another one right would be sheer dogmatism. I am afraid I have to say that such dogmatism is rampant in film milieus.

It may be appropriate to describe the change in attitude which I myself underwent with regard to the Ray films. The first Ray films I saw were the three *Apu* films, in 1961, just as I was on my way to India for the first time. The *Apu* trilogy revealed to me a nation of extraordinary people whom I longed to meet with great respect and humility. For, as a young 'missionary', if I at all shared the arrogance and paternalism so common among Westerners, nothing could have helped me more than the experience of watching the *Apu* films, to realize that there were lot of things I would have to learn from the Indian people before I could dream of being of help to anyone of them.

There was yet another aspect to the experience. If the *Apu* trilogy introduced India to me, it also showed me what cinema can be. That was, in fact, my third 'discovery' of the cinema, the first having been while watching Eisenstein's *The Battleship Potemkin* when I was 16, and the second while watching Robert Bresson's *Un condamné à mort s'est échappé.* And then came the *Apu* films. I was enraptured.

The importance of the *Apu* Trilogy in the late 1950 did not derive solely from its aesthetic excellence. The *Apu* films broke away from a certain ideology and put forward another one, no less Indian — that of struggling individuals who believe changes are possible, and have a will to bring them about. In fact, the very aesthetic excellence of the *Apu* films results from the ideology which Ray has injected into the material provided by the book which he used, in his own words, as an encyclopaedia of rural life. Ray's Apu is individualistic and has no social concerns, it is true. But he is a struggling individual who attains personal freedom, and becomes capable of literally shouldering (Kajol on his shoulders) his social responsibility. A parallel may be drawn here between the endings of the neo-realist film *Bicycle Thieves* and Ray's *Apur Sansar.* While in de Sica's film the son of the poor vainquished man is brought down to becoming a partner in his father's ineluctable defeat and degradation, in Ray's film the son is elevated and introduced by his father into a life of self-respect, joy and freedom.

I mentioned earlier that to me the most cinematic of all Ray films from the trilogy to *Charulata* (1964) was *Charulata.* Later on, when *Aranyer Din Ratri* appeared in 1969 I felt that this film was the best Ray film thus far, better still than *Charulata.* I liked *Pratidwandi* (1970), of course, but I believed *Aranyer Din*

Ratri to be better cinema. However, the later Ray films appeared to me less interesting. I liked *Sonar Kella* (1974) but disliked *Ashani Sanket* (1973). Since it was the same Ray and since *Ashani Sanket* was definitely a 'good' film, what was happening to me?

Paradoxically I liked *Sonar Kella* for its apparent irrelevance, and I disliked *Ashani Sanket* for its obvious relevance. I had reached a point when a 'statement', however true and courageous, about as relevant a fact as the West Bengal famine, was to me irrelevant and even irritating. To my sensibility, a much more questioning approach was required, appealing more to the mind than to the heart. The film, I felt, should have at least thrown some light on the social mechanisms which brought about the famine. In my opinion, the very relevance of the film called for a much less contemplative approach. On the other hand, I thought that *Sonar Kella,* which did not seek to be topical, was relevant to the need for clean, intelligent entertainment. I would not wish all films to deal in depth with social issues. I think there is a real need for entertaining films like *Sonar Kella.*

The reason why I became less interested in the Ray films of the mid-1970s is that at the time I had become increasingly interested in 'cinéma direct'— somewhat like Marcorelles — and when I decided to make a documentary film in 1970, it was in the direct cinema style that I spontaneously chose to make it. Naturally, I greatly appreciated *The Inner Eye* (1973). But there it was not only the direct cinema touches that I liked. What I appreciated most in it was the ability of Satyajit Ray to put his own medium at the service of another art. At last, I saw a film on painting that did not destroy the paintings in order to recreate them into a film! I felt that only a great artist could thus bring somebody else's art to the fore, without, if I may say, 'stealing the show'.

This then was my own response to the Ray films. I should like to emphasize, while concluding that my preferring a certain type of films does not make of these films absolute models. All film is fiction, and all fiction is moulded on a particular ideology.

Hence the 'cinema direct' of the Brault, Rouch, or Leacock types is not the last word in film making. Nor do 'cinema-direct' films invalidate other types of films. The pitfall of many critics who strive for radicalism is to dogmatically erect a particular approach to film as the ultimate and only valid one. Marcorelles, for instance, did just that in his book *Living Cinema.*

If, beyond any matters of sensibility, one wishes to militate for a certain type of cinema to the exclusion of other types, one has to question filmmaking at a much deeper level. One has to raise the issues of the modes of pictorial representation and the modes of narration as ideologically determined and thus as either progressive or reactionary. Moreover, the debate has to be set in a much wider context than that of filmmaking, because it involves all the media of a society, its particular structures, its modes of material and spiritual productions, etc. While this debate is desirable it is also difficult to sustain. And the militant, often aggressive, attitude of those who engage in it causes them to discuss issues with more assertive force than rational arguments.

Unless one is satisfied with shouting slogans to reassure oneself in the night of one's solitude, one has to take stock of the particular moment of history one lives in. For instance, to want all cinemas overnight to do away with story-telling is to live in no history at all — past, present or future. Secondly, while it may be quite reasonable to disagree on ideological grounds with a particular type of filmmaking, one has to acknowledge that perhaps in particular circumstances, another type of filmmaking is not possible. For instance, how to expect the film establishment to pay for the making and distributing of films that directly challenge its existence? I do not wish to say that differences in sensibility are purely formal and of no ideological importance. What I mean is that these differences are perhaps the only ones that can be accommodated within a particular set-up.

However, the fostering of certain sensibilities positively prepares social structures for radical changes, while other forms of sensibility tend to make existing structures more acceptable.

Beyond this, filmmaking offers little scope for revolutionary action. It is only by encouraging subtle shifts in sensibility that films can prepare social changes. To ask more than this from films in our present socio-economic situation may be brave, but sadly unrealistic.[2]

Ray, of course, is well aware of all this. It seems to me, therefore, that the questions he has faced and — as his steady work indicates — answered can be summarized as follows : (a) whether he ought to adjust his approach to the sensibility of a group which, although increasing, is still a minority of his audience; (b) whether the film establishment would permit such an adjustment on his part and; (c) whether, given the relative value of film styles and approaches and their short span of life, he should not keep to his own versatile approach.

Whatever his choice, present or future, Ray continues to be looked upon as a leader by younger filmmakers. All may not wish to follow his approach. (Surely, all would not be able to follow it.) But the attitude of all may be summed up in these few words a young filmmaker said to me recently: 'I do not agree with all the Ray films, but him I respect.' I believe that in this young filmmaker's respect, there was perhaps a little bit of awe and also certainly a great deal of admiration and love.

NOTES

1. Note added for this publication. Ray received seven honorary doctorates from various universities as follows:

1973	Delhi
1974	Royal College of Arts (London)
1978	Oxford
1980	Burdwan, Jadavpur (Calcutta)
1981	Benaras, North Bengal
1985	Calcutta
1987	Rabindra Bharati (Calcutta)

2. See what Ray himself says on the subject during his interview with William Fisher, quoted at the end of Chapter 10.

CHAPTER 19

Humanism in Ray's Cinema*

PATHER PANCHALI established Satyajit Ray as a filmmaker of international standard at the Cannes Film Festival of 1955. In 1961, Ray's *Apu* Trilogy was shown with considerable success at the International Film Festival of Montreal. By the mid-1960s, *Pather Panchali* was one of the ten films most often shown in American cineclubs, along with Fritz Lang's *M,* Sergei Eisenstein's *The Battleship Potemkin,* Orson Welles' *Citizen Kane,* Federico Fellini's *La Strada,* Buster Keaton's *The General,* and Akira Kurosawa's *Rashomon.* However, from 1961 to 1965 few of the other Ray films were shown abroad, for lack of suitable distribution. Then came the films of Ray's second decade, 1965-75. Among the thirteen films made during that time were: *The Hero* (1966), *The Adventures of Goopy and Bagha* (1968), *Days and Nights in the Forest* (1969), *The Adversary* (1970), *Company Limited* (1971), *Distant Thunder* (1973), *The Golden Fortress* (1974) and *The Middleman* (1975). These eight films were shown at international film festivals, and had some exposure abroad. Of them all, *Days and Nights in the Forest* and *Distant Thunder* arouse most interest abroad.

This article examines well over 100 foreign reviews of these eight films, ranging from short notes to substantial critical reviews of nearly 1,500 words. These reviews were written for papers in London, New York, Washington and Los Angeles. The author was not in a position to obtain all the reviews written, but the number of reviews available was sufficient to arrive at certain conclusions.[1]

*Satyajit Ray Film Festival, *The Second Decade,* in aid of Students Health Home, 2–8 May 1979.

The first thing that strikes one upon reading the foreign reviews of Ray's films, written by some sixty critics over a period of ten years, is their general mediocrity — barring a handful of exceptions, like the reviews by Penelope Houston, Judith Crist and Pauline Kael, which are remarkably perceptive, and avoid the general condescending tone that will be criticized presently. The critics responded enthusiastically to Ray's cinema. But in general they had little to say that was helpful for an understanding of Ray's work, especially in the fluid context of changing sensibilities and conflicting ideologies. The mediocrity of foreign reviews is little consolation for anyone who bemoans the poor quality of film criticism in India. But it reminds one of the fact that film criticism, given the conditions in which it is practised and the wide range of sensibilities it calls for, is, after all, a very difficult activity. Furthermore, film criticism is not taught; for good or bad, one just takes up the job. Unfortunately, it's often for bad.

Almost all the reviews under discussion here are so-called 'good' reviews, that is, reviews that praise the works they deal with. Most of them are patronizing. As said earlier, few Ray films were shown abroad between 1961 and 1965. Second, a Ray film is not meant to be a financial blockbuster in the way *Star Wars* recently was. Yet, the *Apu* Trilogy was relatively popular amongst film audiences when foreign critics reviewed Ray's films between 1965-75. The patronizing attitude of most of these critics betrays a lack of confidence in the spectators' judgement, and perhaps some diffidence in the critics themselves. Ray is said to be 'our greatest living film director (. . .) ranked among the world's top five or six directors' (1)* 'one of the greatest of all filmmakers' (4); 'undeniably one of the greatest directors in the world' (26); 'one of the most conscious artists who ever lived' (46); 'one of the two or three best film directors working in movies today' (94: 9); 'His (Ray's) means as a director are among the most intuitively right in all

*Figures in brackets, unless they follow the name of a film, refer to the reviews listed at the end of this Chapter.

movie making' (10). Yet, these critics who affirm Ray's greatness as a filmmaker identify him as if he were unknown. One would not think of calling Kurosawa 'the great Japanese director' or Bresson 'the great French director'. For, anyone who has ever heard of Bresson can be assumed to know that Bresson is French, that he is a great director, and that with a good twenty other filmmakers he is among the top five or six. Why then speak of Satyajit Ray as 'the cinema master of Calcutta' (8); 'a great Bengali artist' (16); 'the great Bengali director' (24, 93); 'the great Indian director' (39, 84, 111)? Moreover, most foreign critics take Ray to be the only Indian or even the only Bengali filmmaker, thus showing their very limited knowledge of the Indian cinema. Some of the critics even emphasize their assertions as to Ray's international status: 'the great, I repeat, great Indian director' (32); 'let there be no doubt, Satyajit Ray is one of the master directors, measured against world competition' (103); 'Satyajit Ray's genius, (I don't use the word lightly)' (110). When Ray is said to occupy such a high position in international cinema, what is the meaning of saying, for instance, that '*Distant Thunder* is a stunning proof that Satyajit Ray is one of the world's greatest filmmakers' (68)'?

Is there any need for establishing that Satyajit Ray is one of the great living film directors when his films are praised so highly? For instance, Donia Mills said of *The Hero,* that it 'is more substantial than *Grand Hotel,* more lucid than *8½*, more absorbing than *Wild Strawberries,* and more enjoyable as a piece of entertainment than any of the above' (88). The conversation of Rini and Ashim by the river side in *Days and Nights in the Forest* is said to be 'perhaps the gentlest, most profound confrontation between man and woman ever depicted in film' (8). Writing about the same film Pauline Kael said, 'Satyajit Ray's films can give rise to a more complex feeling of happiness in me than the work of any other director' (9). She added: 'Underneath their (Ashim and Aparna) love story, and the stories of Ashim's companions, there is the melancholy and corruption of their class and country. In a quiet way, the sub-text is perhaps the subtlest, most plangent study of the cultural tragedy of imperialism the screen has ever had.' And she concluded: 'No artist has done more than Satyajit Ray to make us reevaluate the common place. And only one or two other film artists of his generation — he's just past fifty — can make a masterpiece that is so lucid and so inexhaustibly rich' (11). Penelope Houston felt that 'one would rate this lucid, ironic and superlatively graceful film among the very best of (Ray's) work' (12). *The Adversary* was said to be 'a modest masterpiece' (17), a movie that 'may be remembered as one of the most perceptive and relevant works of the decade' (21). *Company Limited* was acknowledged as a film that 'would have been one of the strongest contenders for the Golden Bear' at the Berlin Film Festival (34). The film was shown out of competition but it turned out to be 'Berlin's biggest treat' (35), which 'would by itself have justified the journey to Berlin . . . one of the most outstanding movies shown at any festival this year' (36), 'a little masterpiece' (38), 'a subtle and unqualified masterpiece' (39), 'one of the most subtle and trenchant studies of the corrosive effect of the ambition on a rising young business executive that has ever been filmed' (40). At the beginning of the London Film Festival where it was shown, when 50 other films were yet to be screened, a critic wrote 'I doubt if the festival has anything more satisfactorily absorbing to offer in the coming weeks' (44).

Then came *Distant Thunder*. Pauline Kael, one of the most articulate and enthusiastic critics discussed in this article, found flaws in this film, but nevertheless she wrote: 'I don't know when I've been so moved by a picture that I knew was riddled with flaws. It must be that Ray's vision comes out of so much hurt and guilt and love that the feeling pours over all the cracks in *Distant Thunder* and seals them up' (47). Most critics felt the film was 'a masterpiece' (48), 'the work of such artistry and craftsmanship as to verge on sheer genius' (55), 'an art object, a thing of beauty in and of itself' (57). 'I've seen no other film this year or last which seems to me to approach it' (62). 'No films are great. Not anymore. But *Distant Thunder* is truly a great film' (65). 'For this movie, . . . Ray seems as close as any filmmaker to the terms of great art' (67). 'No other word but 'masterpiece' will do for (this film)' (70). 'The sweep of the film is so vast that you feel as if you'd witnessed the events from a satellite. You've somehow been able to see simultaneously the curvature of the earth and the insects on the blades of field grass' (77). '*Distant Thunder* is a work of art — perhaps the only work of art in the movies this year' (94: 6).

I wonder if any contemporary filmmaker has received more praise than Ray has, if any film made between 1965-75 has been rated as high as *Distant Thunder* and *Days and Nights in the Forest*. The New York Times of 14 November 1975 (94), announcing *Distant Thunder,* carried a full page of snippets under the caption *Raves.* After a week the same paper had 'more raves' still. Some of these were reproduced above. The term *Raves* has come to mean enthusiastic praise. But at a time when people used words with greater restraint and a finer sense of propriety, the term meant 'an extravagantly favourable criticism'. Surely I do not dispute the greatness of Satyajit Ray or the quality of his work. But in the reviews discussed here, I feel that there is a certain extravagance which, to my mind, is almost offensive to the person thus praised and certainly a sign of mediocrity in the person thus praising.

I do not dispute either the right of a film critic to have preferences: criticism is based on preferences. And a critic cannot be blamed for being articulate in his/her preferences. What I feel objectionable in most of the reviews discussed here, is the tone in which the preferences are expressed. There is no need for condescension towards Ray, no need for a crusade in his support. As a critic rightly said, Ray 'is perhaps the least condescending director alive' (14). Critics might learn, something here from him. In assessing Ray's work there is no place for extravagance either. Are Ray's unerring sense of propriety and exquisite self-control qualities to send one 'raving'?

II

A critical judgement is intuitive and synthetic. It's rarely worked out through rational argument. Yet, there is always in a critical judgement an implied comparison. The implied comparison is often stated in order to create a scale against which the value of the work being criticized can be gauged. Thus, in the reviews discussed here, the Ray films are compared with other works. *Nayak* is compared with *Grand Hotel, Ship of Fools, Wild Strawberries* (1); *The Adventures of Goopy and Bagha* with *The Yellow Submarine* (3) and *The Magic Flute* (4); *Days and Nights in the Forest* with *Tristana* (13), *Ma Nuit chez Maud* (14), *Hatari* (118); *The Adversary* with *Minnie and Moskowitz* (17); *Company Limited* with an Ibsen play, with *A Face in the Crowd* (43); *Distant Thunder* with *Shame* (47, 76, 89), *Cries and Whispers* (89), *The Magnificent Ambersons* (91).

As an author, Ray has been likened in the same reviews to Lewis Carroll, Edward Lear (3); Chekhov (6, 7, 13, 15, 115); Antonioni (7); Renoir (10, 36, 100, 102); Agee (10); Bunuel (13); Rohmer (14); H. James (15); Cassavetes (17); Ford (36); Elia Kazan (43); Bergman (47, 76, 89, 91); Kurosawa (63); Rossellini (102); Dickens, Gogol, Twain (103); Balzac (103, 105); Godard, Ken Russel, Kubrick (113) and Howard Hawks (118). Most of these comparisons are made rather casually, though. And Ray is likened more definitely to Chekhov and to Renoir. But the critics rarely go beyond stating that a particular Ray film (mainly *Days and Nights in the Forest*) is Chekhovian, and that Ray shares *Renoir's* humanism (about *Days and Nights in the Forest, Company Limited* and *The Middleman*). It will be profitable to examine these two affirmations.

First, Chekhov. But will a comparison with Chekhov help understand Ray when it is perhaps true that 'in our times, no playwright is more respected and less understood than Anton Chekhov'?[2] Respect and misunderstanding are indeed comparable in the cases of both Chekhov and Ray. Yet, there is more to the comparison than just that. Chekhov's dramas do have characteristics that can help define the particular qualities of Ray's cinema.

Chekhov is one of the forefathers of the theatre of the Absurd; he obliterated the demarcation line between comedy and tragedy; he excelled in black comedy and wry humour;

he isolated his characters from their social milieus to reveal their private, subjective lives through concrete details which are common to all, and by means of which each one of us projects his innermost self outwardly. Above all, Chekhov had no use for a linear plot in the way Aristotelian drama had. In a Chekhov play hardly anything happens, the play progresses not along a story line, but through a series of concentric situations with increasing emotional intensity so as to *reveal life as it is* in a particular situation, with a particular set of human relationships (that is, these few relationships which a character cannot avoid). Thus, a Chekhov drama does not make a statement about life, but rather directly shows life as it is. Chekhov's dramaturgy, anti-theatrical in so many ways, is not just a matter of style, however.

Chekhov had to wrestle with theatrical conventions in order to render theatre capable of expressing his vision of man. For Chekhov, man is a failure, human life is doomed to fail. Yet, for him, man is great, because in spite of his inadequacy and ridiculous clumsiness, man keeps on trying to live up to the impossible self-image which his spirit constantly produces. And it is this tension between an acute awareness of his helplessness and the indomitable desire to arise above it that constitutes the tragically comic life of man. Chekhov, who was a physician, knew that he was dying of tuberculosis at an early age, and he — like so many of his characters — was tormented by the question: 'What can I do, tell me, what can I do?' And he felt that the question had no answer.

A comparison of *Days and Nights in the Forest* with Chekhovian drama is indeed illuminating. Yet, the comparison has its limits. In *Days and Nights in the Forest,* Ray has detached the protagonists from their ordinary social milieus, he has studied their relationships among themselves; above all, he has revealed their characters through their reactions to a number of incidents. Thus, in terms of plot or story line, nothing much seems to be happening with a beginning, a middle and an end like in Aristotelian drama. And yet, *Days and Nights in the Forest,* perhaps more so than any other Ray film, is crowded with incidents, including acts of violence and a good amount of criticism. But these incidents are not there to advance a story line: they only reveal each character. However, while *Days and Nights in the Forest* is one of the most successful Ray films abroad (in the 1965-75 group of films) it is one of the least successful at home. Why? Probably because it revealed so much that was true.

To the extent that *Days and Nights in the Forest* is 'epiphanic', undramatic in Aristotelian terms, it is the most Chekhovian of the Ray films. Some of the other films like *Company Limited* and *The Middleman* also are 'epiphanic', but they depend much more on the linear development of a central event. They have some other Chekhovian qualities, but these are not exclusively Chekhovian, like the wry humour and the revealing, realistic, detail. Moreover, there are two main differences between most of Ray's cinema and Chekhovian drama. Firstly, Chekhov is always moralizing. To my way of seeing, successfully. Ray hardly ever moralizes. Ray is not a 'moral' filmmaker, not even, in my opinion, in the way Rohmer is in his 'moral tales'. Yet, all his films deal with moral problems. For, in most Ray films, and this is the second difference, the characters change, although this is less true in the later films. In Chekhov, on the other hand, the characters do not change: they are revealed to be what they are. *Days and Nights in the Forest* in this respect is Chekhovian, but where *Company Limited* and *The Middleman* are concerned, there is an exception. In Ray's films, the characters usually undergo change because Ray's vision of man is not Chekhovian. While there seems to be an increasing pessimism in Ray's films, Ray does not see man as a failure, human life as absurd, and the question, 'What to do?' as unanswerable. In other words, Ray's humanism and Chekhov's are not the same. And this brings me to the second important statement which I have singled out in the foreign reviews of the Ray films of 1965-75, namely, that of Ray's humanism which is often compared with Renoir's.

III

I cannot discuss here the humanism of Renoir. I shall discuss humanism with regard to Ray alone. Today, critical judgement hinges on that somewhat muddled question of humanism. In the mid-1950s, *Pather Panchali* was praised especially for its humanism. And since then, Ray's reputation as a humanist endures.[3] But while in 1955, the term humanist was used almost univocally by film critics, shortly afterwards it appeared that the term can, and indeed does, mean many things that are often contradictory. There has been an ideological polarization. Humanism, in the 1950s was mainly idealist, a concern for Man in general, for his qualities, 'eternal' and independent from man's social milieu. Later on, another brand of humanism, which I shall term 'pseudo-materialist', has developed in sharp opposition to idealist humanism. This pseudo-materialist humanism sees man as irremediably entrapped by his socio-economic situation. While idealist humanism knows of no socio-economic conditioning of man, the pseudo-materialist humanism knows of no possibility for man to transcend his socio-economic conditions. A humanism of the latter type, coupled as it often is with a very narrow range of sensibilities, rejects art to the extent that art affirms the universal in the particular.

But the alternative idealist/pseudo-materialist need not become a double bind: either/or, where both sides are unacceptable. The alternative is overcome by a humanism that affirms at one and the same time that man is conditioned by his socio-economic situation, and can transcend these particular conditions to affirm his own universal essence.[4] If this were not so, we would have to reject 'in toto' the art produced by the Greeks, for instance, because of their ideology. The Greeks believed they were right in owning and in making use of slaves. Yet, in spite of this abject ideology, some of the Greeks have been able to depict in their dramas, sculptures and monuments, aspects of human life which we can understand today, and from which we can derive lessons for our existence in our own socio-economic conditions. The Greeks transcended their conditionings, we transcend ours.

The attitude of any person regarding a Ray film depends on that person's humanism. And today, one's humanism can no more be (if it ever was) candid.

One is summoned to commit oneself to man, and to do it in one of a few particular ways. The tension between aestheticizing idealist humanism and sociologizing pseudo-materialist humanism cannot be resolved once for all. And it has been the merit of Ray, against the pressures of ideological terrorism at home, and the allurements of a facile, exotic, fame abroad, to re-define in each of his films his own humanism.

The Adversary was perceived abroad as a film in which Ray had tried to come to grips with the pressure on his vision of man, and of contemporary, local, and social upheavals. By the time *Distant Thunder* appeared in New York, London or San Francisco, however, the ideological polarization I mentioned earlier, had already taken place long before. Many critics were antagonistic to anything that, they feared, might be inspired by idealist humanism. Some of them had even become incapable of an aesthetic attitude in front of a film. They were impatient with any film that did not blatantly broadcast slogan-like messages. And thus, some writers started to feel uneasy with the later Ray films. Was he as 'great' as they had believed him to be? Was not the enthusiasm for the human qualities of *Pather Panchali* an idealist tribute to the film? In retrospect, it is evident that *Pather Panchali* could not but meet with the approval of critics inspired by an idealist humanism. After all, as Bertolt Brecht pointed out long ago, even *The Battleship Potemkin* can give great delights to a 'bourgeois' spectator.[5] But Eisenstein's film is not rejected today because some (many!) bourgeois find it a masterpiece. The value of *Potemkin* and similarly that of *Pather Panchali* is that these films are genuine works of art: they convey through the particular circumstances of their protagonists something of significance to us, in our particular circumstances. The ability of Ray to manifest the universal in the particular is mentioned like a *leitmotif* in foreign reviews.[6]

The main difficulty which the later Ray films have come up against is the politicization of culture at home and abroad. The urgency of the political tasks had caused some persons to wish to enlist all human activities in the service of politics. But art and politics are irreducible. The former is concerned with what endures in man and must be preserved. The latter is concerned with what is transitory and must be changed. Art is autonomous, yet conditioned by the particular. The relationship between art and politics is, therefore, a problematic one. But the one sphere does not deny the other since art can only exist from and through the particular, which is, precisely, the material of politics. But the aesthetic activity, which is essential to the welfare of the human mind, cannot be reduced to 'political, pragmatic activity.'[7]

To the extent, that they have come closer to politics, as in *The Adversary, Distant Thunder* and *The Middleman,* Ray's films ran the risk of calling in the audiences an un-aesthetic attitude, and then of being unsatisfactory from the point of view of politics. The problem was and remains: to arrive at the universal in and through our particular circumstances, which are essentially political. The task facing Ray required intelligence; the result was bound to be interesting. For, as a critic has put it: '(Ray) is one of the few directors working anywhere in the world who is committed to being intelligent and interesting' (22). Indeed, each of his films is an experiment in the delicate art of affirming the human in a film's protagonists amidst their social, often political, existence. Ray's humanism consists in knowing that man is definitely conditioned by his milieu, that at times man does not free himself from that conditioning, and yet that man, not too rarely, transcends his necessary conditioning. In Ray's cinema is also asserted the respective autonomy of art and politics. The films do not ignore politics but remain aesthetic. In this is affirmed the necessity of both art and politics: without the latter life would be fruitless, without the former man would lose his taste for the fruits of life. As he went on producing his films in the period under review — nearly one every year — Ray has succeeded to a remarkable extent in his difficult task. All his films were intelligent and interesting. *Distant Thunder,* however, the most fascinating of all in terms of sheer beauty and sensuousness, had a certain ambiguity most critics have not been able to overcome.

IV

It is because they did not clarify their stance with regard to humanism, and, implicitly, with regard to the relationship between art and politics, that so many of the reviews under discussion were mediocre. Most of them hail Ray's humanism.[8] But each film critic projects in the films his/her own brand of humanism. Is it true, for instance, that 'by stripping his drama of human suffering away from the specific events that caused it, Ray creates (in *Distant Thunder*) a timeless panorama of the vast cruelty man can inflict, even haphazardly, on man'? (66) This statement reminds one of the things critics had to say about de Sica's *Bicycle Thieves* in the heyday of idealist criticism.[9] It's no wonder if the author of that statement adds: 'For two years I have been haunted by the movie's final harrowing cut', that is, the image of the countless famine-stricken, ghostly, people appearing on the screen at the end of *Distant Thunder*.[10] The scene is haunting and 'harrowing' to a person who did not expect or wish the film to establish contact with the reality of the West Bengal famine. But for the spectator whose humanism caused him to wish the film to deal squarely with the famine, its causes and its overall effects, the concluding scene comes belatedly and disappointingly. Critics of this latter category are less numerous, but, without being necessarily more correct, they usually are more articulate in their stance than the former. One of them wrote:

> This (ending of *Distant Thunder*) is strange and disappointing, coming from a director whose best films deal with the evolving social conscience, the psychology of change. Even stranger is the affectation of the art house equivalent of the Hollywood gloss. The horrible realism of hunger, emaciation, and death are eclipsed by the hypnotizing poetry of Ray's camera — the drifting lyricism, the white heat, the slowly changing rhythms, the softly colored images, and the floating, exotic sounds of the countryside. According to the reviewers, it's the latest thing in ambiguity, as if ugliness is more threatening and hideous if it comes gift-wrapped. It achieves the same end — they just starve beautifully, making it so much easier for critics in humanist cloak to be seduced by, rave about and forget (90).

The same critic, who otherwise is an admirer of Ray, complains that the film moves forward so sensuously and lyrically and because all Satyajit Ray's films are invariably rubber-stamped with the critical catch word 'humanism' it's no wonder *Distant Thunder* appeals to critics as varied as Vincent Canby, Molly Haskell and Pauline Kael.

Critics, from naïve idealists to bitter pseudo-materialists, responded variously, as can be expected, to *Distant Thunder.* Yet another factor explains the variety of responses. *Distant Thunder* offered an ambiguity in intention, which Pauline Kael has tried with only partial success to explain. She wrote: 'Ray wants to show how war changes people, but I feel he also wants to make an indictment'. Ray was not concerned with showing, 'how war changes people'. Nor was his main intention to make an indictment, although he attempted one. I believe he wanted mainly to reveal particular characters against the tragic background of the West Bengal famine. This, to my mind, was a dangerous thing to do. The background was too large for the analysis of a few characters, insignificant in terms of the historical background.[11] The background threatened to erupt into the foreground and this is perhaps what caused Ray to attempt an indictment as a way of acknowledging the "background" and controlling its impact on the movie. In my way of seeing, the West Bengal famine of the forties with its millions of victims is too close to us, too imminent as a possible recurring experience, for one to use it as the background for a study of characters. But one can disagree with me on this. Certainly, Ray did think otherwise when he made his film. And perhaps was it this flood of emotion, which Pauline Kael so intensely sensed in the film, that alone could keep in check the emotion that a simple allusion to the terrible famine could arouse in the spectator.

Nevertheless, in spite of their profound emotional reaction to it, a few critics were able to offer a balanced judgement on the film. This is well-summed up in the following statement:

Distant Thunder (and *Company Limited*) combine a basic love of humanity with a desire to change society. To be both tender and committed at the same time is very rare and something that we should earnestly cherish (80).

Tenderness as in Renoir, lucidity as in Chekhov and hope as . . . in Ray. These are, I believe, the three main components of Satyajit Ray's humanism.

When discussing Chekhov, I mentioned that his particular vision of man had called for a particular dramatic form. So also Ray's humanism appears in a particular film form. Most critics have called this form 'subtle' and 'simple'. Indeed, they mention this quality so often and in such a pedestrian manner as to be irritating. They usually speak of a 'deceptive', subtle, and unassuming simplicity. Do the critics mean that Ray's simplicity is his own manner of being complicated? Can these critics be forgiven their intricate and blunt statements about simplicity and subtlety? Ray's simplicity, as Pauline Kael rightly noted, 'is arrived at, achieved, a master's distillation from his experience' (113). And if there is any way in which 'art imitates nature' it certainly is in the simplicity of life and existence. Over the years, Ray has applied his vast talent and indomitable energy to this demanding 'imitation'. Speaking of what she called Ray's 'essential and unfashionable humanism', Penelope Houston wrote:

> There is a debilitating critical notion that humanist cinema is dominated by content — that it is somehow creatively a soft way out. Anyone who thinks this should look closely at *The Middle Man,* at the way the film uses its setting to extend the field of its action, at the sheer narrative adroitness of its transitions, at the control of nuance which suggests that all choices are moral, but that in present-day India they are all too often predetermined. Ray's is not the cinema of the soft option (98).

FILM REVIEWS DISCUSSED IN THIS ARTICLE

The Hero 1966

1. Gary Arnold	*Washington Post*
2. Judith Crist	*New York*

The Adventures of Goopy and Bagha 1968

3. Marie Seton	*Times of India*

4.	Bernard Taper	*The New Yorker*	
5.	Nigel Andrews	*Monthly Film Bulletin*	March 1972

Days and Nights in the Forest 1969

6.	Stanley Eichelbaum	*San Francisco Examiner*	30.10.1970
7.	Kevin Thomas	*Los Angeles Times*	4.9.1973
8.	Renee Renouf	—	23.11.1970
9–11.	Pauline Kael	*The New Yorker*	17.3.1973
12.	Penelope Houston	*Monthly Film Bulletin*	December 1971
13.	Omitted		
14.	Gary Arnold	*The Sunday Standard*	20.8.1972
15.	Tom Milne	*Sight and Sound*	Winter 1971/72
16.	John Rosselli	*Arts Guardian*	22.10.1971

The Adversary 1970

17.	Margaret Hinxman	*Sunday Observer*	1973
18.	Dilys Powel	*Sunday Times*	7.1.1973
19.	Kevin Thomas	*Los Angeles Times*	30.6.1973
20.	Jan Dawson	*Monthly Film Bulletin*	February 1973
21.	Gary Arnold	*Washington Post*	
22.	Jerry Astzy	*New Yorker* (?)	
23.	—	*Variety*	8.9.1971
24.	David Robinson	—	
25.	Dilys Powell	*Sunday Times*	

Company Limited 1971

26.	Derek Malcolm	*Arts Guardian*	
27.	Maurice Speed	*What's On in London*	22.2.1974
28.	David Robinson	*The Times*	
29.	Christopher Hudson	*Spectator*	2.3.1974
30.	Nigel Andrews	—	
31.	Dilys Powell	*Sunday Times*	
32.	Patrick Gibbs	*The Daily Telegraph*	
33.	John Coleman	—	
34.	Omitted		
35.	Jan Dawson	*Sight and Sound*	
36.	Ken Wlaschin	*Film*	
37.	Gary Arnold	*Washington Post*	2.8.1974
38.	Russell Davies	*Observer*	—
39.	Michael Billington	*The Birmingham Post*	—
40.	Judy Stone	*San Francisco Chronicle*	1.12.1975
41.	Tom Milne	*Monthly Film Bulletin*	March 1974
42.	Penelope Houston	*Sight and Sound*	Spring 1974

43.	Ken Wlaschin	*Films and Filming*	September 1972
44.		*Hindustan Standard*	17.11.1972

Distant Thunder 1973

45–7.	Pauline Kael	*The New Yorker*	10.11.1975
48.	—	*Newsday*	2.11.1975
49.	John Crittenden	*The Bergen Record*	27.10.1975
50.	Joy Gould Boyum	*Wall Street Journal*	—
	Howard Kissel	*Women's Wear Daily*	27.10.1975
51.	—	*Newsweek*	17.11.1975
52.	Norma McLain Stoop	*After Dark*	—
53.	Stewart Klein	WNEW-TV	—
54.	Kevin Sanders	ABC TV	31.10.1975
55.	Mary McGeachy	—	—
56.	Joseph Gelmis	*Newsday*	27.10.1975
57 & 58.	Vincent Canby	*New York Times*	27.10.1975
59.	Joseph Lelyveld	*New York Times*	21.10.1975
60–1.	Pauline Kael	*The New Yorker*	10.11.1975
62.	William S Pechter	*Commentary* (USA)	October 1976
63.	David Robinson	*The Times*	11.4.1975
64.	Dilys Powell	*Sunday Times*	13.4.1975
65.	Nick Cohn	*New Times*	—
66.	Frank Rich	*New York Post*	27.10.1975
67.	Roger Greenspun	*Soho News*	—
68.	William Wolf	*Cue*	—
69.	Kathleen Carroll	*Village Voice*	3.11.1975
70.	Judy Stone	*San Francisco Chronicle*	2.6.1976
71.	Norman K Dow	—	—
72.	Derek Malcolm	*Arts Guardian*	10.4.1975
73.	Patrick Gibbs	*The Daily Telegraph*	11.4.1975
74.	David Castell	*The Sunday Telegraph*	13.4.1975
75.	Russell Davis	*The Observer*	
76.	Gary Arnold	*Washington Post*	
77.	Vincent Canby	*New York Times*	27.10.1975
78.	Gary Arnold	*Washington Post*	26.10.1975
79.	Alexander Walker	*Evening Standard*	10.4.1975
80.	Michael Bellington	*The Birmingham Post*	12.4.1975
81.	Margaret Hinxman	*Daily Mail*	12.4.1975
82.	Omitted		
83.	Joy Cacks	(*New York*)	21.10.1973
84.	Richard Galligan	*The New Haven Register*	12.10.1973
85.	Vincent Canby	*New York Times*	—
86.	Omitted		

87. Martin Crayn	*Hindustan Standard*	30.11.1973
88. Donia Mills	*Washington Post*	29.10.1975
89–90. *Schemering Chris*	*Cineaste*	Spring 1975
91. Jonathan Rosenbaum	*Sight and Sound*	*Spring* 1975
92. —	*Variety*	August 1973
93. David Robinson	*The Times*	5.7.1973
94–5. More Raves	*The New York Times*	14.11.1975

The Golden Fortress 1974

96. —	*Variety*	19.11.1975
97. Judy Stone	*San Francisco Chronicle*	15.10.1975

The Middle Man 1975

98. Penelope Houston	*Sight and Sound*	Spring 1977
99. David Robinson	*The Times*	11. 2.1977
100. Michael Bellington	*The Birmingham Post*	—
101. Vincent Canby	*The New York Times*	12.10.1976
102. Derek Malcolm	*Arts Guardian*	10.2.1977
103. Alan Brien	*The Sunday Times*	13.2.1977
104. Patrick Gibbs	*The Daily Telegraph*	11.2.1977
105. Russell Davies	*The Observer*	17.2.1977
106. Geoff Brown	*Monthly Film Bulletin*	March 1977
107. —	*Evening Standard*	17.2.1977
108. John Coleman	*New Statesman*	11.2.1977
109. Omitted		
110. —	*Spectator*	19.2.1977
111. —	*Sunday Telegraph*	13.2.1977
112. Omitted		

General

113. Martin Molina	*The Montreal Star*	6.1.1973
114. John Stark	*San Francisco Chronicle*	15.10.75
115. Ann Leslie	*The Times*	22.1.1973
116. Thomas Quinn Curtis	*International Herald Tribune*	27.7.1973
117. Romard Weinrauf	*New York Times*	3.8.1973
118. Henri Micciollo	In Calcutta on study tour — writing a book on Satyajit Ray — private conversation.	12.7.1979 8–12 April 1972

NOTES

1. I am thankful to Satyajit Ray for lending me his collection of reviews. This collection, however, is not systematically gathered. It is made up of clippings, sent to Satyajit Ray by friends and well-wishers abroad.
2. R.W. Corrigan, 'The Drama of Anton Chekhov', in *Modern Drama Essays in Criticism,* New York, Oxford University Press, ed. T. Bogard and W.I. Oliver, 1965, v, pp. 73-98.
3. 'à la Renoir' for all sorts of reasons, not least among them being Ray's deeply-felt sympathy for most of his characters.
4. See Adolfo Sanchez Vazquez, *Art and Society: Essays in Marxist Aesthetics*, New York and *London, Monthly Review Press*, 1973.
5. Bertolt Brecht: *Écrits sur le cinéma,* éd. de l'Arche, 1970, p. 180. See my *Films for an Ecology of Mind, Essays on Realism in the Cinema*, Calcutta: Firma KLM, 1978, pp. 113-26.
6. For instance, Siegfried Kracauer, *Theory of Film: The Redemption of Reality*, Oxford University Press, 1960, pp. 310-31. 'What seems to me to be remarkable about *Aparajito*', a reader of the *New York Times* writes to the editor of the film section, 'is that you see this story happening in a remote land and see these faces with their exotic beauty and still feel that the same is happening everyday somewhere in Manhattan or Brooklyn or the Bronx'. Of *The Adversary* Margaret Hinxman (17) wrote that it 'speaks more dearly to an alien Western audience than any number of alarming news-reels or lectures'. Also (28), (44), (63).
7. Gregory Bateson, *Steps to an Ecology of Mind*, New York, Ballantine, 1972, p. 146: 'the mere purposive rationality unaided by such phenomena as art, religion, dream and the like is necessarily pathogenic and destructive of life'.
8. (17, 23, 32, 37, 48, 49, 50, 54, 57, 72, 73, 74, 76, 79, 82, 83, 84, 92, 98, 99, 113). And here is a platitude of the idealist type: '*Distant Thunder* shows us Man — his simplicity, his contradictions, his tenacity. It reminds us of our own humanity, which may not be entertaining but is certainly enriching.' (49).
9. My *Films for an Ecology of Mind,* pp. 48, 86.
10. I am not aware of any critic mentioning that this scene is reminiscent of the opening of Abel Gance's *J'accuse* (1919 and 1938). In Gance's 'harrowing' film, the soldiers killed during the wars of mankind rise and walk towards the audience silently accusing them. Gance was surprised that his film did not stop World War I or prevent World War II.

11. If I may mention a much less important film to illustrate my point, I would say that in *Medium Cool* (1969) Haskel Wexler did pretty much the same thing. He used the Chicago convention as a background to an ordinary story. He went to the excess of incorporating shots of actual riot scenes into a sentimental love story.

CHAPTER 20

Satyajit Ray's Faith in Youth*

IF IT WERE possible to bring together all the film characters that Satyajit Ray created in nearly forty years, surely some two hundred of them would turn up, including men and women — from babies to very old persons. Babies like Apu and, later in the *Apu* Trilogy, Apu's own son, Kajol. But also the baby yet to be born that Charulata dreams of, old people like Auntie Indir in *Pather Panchali*, or the great-grandfather in *Shakha Proshakha.* Between these extremes you have a good number of elderly men like Biswambhar in *Jalsaghar*, Kalikinkar Roy in *Devi*, Indranath Chaudhuri in *Kanchenjungha.* The majority of characters, though, would consist of young adults. But there would also be some marvellous youths. Like, of course, Apu in *Aparajito* and *Apur Sansar.* Apu is too well known for me to discuss him here. Besides, he ends up being a young adult. I would like rather to discuss four other young characters that remain young until the end of the film in which they appear, but who nonetheless undergo an irreversible process of growth. Youth is a period of transition. A youth is no more a child and not yet a young adult. One is on the move between childhood and adulthood. The first two Ray characters I wish to discuss now are those of Siddhartha in *Pratidwandi* and Mrinmoyee in *Samapti.* The depiction of their growth constitutes some of the finest fragments of cinema not only in Ray's entire work but in international cinema as well. Ray is at his best when he depicts the evolution of a character. The two other youths I want to introduce form a couple, soon to get married, in *Gana Shatru*, Indrani or Ranu, Dr. Gupta's daughter, and her fiancé, Ronen.

*Lecture delivered on 19 December 1992. Appeared in Santi Das, ed., *Satyajit Ray: An Intimate Master,* 1998, pp. 62-78.

In the depiction of these characters can be seen the love of Ray for youth. And in their positive growth can be seen Ray's faith in youth. Young people, he seems to say, deserve to be loved and one can put faith in them: they will come up to their responsibilities. This is true especially with regard to Siddhartha and to Mrinmoyee. When it comes to Indrani and her friend, Ronen, the roles are reversed: it is they, the two youths, who help the adult hero to grow, and, of course, they too grow in the process of helping Dr. Gupta. And in this too is seen the limitless faith of Ray in youth.

SIDDHARTHA (*PRATIDWANDI*)

In the film *Pratidwandi*, Siddhartha is a young man of 25, almost an adult but not quite so. Like in the case of many urban youths, his adulthood is delayed by his college and university studies. But the death of his father suddenly puts an end to his student's life. He must now find a job. He is called for an interview. Siddhartha's youthfulness is revealed by the manner in which he answers the questions put to him by his interviewers. He is not one to give the answers that are expected of him. True to himself he will say only what he thinks must be said. He does that, and, of course, he does not get the job. Later in the film, he acknowledges that he has to be more careful.

Siddhartha must find a job, but also he must find himself. Both the tasks are difficult. In the case of the job, it's obvious. There are very few jobs available, and to get one, it is often necessary to compromise. The matter of Siddhartha's identity is infinitely complex. He defines himself in relation to his younger brother, Tunu, and his younger sister, Sutapa. Tunu, like Siddhartha himself a few years earlier, is committed to political and violent action. But Siddhartha is not a man of action, he is a dreamer. Tunu tells him at one point, 'There are two sorts of people: those who think and those who act. You think, I act.' Sutapa has a job and, with great pragmatism, she does whatever is required of her to advance her career. Siddhartha is not an activist, and he is honest. Therefore, he can follow the ways of neither his activist brother nor of his dishonest sister. As he goes in vain from one interview to the next, he meets Nareshda, an old acquaintance of his political days. Nareshda, with obvious sympathy for Siddhartha, tries to help him with a piece of advice. 'If you do not want to engage in political action, then you have to take up a job of sorts. It's a life requirement.' Siddhartha has enough of being lectured to. Yet, he respects Nareshda. He does not quite refuse the offer of help from his elder, but he shows no enthusiasm in taking up a job outside of Calcutta. It is significant that Ray himself has spoken these words of advice to Siddhartha. It is said that Ray had to lend his voice because at the last moment the person who had been selected for the role did not sound correct. Even then, in lending his voice, to Nareshda, Ray has identified more directly with the advice given to Siddhartha. Besides, the face of Nareshda is never seen. Only his back is seen and just a little of the side of his face. Satyajit himself could have sat in front of Siddhartha. The words of Nareshda in Satyajit's mouth are words of reason. And it is reason that will help Siddhartha grow. Not just dreams and feelings, however lofty.

The change in Siddhartha, his growth from a youth into a young adult, occurs after his aborted interview, the second in the film, when outraged by the decision of the interviewers to pause for lunch, he enters their room, overturns their table, and walks out. The change that follows must have taken place over a period of at least a few days. That is, from the time he leaves the place of interview to the moment he finishes writing a letter to Keya, his girl friend. But the filmmaker takes only a few moments to show the change in his film. Besides, how do you show a change of mind? Here Ray uses the resources of the film medium superbly. As Siddhartha leaves the interviewers and walks out, there is a rapid lateral movement of the camera on wall posters, suggesting the intensity of Siddhartha's reaction. A lateral movement of the camera showing fields from within a train immediately follows this. But this second movement is gentler, and it shows an open space. The quality of the movement is different. There follow a few shots of Siddhartha, sitting in the moving train, entering a hotel, sitting in his room, giving an instruction to the bearer, hearing the sound of a bird, walking out on to the verandah to listen to the bird. Meanwhile on the sound track, from the shot when Siddhartha is seen in the train, is heard his voice saying the words of the letter he is writing to Keya. In these few shots, the profound change in Siddhartha is revealed: a love is born, a responsibility (the job) is taken, and then, then only, can the bird be heard. The bird symbolizes Siddhartha's childhood. His innocence, his wholeness and harmony with nature. During the past few years he could not hear it. He didn't even know the name of the bird, nor could he imitate its song. He just remembered having heard it. Thus, by accepting his responsibility, Siddhartha opened himself to love, and regained the innocence of his childhood.

Of course, there is much to discuss about Siddhartha. Is he not a typical middle class intellectual? Is he not a bourgeois? Especially in the context of the political life of the early 1970s, is he not utterly a-political? Whatever the answers to these questions, Siddhartha of *Pratidwandi* represents a type of youths the like of whom could be found in Calcutta at the time of the film. After a gap of over twenty years, chances are that there are, even today, Siddharthas among us. Tunu and other similarly committed youths — like Amulya in *Ghare Baire* — are described with evident sympathy, but they do not represent Ray's own option. Siddhartha is closer to Ray. And Ray believes that finally the Siddharthas can grow into mature human persons, loving and responsible. Ray does not propose Siddhartha as a model to be imitated by other youths. He just expresses his faith in the Siddharthas of West Bengal.

MRINMOYEE (*SAMAPTI*)

Mrinmoyee has little in common with Siddhartha, except that like him she grows into a young adult. She is illiterate. She is a tomboy. But she is lovely. As Amulya returns home after completing his studies, a degree-holder and a perfectly urbanized gentleman, he cannot help falling in love with her. Accordingly, he rejects the marriage planned by his mother. He has it his way. The marriage with Mrinmoyee takes place. But on the night of the marriage, the bride is not with her newly-wed husband. She spends the night out, looking after her pet squirrel, Chorky. When on the order of her mother-in-law, Mrinmoyee is locked up in the nuptial room, she throws a tantrum, and scatters pieces of furniture in the room, including Amulya's books. Amulya has to intervene, he orders her very gently, yet firmly, to collect the scattered books. 'Did you have to pick on my books?' he asks. As the girl comes to her senses, he tells her not to worry, that he is leaving for Calcutta, and that she will be sent to her mother's house. Whenever she needs him, she can write to him, he will come.

After Amulya's departure, a profound change begins to take place in Mrinmoyee. But, again, how do you show a change of mind, and especially a change of heart? Ray does it in three shots. They constitute a marvellous moment of true cinema. One. Mrinmoyee is seen, almost in close-up, lying on her bed. Her younger brother, long time companion of her childish pranks, offers her a fruit — probably stolen — but she refuses it, she is not interested. Two. The previous shot dissolves into an almost identical one. But the tone is darker. Time has passed by. Mrinmoyee's mother pleads with her to make her eat, but to no avail. Three. Another dissolve. This time the shot is bright. Mrinmoyee is still lying on her bed. She is smiling, her thumb close to her lips. Her small brother announces that the pet squirrel Chorky is dead. He holds the dead animal by the tail in front of her face. She tells him to cremate it by the riverside. He asks whether she will come. Without any hesitation, she answers, 'No.' The transformation has taken place. The next moment she is seen writing a letter. The rest of the film will bring this transformation to its logical conclusion.

From the start, Mrinmoyee is madly in love with Amulya. But she is yet a child. The sexual reverberation of her love is suggested by scenes like the stealing of Amulya's shoes, the placing of her bridal ornaments in the horn of Amulya's record player on the nuptial night when she runs away, as if to say that she belongs to him, but needs some time. At another point in the film, seeing a barber cutting the hair of a client, she gets the idea of cutting a bunch of her own hair in a gesture of self-mutilation which suggests her refusal to become a woman.

As in the case of Siddhartha, it is possible to question the very character of Mrinmoyee growing to womanhood. Although Ray has contributed some of the finest images of women on the screen, he was no feminist. It could be argued that the growth of Mrinmoyee is finally an acceptation of male domination over her. She grows a woman within the context of her own society. What she is shown to grow into is an adult relationship with an adult man. But in the context of his film, Ray was concerned with showing her evolution from childhood to early womanhood. It is as if Ray's social milieu forced him to skip over a phase in the growth of the girl and show her as a young adult.

The presence of death in the two films, *Pratidwandi* and *Samapti*, may perhaps come as a surprise in films dealing with youths. The story of Siddhartha is neatly bracketed by death. The film opens with the funeral rites of Siddhartha's father. The film ends with the sound of a funeral procession for an unknown person. In order to understand the significance of death here, it helps to consider the attitude of Ray towards death in his films. In the *Apu* trilogy, for instance, at least five of the people closest to Apu die. But death does not dominate life. Rather, it is part of the life process. Life endures. And Siddhartha outgrows the shock caused by his father's death, and hence he can face life with serenity, accepting the fact that death is part of life. The death of the squirrel Chorky is symbolical of Mrinmoyee's own death to her childhood and her being born a woman. One cannot cling to childhood. One must let go. On the night of her marriage, Mrinmoyee was still attached to her own childhood represented by Chorky. Only when she grew detached from the pet animal was she free to love her husband. Similarly, as was noted earlier, when

Siddhartha accepted his responsibility by taking up a job, he heard the song of the lost bird.

INDRANI AND RONEN (*GANA SHATRU*)

Gana Shatru is perhaps the film that was most misunderstood in Calcutta. Largely because of a comparison between the film and Ibsen's play. The Calcutta public is too much of an expert in theatre to receive a film made 'after' a play by Ibsen without comparing both film and play. Moreover, there may have been a certain malaise among part of the public: the film is one of the most topical of Ray's. Topical, even political.

Within the framework of this brief presentation I cannot give an exhaustive reading of this marvellous film. Besides, my subject is well defined: Satyajit and his faith in youth. Ray's love and admiration for youth has been demonstrated by the depiction of Siddhartha and Mrinmoyee. In *Gana Shatru*, he goes much farther. Towards the end of the film, Dr. Gupta has come to believe that everything is over, he will not be able to speak out the truth. At that moment, when he sinks into despair, his daughter and his future son-in-law bring him the assurance that all is not lost. He asks them, 'Then, there is still hope?' They answer, 'Yes, of course.' Dr. Gupta who has been deluded by his own brother, by the publisher and the editor of the local newspaper, immediately believes in these young people. What he will do later on with their help is of little importance. Thanks to them he will continue to speak out. Indrani and her fiancé will themselves see to it that Dr. Gupta's article is published. At that very moment, a group of youths, Ronen's theatre group and other friends, are outside the house and they shout slogans that can be heard in the living room of Dr. Gupta, like an echo of the words uttered by the young couple inside. Thus, the home and the world are linked in a masterly manner. In *Ghare Baire*, Nikhilesh and Bimala expressed their politics in their private love, so also in this film the intra-familial relationships extend outside of the family in the world of politics.

In an interview with Andrew Robinson, Satyajit Ray had said that if he had to stop making films, he might consider writing his autobiography.[1] Ray did make three films after that interview, but it is difficult not to read elements of an autobiography in these films. In this case, it is as if Ray had created an occasion for two young people (including indirectly his own son) to declare themselves, to speak out, 'Yes, you may have faith in us'.

Ray's faith in youth was part of his faith in man. While making his film *Rabindranath Tagore*, in 1961, Ray had quoted a passage from 'Crisis in Civilization' where Tagore expresses his disappointment regarding the West. But Tagore had added: 'And yet I shall not commit the grievous sin of losing faith in man.'

In his own way, Ray has expressed his disenchantment with contemporary civilization, but he too, like Tagore, has expressed his faith in man in his last three films, the Heart Trilogy, especially in the very last, *Agantuk*.

NOTE

1. Andrew Robinson, *Satyajit Ray: The Inner Eye*, London, Andre Deutsch Ltd., 1989, p. 346.

PART FIVE

Interview

CHAPTER 21

Satyajit Ray on Scriptwriting*

FILM DIRECTION AND SCRIPT WRITING

When I started making films, I felt that the greatest weakness of the Bengali cinema was the scenario. I think the situation has not changed much since then. Of course, there are a few exceptions: among Bengali filmmakers, Ritwik Ghatak and Mrinal Sen have directed films that contain long stretches of excellence.

The artistic mind, in India, is not used to the idea of an unchangeable formal structure existing in time. Our principal art form is music, and our music is improvised. A musical performance can last anything from one to three hours, according to the musician's mood. But you can't make a film like that. Many of our novels have not got the type of structure you can analyse. The novel *Pather Panchali*, for instance, is discursive, episodic. It is almost too life-like in its rhythms and pace. There have been some remarkably-structured novels, written by men like Bankim Chandra Chattopadhyay, Manik Banerjee and Tagore, occasionally. But the general tendency is a kind of episodic, discursive approach to story telling, and this has never worked in the case of films. As a result, our films have remained shapeless and unsatisfactory.

The cinema was born in the West, and there has always been a deep affinity between the cinema and Western musical tradition. It is significant that most of the great pioneers of the

**Film Eye*, a film journal of the Ruia College Film Society in collaboration with Ruia COHSIP, vol. 1, December 1978.

cinema were musically conscious. Think, for instance, of Griffith, who was constantly referring to Beethoven, and of Eisenstein. Western music has definitely had some influence in the evolution of the form of the film in the West. Now we don't have that kind of tradition here. In my own case, from the age of fifteen, I have been familiar with Western music, the sonata form, the whole classical school, and the romantics. I think one has to have this feeling of a pattern existing in time, a pattern that can be comprehended only over a period of time, which is rigid, unchangeable, and which has a satisfying shape and rhythm.

In the West, and even here, directors rarely write their own scripts, with the exception of men like Bergman, Fellini, Antonioni, and a few others. Most directors who write their own scripts employ writers for the dialogue. In my view, a director should be his own scriptwriter. For, after the basic conception, the primary composition is the scenario, and if somebody else writes the scenario for the director, that part of the credit for the complete film should go to the scenario writer.

Some filmmakers may give the impression that they do not use a script but improvise. In fact, one never knows whether a film is improvised or not. The director may have given certain scenes a great deal of thought at home. It may not be on paper, but this comes to the same thing. Even if you do improvise, the moment you set the camera, you stop improvising. You can tell your actors to improvise their dialogue; but you're not necessarily going to keep every thing in. You are going to cut something out. At some point or other, you're in to introducing a certain element of order into your material. Whether it comes before you start shooting or at the time of editing can make some difference, but not a great one. Griffith never had a written scenario. He always had it in his head. He knew what he was going to do. Of course, you can do that. You can even go with a blank mind and do anything you like. (I have seen ostensibly improvised films, like *Shadows* by John Cassavetes). I would not mind doing this once in a while to see what you can achieve but this can be very costly.

SCRIPTWRITING FOR ME

I have been writing my own scenarios ever since I started making films. Even before I made my first film, I used to write screenplays as a pastime. I would take up a novel, which had been announced for filming by somebody else, write a treatment of that, and compare it with the film. I found this most instructive. It has been, and it remains, an absolute necessity for me to work on a script, really speaking, but it was all in my head.

In the old days, say up to *Charulata*, I always went out of town to write my scenarios. I used to go to a lonely seaside place — maybe Gopalpur or Puri. There, I worked alone, without any assistance, with not even my wife and son to accompany me. In such lonely places, I work much quicker and can produce much more work. I can keep at it sixteen or seventeen hours a day. Of course, when I left, I knew what story I wanted to make into a film. I never took longer than ten days to write a scenario. After that, there remained only to brush up and improve the dialogue. Nowadays, I am getting used to the noise here. Somehow, I can cut it off.

One of the reasons why I have written my scripts from the very first film is that I could not think of any one I could turn to. And at the beginning, I would not have thought of making a film without a script. Even now, I prefer to write my own scenarios for various reasons: first, I have an orderly method of work, that is, my mind works like that; secondly, you spend more money if you don't have a script, and you can't afford that. My shooting ratio for *Pather Panchali* was seven to one. It was only two and a half to one in *Kanchenjungha*. That was the lowest ratio I ever achieved. My usual ratio is about four to one. But *Kanchenjungha* was in colour, therefore more expensive, so I was more disciplined; and also, I had very fine actors, among whom was the late Chhabi Biswas, an old timer. The actors had learned their lines and were ready when they faced the camera. The new actors, also, were wonderful. I once read an interview of Antonioni in which he said, with some satisfaction, that his ratio was ten to one. In fact, one would not mind shooting a high ratio of footage to get the kind of perfection one wants. But sometimes you just have to stop, for other considerations. If, however, it was something which, if not perfect, would really matter, then you went on shooting until you got it.

I had to go up to ten or twelve takes for a correct synchronization of movements in *Pather Panchali.* We had a shot where Apu and his sister Durga start running after a candy-man, a confectioner. In the shot where they first spot the candy-man, the children were seen in the foreground. Behind them, in the background, was a dog. The children had to run and go out of frame while the camera kept on shooting at the dog. Someone was supposed to call out to him. But he was an untrained dog and would not go back at the right time. So we kept on trying again and again. There is no cut there in the finished film. It had to be in one shot, otherwise it would not be interesting. In the same shot the dog gets up and follows the children who follow the candy-man, and, in a later shot, their reflection is seen in a pond. I had one of the children put his hands behind his back, holding some sweets, so the dog followed them.

My method of work has grown out of certain considerations. We operate in a very small market and we have a very special kind of audience. In my case, the potential audience is even smaller because I make very personal films, sometimes rather serious films, and they are always somewhat different from the usual run of films. And yet, you make films first for your own audience. I cannot ignore my audience here. My audience means not only the audience in the city, but also in the suburbs, the lowest common denominator. The problem is to make a film that they will not entirely reject, and at the same time, one that will be accepted at Venice, Cannes or Berlin, and later on also in Europe generally. This is a very sophisticated audience. If I ignored only them I could be freer. If I ignored my audience here and made films only for the West, if I made them as subtle as possible, if I treated more difficult subjects, more adult, let's say more frank, more sophisticated, more complex subjects, then I would be doing different films, taking up different stories.

Besides, when you make films, most of the time you are using somebody else's money. Immediately, certain responsibilities come to you. You are always waiting for the next man to come to offer you the required money. When one comes, you realize that this man is investing lots of money that he hopes to get back. So, I generally tell my producers beforehand what to expect from my films. When I made *Charulata*, I told my producer: 'This film may win prizes abroad, but I don't know if you will make a profit out of it.' He said: 'I don't mind, I like the story, make it.' But if he had said: 'No', I would not have made the film. I made it very clear in other cases also, like that of *Devi*. In the case of *Jalsaghar*, I told my producer: 'This is going to be a fairly important film, I think. You may find a market abroad, but I don't know about my own audience here, because they have not been tested.'

OVER THE YEARS

My method has not changed very much, except that over the years I have acquired a certain proficiency. I think the process has remained more or less the same: first the outline, then the breakdown. Writing the dialogue has improved enormously; I think one always overwrites at the beginning. Even now, I find occasionally — not as frequently as before — when a scene is being shot, that they are talking too much. Maybe a gesture here, a gesture there, will take the place of words that you can drop. The general tendency is to overwrite, to put too much. That's because your visual imagination, is not working to the same extent while you are writing. You have to get into a state where you just live the scenes and imagine the actors living them, surrounded by the props in this or that location, getting up, moving about.

Generally, when you start writing dialogues, you imagine the actors are just talking, which is not the case. That's why I never rehearse, except on location, or, in the studio, when the set is ready with all the props and everything, so that I know precisely how the actors will move, what they will do, etc. In fact, every action affects the words. Sometimes your mind is distracted momentarily, and you repeat something you said just before. And so, everything in the scene, in the shot, has to be taken into consideration, even the season of the year, because, for instance, in winter you talk in a different way from summer. You're more relaxed at certain times. Your state of mind, the props surrounding you and the business that you're performing, whether you are just sitting idly or active in some work, all this makes for different types of dialogue. So, I think my dialogue is becoming more and more life-like. This is not naturalism, but a kind of selective realism, which works only for a particular scene, and with a dialogue the actors find very easy to say. I have discovered that a dialogue which is easy to speak improves the acting, because the actors know that what they are saying comes naturally, not like rhetorical speech.

I have also made progress with regard to the structure of my films. For instance, in *Pather Panchali* and in *Aparajito* there were things that had to be cut out at the stage of editing. These things seemed redundant, or weak, and unnecessary. That would obviously mean that the script was not perfectly conceived. On the other hand, in some cases, I could shoot only parts of some scenes because of lack of money, so the unprinted bits had to be left out. Some of these were very good scenes. Had they been completed, they'd be in the finished film. But they were not. The trilogy had a very special character in the sense that it was not a story: it had a kind of biographical quality to it, and this needed a different kind of script. If you had a plotted structure, that would need another approach. Since the trilogy, I have not attempted anything on the same lines, that is, a film with the quality of a biography, with the flow and rhythm of life rather than that of a plotted story.

HOW I WRITE A SCRIPT

If I am working on somebody else's story, then to write the script means, first of all, casting the story into the form of a film. It then becomes a slightly different story, with a different rhythm and a different sequence of events to it, unless the original story happened to be very close to a film treatment, which is very rarely the case. So, often a considerable degree of adaptation is required, and I do that adaptation. I cast the story in the form of a screen-story. But this is never for me a literary effort. It's something that I have to do, which I wish I did not have to do. Anyway, it's a form of writing, which I don't think of as a literary effort at all. It's just a kind of an outline — a block treatment, as the term goes — and as brief as possible.

In script writing, everything works as long as the final product is satisfactory. I don't think you can frame strict rules any more. A certain degree of grammar is necessary, and you learn that by looking at films more than anything else. That's the way we learned. We used to go to movies which we liked, even to movies we did not like, more than once — the bad movies, to see what was wrong with them, but the good movies we could see five, six, or seven times. I even started at one time to take notes in the dark. But when it actually comes to shooting your own films, all that may be at the back of your mind, but I think your style, your editing method, your set-ups are all dictated by your material. You are not applying rules there. The material of your story, of your subject matter, guides you. Such rules as 'don't cut from extreme long shot to close-up', all that is gone. Nobody takes that seriously anymore, because emotional continuity is much more important than continuity of external movement.

I visualize everything very closely, so all I have to do is to convey what I have in mind. Often, I express it pictorially. This is essential. I think that all the directors who have a sufficient degree of control over their material do the same thing. I do small sketches for my shots. That is the final stage of the shooting script. This is not a typewritten thing that I distribute to my crew. It's a series of drawings of shots, with notes, the dialogue and camera movement. It also shows the frame and the magnification. That is good for discussion with the art director and the cameraman.

Music does not come right at the beginning. But at the time

of writing the scenario, I become aware of certain situations I know might need music. If a certain theme or motif presents itself, I note it down in my script, sometimes in the margin. Suddenly, a line of melody comes and it strikes me that it would suit a certain situation. I generally use music in a leitmotif sort of fashion. It's not a new piece of music for every situation, but it rises out of certain thematic material in maybe one or two main themes. I produce variations on them, like in the film *Charulata.* This process is very clear there. I also have a separate notebook with staff notation. In that book I keep noting down themes, not necessarily for a particular film, but for some film in the future. These are just musical ideas, like a sketchbook. I have three or four such books full of musical ideas. They are usually fragments of melody, sometimes with notes on the instruments that would probably be most appropriate. For, a melody is not suitable for all instruments. Sometimes the idea comes only as a bare line of melody; sometimes it comes dressed in a certain orchestral colour.

THE BREAKDOWN

The breakdown has to be planned very carefully: which scene to shoot first, which set, which location to shoot first. It is a fairly elaborate thing: there is the question of finding the right locations, of discussing with the art director what sets to build.

The question there is, of the availability of the studios, if you are going to shoot in a studio. If it is entirely on location, as in *Pather Panchali,* we have to find a location, we have to find actors, and then we decide on the manner of shooting, which scene to tackle first, etc. Then, I start doing the breakdown in terms of shots. With location work, this is kept fairly flexible, because one always gets ideas on location. You change your camera viewpoint, you change for better light; suddenly a breeze blows and you perceive a better angle for a certain shot, so you change the angle. Sometimes you do tracking shots instead of static shots, or vice versa, depending on how your trolley is functioning. If it's giving trouble, then one long tracking shot can be broken up on the spot into five shots.

Shooting in the studio becomes a more rigid affair, because you have sets there: you usually have only three walls to them, so your angles are limited; you have to light up for a certain angle and then finish that angle and go on to the next one.

In my script, I also leave room for improvisations in the dialogue. If you're working with non-professional actors, sometimes certain words, certain lines of dialogue don't come naturally to them, so you constantly modify; you simplify; you increase or decrease the number of words.

FROM STORY TO SCREENPLAY

Sometimes, in the process of turning a story into a screenplay, I find that certain characters begin to change. Then scriptwriting becomes, a process of criticism of the original, because, as you think deeply about the lines of development, some characters do not seem any more to behave in a convincing manner. So then starts a process of modification and the conclusion becomes slightly different from that of the original story. This happens all the time. Sometimes you discover a serious basic flaw in the original story and you abandon the whole thing because it is not what you had thought it was. It has happened once or twice in my experience — not recently though; earlier on. Something which I had read years ago, and which had struck me as a wonderful story, I would read it again and start treating it in terms of the screenplay. Then I'd find that there were flaws in it, which maybe the original author did not notice or which you don't mind in a literary work. But in a film everything is more concrete, and the time span is so brief and continuous, that you are more alert somehow, and therefore, certain things strike you as being wrong, or maybe not quite properly drawn.

If a story once read sticks in the mind, I usually read it again. It is usually in a second reading that the real worth of a story as film material emerges. If I begin to see the sweep of the film in it, a third reading usually helps make up my mind. After that, I never touch the story again. I even forget it sometimes. It does not matter to me whether I am departing from the original, even if it is a hallowed Tagore story. Sometimes the whole story, with everything in it, stays in your mind; then, of course, it's already almost a film, and you don't have to work so hard. But you still have to find the cinematic equivalent of certain literary things.

In *Charulata*, the first seven or eight minutes of loneliness correspond to twenty pages of writing. I could see that the essential thing to establish in the beginning was the loneliness of Charulata. But what is loneliness? Loneliness is lack of company, which means lack of communication. One has to find the cinematic equivalent of Charulata's loneliness. Without taking recourse to commentary or words, just show her loneliness: what can a lonely woman do? How does she spend her time? Is she still useful? There are two kinds of loneliness: the loneliness of old age, and the loneliness of youth when there is still the desire for company. So this was the initial situation in *Charulata,* and I worked on that. It did not matter to me at all that I was omitting the first twenty pages of Tagore, because I knew I had the substance. This is what I had to establish in order that the rest might follow logically: the coming of the brother-in-law, the falling in love, the husband . . ., etc.

Even with that kind of freedom in adapting, at the time the film is finished, I know I have made a story by Tagore into a film. It is an interpretation, a 'trans-creation', not a translation. Without Tagore, there would be no *Charulata.* After all, he set me off, he was the reason for it. There is a lot of the original in the film. A certain state of mind which the author describes beautifully with words, you can't do that in films. You have to use a different method. Tagore is a great poet, a great writer. He uses wonderful language to describe loneliness and all the small things that go on in the mind. All the time, you have to find something for Charulata to do to establish her state of mind. That is the challenge of the cinema.

Now, when you take up a story, you do not necessarily like the whole of it. Maybe one strong situation, or certain things strike you, which you want to put into film. But if you were to do an original story and use these situations or things, you would be plagiarizing. So you get in touch with the author and tell him. 'I'm going to make a film of your story and I'm going to do my own treatment. I am going to make the necessary modification.' He agrees, and he is paid for it. He sells the rights. In *Mahanagar*, a lot of things in the original story come in the film. But it is a short story to begin with, so you start developing it. You start from the situation that fascinated you in the beginning: the wife having to go out and work to add to the family's income. That's your starting point. And then, of course, you have the inevitable psychological development of husband and wife suddenly feeling this situation, of the husband's feeling of inferiority, with all the psychological complications this involves, and then the child, and the conservative parents. These elements are all these in the original story.

[Here Satyajit Ray mentioned the case of Postmaster, a story by Tagore. Ray altered the end of the story to make it suit his own feeling about it. That passage is reproduced in Chapter 18.]

There are other similar changes in my other films — in the *Apu* trilogy, for instance. The trilogy was not originally planned by me as a trilogy. When I made *Pather Panchali*, I had no idea of making *Aparajito*, because, at that time, I could not think beyond one film. There was no knowing how the public would react. After the success of *Pather Panchali*, I thought of making the second part. Even then, there was no question of the third part. *Aparajito* was followed by *Jalsaghar* and *Parash Pathar*. Only after *Aparajito* won the Venice prize did I suddenly think of making a third Apu film. When I made *Aparajito* I naturally had *Pather Panchali* in mind, but they were not meant to be seen in a single programme, as a totality, as a six hours-long epic. But I used certain recurring symbols, like the train, and the musical motifs of *Pather Panchali* come back in *Aparajito* and also in *Apur Sansar*.

At the end of *Pather Panchali*, a snake is seen crawling into the deserted house of Apu's family. That snake is not in the book. I needed something more than just the family leaving. I wanted to stress the fact that the house was deserted. I could simply have shown the house with no people around, but the snake entering the house clinches the matter.

In *Apur Sansar*, when Apu learns of his wife's death, he hits his brother-in-law who has just delivered the news to him. That needed some thought, because I was trying to put myself in the place of Apu. I was not familiar with such a situation in real life. It was difficult to tell what would happen, and the more deeply I thought about it, the more I felt that, for a man like Apu, it was natural suddenly to hit the person who brought him such bad news. It seemed to me a psychologically convincing thing to do. As this does not occur in the book, this part of my film was strongly criticized. I thought the criticism ridiculous. I was myself convinced that the gesture was the correct one, and my actor shared my conviction.

THE CHOICE OF SOME OF MY STORIES

The *Three Daughters* was undertaken as a tribute to Tagore. It was his centenary year. I had made the Tagore documentary, and I thought I should do some short stories as well. I did *Monihara*, the ghost story, because I am very fond of ghost stories. Of course, you would not do a ghost story today and take it seriously.

This is a different age. But then you want to play about with the film medium also, because, after all, you only have one lifetime, so you do as much as you can. Not many others do that. Everything has fallen into a rut, so why not explore while there is time for it.

There are only two instances where circumstances forced me to take up a film. *Abhijan* and *Chiriakhana*, the detective story, were not things of my own choice. There are wonderful aspects to filmmaking, like working with wonderful actors. If the location is exciting, if you have a good crew, then you are in it in no time. You get involved in it. You enjoy the process of making the film. Then, you forget about whether the story was worth it or not. You give it all you have. Something like this happened in the case of *Abhijan*. This was based on a novel by

Tarashankar Banerjee. A group of friends wanted to make it into a film. They asked me to write the scenario for them. I did so. Then they asked me to see the locations. I went and found that extraordinary place: an area of one square mile covered with rocks. This was not in the original script. I put it in. Then I helped them to select the spots for shooting. Finally, I took over, at their request. I made changes in the scenario and I gave more thought to it, because, at first, it was a popular treatment of a popular story. I gave as much depth to it as it would take. It was one of those adventurous, plotty novels, so I could only do this up to a point. Then I concentrated on the acting, because there were acting possibilities in it, and I had wonderful actors, and wonderful locations. Such things are great fun. I love working, I love making films regardless of what I am making.

The rights to make *Chiriakhana* were purchased by some friends, and they asked me to help them. It was a weak detective story. Detective stories don't make good films anyway. You only wait for the revelation of 'who did it', and once it comes there is nothing else; and then at the end you have a long lecture. I do not like detective stories in films. A thriller? Fine — you can create good suspense with that.

Abhijan and *Chiriakhana* were not of my own selection. I would not have made them anyway. But at the time of *Chiriakhana* I was myself in a very awkward position. My producer had just walked off *Goopy Gyne*; we had recorded the songs, and we went to Rajasthan, looking for locations. Suddenly, he was panic-stricken. He said, 'No.' I was completely left in the lurch with nothing to do, and I don't like to be idle too long. Then there came this offer of a detective story. Again, there was an interesting cast: these friends who had purchased the rights of *Chiriakhana,* and I just took it over.

THE USE OF COLOUR

If colour could be controlled sufficiently, one would, perhaps, make everything in colour. But colour, in its present state, tends to prettify things a little. Also, you are constricted by the fact that you are using three primary bases. Even if you can control one of them, the others will be producing their natural combinations, which you cannot control. The trouble is that it's not like paint, and that keeps worrying me.

In *Kanchenjungha,* I deliberately chose colour, because I felt it would be very interesting. This was a two-hour story with no lapse of time. I had the characters wear the same clothes all the way through. Since they split into groups you had this very interesting effect of having a different colour combination for each group appearing by turns. It works formally; I planned the story in such a way that even the landscape underwent certain natural changes. At one point of the story, you have the mist coming in, and everything, for a certain length of time, is subdued. You see through the mist, and all the colours are automatically muted. No laboratory tricks are involved here, just nature helping you. Finally, the mist rises, but by that time the sun has gone down. Everything has a kind of reddish glow. (For that part of the film all the scenes were shot after five o'clock.)

The story starts on a sunny day. Then clouds come, the sun is obscured, so that you have another chromatic range altogether. Then, the mist comes, that gives a third quality. Then the mist rises, the clouds go, but the sun is so low that everything is muted again. These changes were wedded to emotional states.

The colours of the dresses were chosen very carefully with psychological effect in mind. What sort of a colour would this kind of a girl wear on this particular occasion? The two sisters were differently dressed for psychological reasons. The latter had a gray suit and a little red handkerchief sticking out of her pocket, showing her pride, and a yellow walking stick. This film required a tremendous amount of planning. I had a map drawn of the Darjeeling area where we were supposed to shoot. This was included in the script itself, and the various locations were all marked. The time of shooting in each location was also indicated. Suppose we were shooting in location C and suddenly the mist came, we had to run to location D for some shots in the mist there. Everything was within a half-mile radius, and it was planned so as not to waste time. That's why we could shoot 26,000 feet of film in 26 days, shooting everyday. So in 26 days, less than a month, shooting of the film was finished.

One does not imagine *Aparajito* in colour. Benares would be so gorgeous with pretty colours that the whole mood would be destroyed. The director should have the freedom to switch from black and white to colour. Some have done it already. I did it in *Goopy Gyne.* That was a film of magic. There is a kind of in-joke when the two princesses refuse to look at the two boys, Bagha and Goopy. The boys were shy, and the princesses probably thought they were ordinary boys, so Bagha had the brilliant idea of turning himself and Goopy into princes. Both clapped their hands and everything turned into colour. Then the girls looked up. This was attractive. They refused to look at black and white, but, given colour, they looked. This had some psychological implications.

PART SIX

Satyajit Ray and the Film Societies Movement in India

CHAPTER 22

What is Wrong with the Indian Film Societies?*

IN AN ARTICLE published in 1985,[1] the late Ajoy Dey, then Secretary of the Federation of Film Societies of India, stated that at that time there were 225 film societies in India. Of these, 77 were in West Bengal, of which nearly 30 were in Kolkata. Thanks to these societies, films were shown to keen audiences, discussions were held about these films and about cinema in general, and articles were published in magazines. The film societies supported particular good films. There was a film societies movement. Ajoy Babu was quite happy. And rightly so. But today, would he be happy? What would he write? I can only hope that he would write something on the lines of what I am about to say.

THE RISE AND FALL OF THE INDIAN FILM SOCIETIES

Let me start with 'Purano Sei Diner Katha'.[2] The year is 1948. A young artist. He is hardly 27 years old. He has not made any film; he is not a film critic. Yet, he thinks seriously about the Indian cinema. He feels that there are film classics among the Indian films, but he wonders why Indian cinema has not gained a prominent place within the international cinema. He further wonders why Indian films do not play a greater role among the Indian masses.

Our young artist found an answer to his own question. He wrote that answer in an essay he entitled 'What is Wrong with Indian Film?'[3] The young writer's name was Satyajit Ray.[4]

*2004.

He had reached the following conclusion:

> The raw material of the cinema is life itself. It is incredible that a country which has inspired so much painting and music and poetry should fail to move the filmmaker. He has only to keep his eyes open and his ears. Let him do so.[5]

Thus, in 1948, Satyajit Ray dreamt of an Indian film. An Indian film that would be an important part of the Indian culture. Because that Indian cinema would spring from Indian life. To get that new Indian cinema you needed a new type of filmmaker and a new type of film viewer. If in India filmmakers and film viewers suffered from any ailment, then Satyajit Ray had but one remedy for both: 'open your eyes, open your ears and learn from life'.

That is why Manikda started to work on two parallel fronts: making films, and spreading film education. In nearly 45 years he made about 35 feature films. At the same time as he started to make films, he created the Calcutta Film Society. Later on, and until his death, he was the President of the Federation of Film Societies of India. In that position, he contributed immensely to the spread of film culture throughout India. While Manikda and others created films based on Indian life, the film societies showed films, they held seminars, published film journals, and supported 'good', relevant films.

That combined effort of filmmakers and film societies had a deep influence on the film viewers. As a result, a new form of film criticism began to be published. In fact, there was a need of a new film criticism. In his 1948 essay Manikda had written that inadequate resources had done harm to films, but, he added, 'I have no doubt that equal harm has been done by critics who keep peddling muddled notions about the art form.'[6]

That was in 1948. Nearly fifty years later, in his 1985 essay, Ajoy Dey could write: 'The journals of Calcutta Film Society, Cine Club of Calcutta, Cine Central, Calcutta Cine Institute, North Calcutta Film Society and Cine Club of Naihati carried articles and reviews on cinema. . . . A new type of film criticism emerged through these film society journals.'[7]

The work of the film societies in Kolkata and in India

generally was quite successful. However, to have a more complete picture, one should mention the unique contribution to film education of the Film and Television Institute of India and of the National Film Archive of India. The Archive, along with several foreign missions, was one of the main sources of films shown by the film societies. In addition, ever since the mid-1960s the Archive offered every year a one-month course in film appreciation. I myself attended one such course in 1967.

That situation has changed. The activities of the film societies are much less intense. But, above all, the film societies have ceased to come out in support of good films. That was shown especially with regard to the last films of Satyajit Ray, the films I like to call the 'Heart Trilogy'.

Where were our famous film societies when Satyajit Ray, their president and leader, literally snatching time out of the hands of death, made his film *Gana Shatru*— his ultimate hymn to joy? Critics mislead the public with their trivial discussions. One critic who had a grudge against Manikda sneaked into a private preview of *Gana Shatru* and, before anyone else could see that film, he wrote a scathing review of it. Where were our famous film societies when Satyajit Ray shared with the public his reflection on his life as an artist in *Shakha Proshaka*? Could not the film societies of which Satyajit Ray was the President, and for whom he had done so much, come out to help people appreciate this gift from the master?

Where were our film societies when Satyajit Ray made *Agantuk*? In that film he expanded on the message of Rabindranath Tagore, 'Sabhyatar Sankat' (Crisis in Civilization), and he offered the Indian and world public his own reflection on today's civilizations and barbaric ways.

When critics argued with me that the film did not have the perfection of earlier Ray films, I reminded them of Manikda's poor health. Their reply was that he did not have to make a film. It is as if one commented on the quality of the voice of Rabindranath Tagore when, at the age of 80, he read in public his essay 'Crisis in Civilization'. Would one say that Tagore did not have to read the essay?

I emphasize the poor critical response to Ray's film to show that both the filmmakers and the film viewers need assistance: the former to help their films reach the public, and the latter to help them appreciate — you might say, reach — the films. Unfortunately, that assistance has not been provided by the film societies even in the case of the maestro.

What is wrong with Indian film societies? The question Satyajit Ray raised some fifty years ago about Indian films must now be raised about Indian film societies. Raising the question is to continue the work of Satyajit Ray to spread film education. Ray had written: 'One of the most significant phenomena of our time has been the development of the cinema.'[8]

Fifty years have passed since Ray wrote these words. Today, the most significant development is that of electronic communication. Film still exists, but along with it are video, television and the World Wide Web. That is why we now need a 'New Wave' for our old movement.

A 'NEW WAVE' FOR AN OLD MOVEMENT

The Indian film societies that were doing such a marvellous job have progressively become stagnant. That is because they have not followed the mantra formulated by Satyajit Ray, 'Open your eyes, open your ears.' Because they do not open their eyes and ears, the film societies do not realize that the media scene has changed. And even cinema itself has changed.

It is not the first time cinema changed. Looking at the history of the cinema, one can see that film has changed several times. Each time, self-styled prophets of doom have proclaimed, 'Cinema is dead.'[9] Cinema, however, is not dead. Cinema is not dying. The cinema that many of us used to see not so many years ago, that cinema is no more. But cinema itself is quite alive. Open your eyes, open your ears. Otherwise, the film societies will become irrelevant, and it is of them that we shall say, 'the film societies are dead'.

Some of the changes that have taken place: The main change is that cinema is no more the important medium it used to be. It remains important, but along with other media. That the cinema is less important can be seen from at least three points of view. First, ideologically. Cinema still creates on the screen of the viewer's mind the dream from which the viewer understands his or her life more profoundly: memory of the past, image of the present, blueprint of the future. Cinema never was alone to create these dreams. But today, television too projects powerful dreams in the mind of the viewers, through the news, advertisement, serials, telefilms, and, above all, music television. Add the so-called mobile phone, constantly intruding in the psyche of the mobile user.

Second, aesthetically. At any one time film aesthetics is consonant with the dominant socio-economic system of its time. For instance, the aesthetics of classical cinema (1940-60) was consonant with monopoly capitalism. At that time, space was very important. Colonial powers were appropriating new places to extend their markets. Today, another phase of capitalism has set in: transnational or late capitalism. Now space is not as important as it used to be. Hence, in current film aesthetics real or realistic space is ignored. You can see that in music television, especially foreign music television.

And, third, financially. Even though the production of a film involves huge amounts of money, at times other media can bring in more revenues than cinema.

The objective of the film societies and of film education: In 1970, when I wrote my book *Chitra Bani*, my aim was to contribute to an understanding of society. I used to say, 'If you want to understand society, study the communication media. And if you want to understand the media, study films. Open your eyes, open your ears.' Indeed, the study of film has long been the royal road, or *marga*, to understanding society.

Today also, my objective is to understand society. Today also, I say, 'If you want to understand your society, study its communication media. And if you want to understand the media, study not only films, but also the news, advertising, media sports, serials, telefilms and, above all, music television.' For, to understand films, you need to understand the other media. For instance, you will find that the style of media sports can be observed in films, like *Lagaan*. Again, the exuberance of music television is felt in films, like *Kuch Kuch Hota Hai*. But that is not enough. Today, if you want to understand the media, you have to study the phenomenon of Internet.

At one time, one went to see films on a large screen in a cinema hall. Now films come to you through television in your home. We soon got used to see films on a small screen. We perhaps did not notice that the film experience from large to small screen had changed completely. Indeed, to go to see a film in a cinema hall, and to see a film at home on a small screen are two different experiences. Just think of *Lagaan* on your TV monitor after you have seen it in a hall on a large screen with a Dolby sound system.

Thus, there was the 35 mm film, then the 16 mm film, then the 8 mm, then Super 8 mm film. Then came the videocassette. Then came the compact disc, and finally the Internet. One will soon be able to see any film on one's computer, and on one's cellular phone. Already, you can see feature films on a pay per view basis. As I said, we used to go to the movies, but now the movies come to us. In that reversal, a profound change has happened in our film experience. This is the era we are living in. In this new media environment, what can the film societies do?

A militant programme for film societies: The media environment has changed. Therefore, we need to do something new if we are to participate in social life meaningfully. Earlier, in order to spread film education, it was necessary to show films. Today, it is less necessary to show films, because films are in the hands of many people in the form of video cassettes or discs.

Moreover, film education does not suffice. We need media education. And to spread media education, we need a new form of action. It will be great if our film societies can do that work. If they cannot, a new type of societies will have to be created. I firmly believe, though, that our film societies can do the job of spreading media education, for a renewed film education.

In addition to film seminars and film festivals, therefore, we shall have to organize other types of seminars or workshops where advertising, media sports, serials, telefilms, music television will be discussed. We shall have to also consider the communication rights of the citizens as they are formulated, for instance, in the 'People's Communication Charter'.[10] We shall have to also consider the role of community radio. We shall have to discuss the Internet. Not only discuss the Internet, we shall have to use the Internet in our work. All this, in order to discuss films in more depth.

One more thing will have to be done. Film societies will have to come out in support of particular films, relevant to contemporary society. For, the responsibility of film societies and of film critics is to help both the film's maker and the film's viewer.

Unfortunately, there are still many who think that the duty of the film critic is to find faults in a film. On this subject, an Indian theatre expert has written that the production of a play involves so many technical details that, 'no play can be devoid of any merit or totally free from faults. Hence, faults in the production of a play should not be made much of'.[11] The name of the author: Bharat Muni. His book, *Natya Shastra,* was written over 2,000 years ago. Can we not receive that two thousand-year-old advice?

History shows that film societies were at their best when they supported particular films. That is, films that were relevant to contemporary society. But what is a relevant film? Any film that helps me to understand my society is relevant to me. Any film that develops my sympathy and even love for people is a relevant film. Film societies were attractive when they supported films relevant to the viewers. In other words, film societies in India and abroad were vibrant when they were militant and defended a cause.

CONCLUSION

At the beginning of this presentation, I asked, 'What is wrong with Indian Film Societies?' What is wrong is that they don't open their eyes and ears. If they only open their eyes and ears, they will receive inspiration from Indian life, and with that inspiration they will begin to do new things. And, while singing *purano sei diner katha,* India will take a special place, at least in the field of film and media education, in the international community. *Bharat abar jagata sabhay shrestha asan pabe.*'[12]

NOTES

1. Ajoy Kumar Dey, 'Film Society Scene in West Bengal', in West Bengal Film Centre, 1985, pp. 30-2.
2. From a song by Tagore, 'Remembrances of Days Past'.
3. It can now be seen that the title of my essay is a homage to the late Satyajit Ray and to all those who, following his inspiration, worked for the spread of film culture in India.
4. Satyajit Ray, *Our Films, Their Films,* Orient Longman Limited, 1976. pp. 19-24.
5. Ibid., p. 24.
6. 'While it is true that inadequate technical resources, erratic financing, slackness in writing and direction and acting, have all contributed to the general poor quality of films that surround us, I have no doubt that equal harm has been done by critics — which in films, means anybody with access to print — who keep peddling muddled notions about the art form.' Ibid pp. 12-13.
7. Ajoy Dey, 'Film Society Scene in West Bengal', p. 31.
8. Ibid., *Our Films* ..., p. 19.
9. For instance, British artist and filmmaker, Peter Greenaway, July 2002.
10. See http://www.pccharter.net/
11. *Natya Shastra*, 28: 47, Ghosh's edition, pp. 522-3. The *Natya Shastra* is emphatic on the role of the critic and the public, respectively. 'Playwrights and producers should take the people as their (ultimate) authority (as regards the rule of the art)', xxiv: 126. See also 120-1, and xxvii: 39.
12. From a song by Tagore: 'India will again occupy an important place in the assembly of nations.'

CHAPTER 23

The Film Societies and the New Media*

INTRODUCTION

I CONSIDER IT a great honour to deliver the 2005 Ajoy Dey Memorial Lecture. I am honoured. I am also very happy. For at least four reasons. First, I am happy because I had the privilege of knowing Ajoy Babu. I appreciated his commitment to the cause of the film societies in India. And, over the years, we became good friends. Second, I am happy because to work for the film societies movement is to continue the work that the late Satyajit Ray had started with his colleagues in the late 1940s. It is perhaps not sufficiently known that while Ray was concerned with creating films, he was also concerned with educating film viewers. He educated the viewers by his very films, and by his support to the film societies and to any film education programme. Third, I am happy because I am a film society enthusiast, and cinema is dear to me. Fourth, I am happy, because I believe the film societies are at a crossroads. And they have a bright future. This modest presentation may perhaps suggest an orientation that can help the film societies to proceed, and to discover the marvellous task ahead of them.

THE FILM EXPERIENCE AS A DISCOVERY OF THE WORLD

I said that I am a film society enthusiast, and cinema is dear to me. I would like to develop that statement. I have been a film society man for over 50 years. And I am still a film society

*3 August 2005. This chapter draws largely from my book *Cyberbani: Being a Human in the New Media Environment*, 2005, pp. 193-208.

man. Before joining a film society for the first time, I had seen countless movies as a schoolboy. We were shown serials — mostly 'B Westerns', cowboy films. We loved them. I still remember vividly a scene where a good cowboy is riding on his horse in a prairie. Next to him, riding on her horse, is his beloved. As they pass next to a steep cliff, from on top of the cliff, Red Indians throw a lasso, and catch the girl. They begin to pull her up. By the time the cowboy realizes what has happened, he has gone some meters away. So, he turns back and rushes towards the cliff. He pulls his pistol and with one shot hits the rope and cuts it. Quite a feat! But that is not all. As the bullet cuts the rope, the girl falls down, in the arms of the riding cowboy who rushes away with her, to the amazement of the Red Indians and the delight of the audience. We, kids, knew that what had happened was impossible, but we enjoyed it all the same. It could have happened. In other words, we experienced what Aristotle had long ago defined as the 'plausible', that is, something practically impossible that could yet happen. The plausible titillates the imagination.

At the first film show I attended as a new member of a film society, I was quite surprised when our leader stepped on the stage to introduce the film. I had no idea that a film could be introduced. Still I listened. And my first film as a film society member was *The Battleship Potemkin.* The film had a tremendous impact on me. I discovered that film could be used with a purpose. Not just to entertain. Each film I saw afterwards, whether on my own in a cinema hall or at a show of the film society, was a new discovery. Discovery of an aspect of the world and, at the same time, discovery of the film medium. The filmmakers who impressed me most at the time were Luis Bunuel and, even more, Robert Bresson. I progressively discovered that any film I watched was not on celluloid, not on the white screen. The film was myself — not the whole of me, to be sure, but myself nonetheless — that is, myself in a certain emotional state, in a certain state of awareness. That is why, films remain parts of ourselves: they are our own mediated experience of the world. For, the films we talk about are the films we have lived. We have no other access to films than our experience of them.

The importance of film in my life culminated when I was twenty-six and, in one sitting, I saw for the first time *Pather Panchali, Aparajito, Apur Sansar,* the entire *Apu* trilogy. What a discovery! Durga, Apu, Sarbajaya, Harihar and Pishima, the unforgettable Indir Thakrun. Ray introduced Bengal to me. He led me into the world of Apu. And with what love! I finally arrived in Kolkata. I felt at home. I already knew the Durgas, Apus, Sarbajayas, Harihars and Pishimas of Bengal. Similarly, suppose you decide to go to live in Italy, and just before leaving, you see *Bicycle Thieves,* would you not be filled with love and respect for the Italian Brunos and their sons?

In order to work for film education, I took a master's degree in Theatre Art (Film). In 1970, I eventually founded the Chitrabani centre, with Satyajit Ray as co-founder. Ray remained the adviser of Chitrabani until the end of his life.

Then, in 1974, I wrote *Chitra Bani: A Book on Film Appreciation,* with foreword and cover design by Satyajit Ray, with essays by Kironmoy Raha, Kabita Sarkar, and Ramesh Sharma — of *New Delhi Times* fame. For me the objective was to understand society — and play a meaningful role in it.

Today, after over 30 years, I still hold that the 'royal road to understanding society is the study of the communication media'. But is film still the royal road to understanding today's new electronic media? And here is, I believe, the crossroads where the film societies are standing, ready to move ahead. For, film can yet be the royal road to understanding the new media and society itself.

FILM AND THE NEW MEDIA

A moment ago, I insisted on the place of film in our lives, that is, up to some years ago. My insistence on the place of film in our lives was to prepare the ground for a reflection on the place of the new media in our lives today. Sure, film is there — for instance not a few of my students see at least one film a day! Few film society members could claim the same. But then, how do my students see those films on STAR Movies or the HBO channel? Some of them acknowledge that they spend close to 8 or 10 hours a day using the media. How do they relate to the media? My answer: they are like a fish in water — totally unaware of the water, as long as it is in it. Similarly, we become aware of the media when, for some reason, we are deprived of them. Exercises in media awareness would be to occasionally cut ourselves off for a little while from one or another media, and see what happens. You will find that each of the media requires an increase in awareness. I mention only two cases.

Case One: the telephone. The cellular phone is popularly called mobile. But it is not the phone that has become mobile, through being moved around by its user. It is the mobile user that has become a telephone, a mobile telephone. Permanently hooked. When I don't feel annoyed at the disturbance of the mobile phone, I feel sorry for the user. What slavery! What lack of self-control! Yes, of course, a mobile phone is a marvellous instrument. But it is an example of what Ignacio Ramonet has called the 'tyranny of communication'.[1]

Case Two is more directly related to our subject, film. To understand the specificity of the film experience, we shall compare it to the experience offered by four media: a folk drawing, a photograph, a cinema scene and a cyber image. We shall do an exercise in what scholars call 'an existential phenomenology of image representation'.[2]

Suppose we want to represent a pond that exists in the world, say, a square pond surrounded by a row of trees. By representing it, we make it present anew in a mediated manner. First, let us take a folk drawing like those we have on a *kantha* or hand-made blanket, often covered with drawings. I take a folk drawing, because usually folk drawings do not use perspective. Thus, on a *kantha,* a square pond surrounded by trees would be represented as a square with trees perpendicular to the sides of the pond. But a photograph would show the same pond in perspective, that is, from the viewpoint of an individual onlooker. The horizontal sides of the pond would be parallel, but one horizontal side would be to the right or to the left in comparison with the other horizontal side, that is, not exactly above it. As for the vertical sides, they would of necessity, be oblique. The photograph does not represent the pond as it is, but as it appears to an onlooker at a certain point. Thus, the folk drawing invites you to look at the pond objectively, whereas the photograph invites you to be present to the pond from a subjective point of view. By representing the pond in their specific ways, the media of folk drawing and of photography invite you to be present to the pond in two different ways. In other words, the two media mediate your presence to an object in the world in two different ways. Most of us are unaware of the mediation of the media. Like a fish in the water.

Now, film. Should an incident occur in or next to the pond, various shots of the pond would represent it in perspective, thus in a subjective view — since film is moving photography. But the various shots or views of the pond would constitute a mesh of looks at the pond. Some of the looks would be the looks of the protagonists in the film. Some other views would be those of an imagined narrator. But some views would be no one's views, as it were. The film medium invites you, the onlooker, to make these views yours. As you do that, you become, what Nick Browne has called 'the spectator in the text.'[3] The experience of being in the text is well exemplified by the film *Incident at Owl Creek*. In that film, many shots show us what the hero, Farquar, sees, but not exactly from his point of view. The shots are the views of someone not seen but standing just next to Farquar. The spectator is invited to assume these views and, in so doing, to enter into the text not just as an observer, but as a participant.[4] Both the folk drawing and the photo keep you out of the representation, cinema can draw you into its particular representation.

When you come to the image on your TV screen or on your computer monitor, you find that the image has no depth. For instance, on your computer monitor you can open, say, eight windows, each one on top of the others. But if you close one window, you do not get deeper into the screen. The eight windows are virtually on the same surface at the same time. The cyber-image has no third dimension. Moreover, it is detached from the world, that is, it does not necessarily refer to a real object, actual or imagined, in the world. Indeed, it is the world, just there in front of you. Whereas the folk drawing, the photograph, and the film scene invited you in your body to be present to the world, a three-dimensional, material, world, the cyber-image needs neither your body nor the material world. It is just there, a world of its own, made of infinite links, with nobody to inhabit the network.

There is a strong tendency to personalize the cyber-image and to speak of interaction. But out there, in the cyber-world, there is no one who can feel or love. As Frederic Jameson has put it, in that world you don't have feelings, but intensities. A sort of spontaneous excitements. That's far different from the real world I discovered under the lead of Eisenstein, Bunuel, Bresson, and Ray. Do I want now to let go of my body, to get networked in the cyber-world? Do I want to get wired? (The mobile phoneman or woman is wired. You can be wired to your computer too. TV sets can be implanted into your eyeballs. Hooked, permanently.) Once you are wired, the cyber-machine computes your use of the telecommand and draws your profile: what you like, what you dislike. Next, it feeds you with what it 'thinks' is good for you. Fully wired, you can forget about the world, about the problems that plague the body, like hunger or AIDS. You're floating, as it were, on the surface of the net.

Now, what happens to the film *Charulata* when shown on a TV screen? Does it become a cyber-image? For most viewers of the film, Charu refers to Madhabi Mukherjee, although viewers know that the film is not the world, and Charu is not Madhabi. But there is an unbreakable link. On TV, does the film *Charulata* retain its moorings in the real world? Or is it that film, as a whole, becomes slowly (rather quickly!) absorbed in the cyber-world? Are not films made more and more to suit the requirements of the small screen of TV? There is nothing wrong in a movie image becoming a cyber-image. But, then, what happens to the film medium?

Whatever the usefulness of photography, it did not replace or supplant drawing and painting. Similarly, cinema did not wipe out photography. The question facing us is, 'will the cyber-image repress film?' The best way to ensure that the new electronic media does not wipe out film is for film users to grow more and more aware of the new media and its characteristics. For that to happen a new type of media education is required. This is the object of the next part of this chapter. But I would like to raise a question already at this point: while taking into account the new expectations created in the mind of the spectator with regard to visual style through exposure to the intense visuality (or visualness) of television,[5] could not the film societies help the spectator appreciate the modes of representation of drawing, painting, photography, and conventional cinema?

FROM *CHITRA BANI* TO *CYBERBANI*: FOR A NEW MEDIA EDUCATION

As I mentioned, thirty years ago, I wrote *Chitra Bani*.[6] That was a contribution to *film, media, and social* education. Today, in 2005, I have just written *Cyberbani: Being a Human in the New Media Environment*.[7] Whereas *Chitra Bani* had a foreword and book design by Satyajit Ray and included essays by well-known film scholars, *Cyberbani's* illustrations and book cover were designed by a graduate student. The book also includes an essay by another graduate student. You see the shift. A new media education, like the media themselves, is participatory, and invites the addressees to have their say. A new education does not assume that the one being educated is a *tabula rasa.*

Not only has the film environment changed, but film also has changed in the last few decades with the advent of the new media. I mention six areas:

- Film used to be shown to large groups of viewers on a large screen. Now, films are mostly shown on a small screen to individuals or small groups. We need to ask ourselves what might be the effect of the small screen on the film experience.

- Film has absorbed elements of TV aesthetics (e.g., Ravi Ojha's *Abar Ashbo Phire.* There you have shots of two protagonists speaking together, yet not looking at each other, but looking towards the camera. One can understand that in representing the actors the way television does, and not with the conventional over the shoulder shots, one saves a lot of time and effort. But more importantly, one makes it possible for the TV viewers always to properly see the faces of the protagonists. But one wonders why should such shots appear on the large screen of cinemascope. The viewers are so used to these TV shots that they do not find it odd if not ludicrous that two protagonists should talk together without looking at each other, except once in a while.
- Films often deal with global themes (e.g., *Kuch Kuch Hota Hai*).
- Films are produced with new technologies, in particular the small hand-held camera. That fact had made Samira Makhmalbaf exult: 'Now,' she claimed, 'the artist regains the centrality of the filmmaking process.'[8] Yet, a question arises: should a director hold in one hand the entire filmmaking process? Is not filmmaking so complex as to demand the collaboration of at least a few creative artists?

  On the other hand, we hear the startling story of Jonathan Caouette who, without ever going to a film school, shot an enormous amount of video footage. Then, with the help of a friend, he discovered iMovie, and he remixed his footage. 'The result was a film that was the hit of Sundance and Cannes in 2004: *Tarnation.*'[9]
- Films are distributed and consumed in new ways (e.g., the DVD, the cellular phone, the multiplex).
- The film image appears amidst a flow of images that have different characteristics — in particular they are not linked to literature, theatre, painting and, in general, to narrative

tentative, open to questions and corrections, more participatory. I would welcome the change.

CONCLUSION

As for the rest, like, the need for new structures in our film societies, the need for greater use of the Internet, more networking, more social programmes, new forms of membership, I am fully confident that these aspects will be taken care of in due time. The film societies are at a crossroads, ready to move towards a bright future.

In support of my optimism, I would like to mention the initiative taken by two young filmmakers cum scholars, Indranil Chakravarty and Chandita Mukherjee. They are creating a postgraduate programme in New Media, based in Mumbai. To discuss that programme, they have launched a series of discussions on a new media pedagogy, titled COSMOS New Media initiative, to explore the impact of technologies of communication on culture, and relocate creativity in the arts in the changing cultural paradigm. During a session of COSMOS, held in June 2005, Indranil Chakravarty said:

> We are trying to create a kind of atmosphere where we can get students to think. We are really very worried whether we will get those kinds of students who want to learn or share the kind of ideas that we have.
>
> We need our own kind of library, to set up an audio-visual archive..., obviously an equipment store and shooting studio. We can think of new ways of defining space, a classroom that can alternate as a shooting studio. We have to redefine the Internet café to see how it works as a learning space . . ., etc. The bottom line is that students should enjoy what they are doing. And we want to have fun while teaching also.[12]

It is heartening to know that the film societies will not be alone in their effort to spread a new type of media education.

NOTES

1. Ignacio Ramonet, *La Tyrannie de la Communication,* Paris, 1999, Éditions Galilée.

2. Vivian Sobchack, 'The Scene of the Screen: Envisioning Cinematic and Electronic Presence', in John Thornton Caldwell, ed., *Electronic Media and Technoculture*, Rutgers University Press, 2000, VIII, pp. 137-55.
3. Nick Browne, 'The Spectator in the Text', *Film Quarterly*, Winter 1975/76, pp. 26-38.
4. That film is discussed at length in Gaston Roberge, *The Ways of Film Studies: Film Theory and the Interpretation of Films*, Ajanta Publications, Delhi, 1992, pp. 169-75.
5. John Thornton Caldwell, *Televisuality, Style, Crisis, and Authority in American Television*, Rutgers University Press, New Brunswick, New Jersey, 1995, xiv.
6. *Chitra* means image and *bani* means word. It is a close equivalent to 'sight and sound'. My book on film appreciation was called *Chitra Bani,* in two words. But the media centre I was associated with was called *Chitrabani,* in one word.
7. *Cyberbani* alone will not suffice. Fortunately, new books are being published as I write these lines. For instance, Rajiv Mehrotra, ed., *The Open Frame Reader: Unreeling the Documentary Film*, Public Service Broadcasting Trust (India), Rupa & Co in association with PSBT, 2006, 162. In that book, see Subha Das Mollick, 'The Third Revolution', pp. 87-97.
8. Samira Makhmalbaf, born in 1980, was the youngest ever filmmaker to have her feature film shown in the competition section at the Cannes film festival. That occurred twice, in 1998 and 2000. In 2000, at 20, she delivered the keynote address at a seminar organized at Cannes on the future of cinema. It was during that address that she praised the new technology.
9. Lawrence Lessig, 'The People Own Ideas!' in *The Technology Review*, June 2005. Jonathan Caouette's *Tarnation,* a documentary on growing up with a schizophrenic mother, a mixture of snapshots, Super8, answering machine messages, video diaries, early short films culled from 19 years of life. (*Yahoo! Movies.*)
10. *Span*, July/August 2005, p. 29.
11. Ibid., p. 33.
12. *The Transcript*: New Media Pedagogy: the Offline Meet., Rachna Sansad, Mumbai, 17 June 2005. http://groups.google.co.in/group/e-XploreCOSMOS

APPENDIX

Elements for a Film and Media Educational Programme

We have to cultivate various skills and attitudes. I mention seven.

i. Hope and Joy

> Without a minimum of hope, we cannot so much as start the struggle.
>
> Paulo Freire[1]

At times, one may feel, quite rightly, that one cannot *do everything* that must be done. Yet, one must be prepared to *do everything* that one can do. For, what one can do cannot be done by someone else. And, hence, if I do not do what I can do, something will be missing in the revolutionary movement. A drop of water in the ocean? Maybe, but as philosopher and mystic Blaise Pascal said, more or less in these terms, 'The ocean is changed for one drop of water added to it or removed from it.'

Similarly, Vaclav Havel once wrote in *An Open Letter to Dr. Gustav Husak*, that the liquidation of one little cultural magazine 'can cause the social organism much greater damage than would appear at first sight'. He compared the magazine to a vitamin, essential for the health of the organism. So also, each one's contribution is essential, even if it appears insignificant. Hope rests on that certainty.

ii. Network spirit

Networking must become a habit. For, the fact of joining a network, that is, a group of interrelated persons, strengthens us by the awareness of not being alone. It inspires by the dedication we see in the network. And the original initiatives we witness there trigger our creativity. Moreover, a network invites an equalitarian, participatory, and free approach. That is not automatic, of course, but networks constitute milieus in which these attitudes are valued, rewarded, and called for.

iii. Self-discipline

First, once in a while, one has to pause, to stop, and to disconnect oneself from the media. It is suggested that once a week, perhaps, one does not use a particular medium, the newspaper, for instance. One should also use one's cellular phone with discretion, that is, with what some people now call *netiquette* (Inter N(et)+ETIQUETTE). And there are other aspects too: for instance, one should not indulge one's cravings through television or computer. As we discover painfully, the new media offer occasions for all types of addiction.

One should occasionally examine one's daily routine, and see if the time devoted to the media is fruitful. One should examine whether one expends the effort required to benefit from the facilities offered by the new technologies by way of information, communication, or word processing. In all these exercises, the aim is the same: remain in control of oneself.

iv. New intellectual skills

The very use of electronic technology — of the computer, for instance — invites us to develop new skills. This does not mean that the computer is our master.

> Social interaction is far more complex than anything a computer programme can deal with. This is true in the general case: computer programmes cannot react to emotional realities or cope with the irrational, cannot be tactful or fall in love. However, there is an important subset of interaction that very closely corresponds to what we use computers for: the coordination of production processes, which includes all practical communication. (. . . In particular,) computers have better attention to detail than we do.[2]

v. New understanding of the cultural milieu

Since the cultural milieu changes constantly, one needs to keep probing one's environment the better to understand it. Besides, not only does one's milieu change, but one changes too. Networking, in particular, can be a great help to keep in touch locally and globally.

vi. Conscious, creative involvement in one's daily routine

> Every one is a space designer and we all use our spaces and interfaces differently. We place posters on walls, paint them light blue or orange, position furniture in rooms, make love in kitchens, use 'bedrooms' as 'offices', sing opera in the shower, spray particular fragrances in our bathrooms and use staircases for arguments, games and romances. (...) Yet, most people do not think of themselves as being able to 'design'.[3]

The same can be said of communication in general. We leave it to professionals, failing to notice that we communicate the whole day, day after day. One area that is most neglected is that of conversations. Yet, again, conversations give us the opportunity to constantly 'programme' ourselves according to our interlocutors. Here we have—or can have—real interactivity.

That is, if we allow 'the other' to reach us. In other words, if we really 'receive' his/her message. If you observe around you, you will be surprised to see how few people 'receive' the other's interventions. Most use them to trigger their own repartees. It is as if the other placed stones in shallow water for us to walk on — stepping stones, indeed —, oblivious of what the stones were or even what they looked like.[4]

vii. Spirit of freedom in front of the media and in the midst of consumerism

In addition to self-discipline, as mentioned in 'iii' above, there is need to frequently posit — in some instances, regularly — small actions which I call 'personal sacraments', that is, for the one who posits them, actions that effect that which they mean. If, for instance, I occasionally abstain from a particular soft drink, I affirm and enact my freedom with regard to it. And my abstention is in no way a hostile act. It permits me to experience my freedom in peace and joy.

One might wonder: all that has little to do with film. My answer: film is part of the new media. If the above education is required for the new media, it is required for film also. For instance, if one watches one film everyday, what about the need for self-discipline? If one spends two hours on the phone daily, what about cultivating conversational skills?

And what about Satyajit Ray? There was not a word about him in this entire presentation. True. But his inspiration is there. And am I stretching the point if I quote again here what he told me and also wrote, when I informed him about a film course that had just taken place (Chapter 3, concluding words):

> I find it most heartening that such an event (the film course) has taken place. I have been hoping for a long time that something concrete should be done about the dissemination of film culture among the young people in our country. This course is surely a step in that direction. I hope that the enterprise will continue (29 April 1990).

Yes, the enterprise continues. And I find it most heartening that it does.

NOTES

1. *Pedagogy of Hope: Reliving Pedagogy of the Oppressed*, New York, Continuum, 1996, pp. 8-9.
2. H. Abelson and G. Sussman (in *The Structure and Interpretation of Computer Programs*) quoted by Benjamin Geer, in his *The Engineering Approach to Social Processes.* http://www.open-organizations.org/view/Main/Engineering Approach?skin=print
15. Usman Haque, 'Hardspace, Softspace and the Possibilities of Open Source Architecture' (2000) in NicePaper no. 2, 2004, pp. 4-5.
16. Gaston Roberge, *Communication Cinema Development: From Morosity to Hope*, New Delhi, Manohar, 1998. See 'Monologue on Dialogue —The Fine Art of Conversation', pp. 86-9.

Conclusion

CHAPTER 24

A Journey to the Cave of the Heart: 'Amar Pather Panchali' (*My Song of the Road*)*

ON THE OCCASION of the anniversary celebrations of Satyajit Ray's *Pather Panchali* and of Bibhutibhushan Bandyopadhyay's book of the same name, I would like to tell the story of the long lasting effect on me of *Pather Panchali*. In doing so, I will speak about myself to some extent. But then, does not anyone speaking about somebody else's work say a lot about him/herself, even though not always explicitly? I dare hope that what I shall say will be a tribute to both Satyajit Ray and Bibhutibhushan Bandopadhyay for what they were and for what they have given us in *Pather Panchali*, the film and the book, respectively.

INTIMATION OF THE JOURNEY

The first intimation of an eventual journey to India and ultimately to the 'cave of the heart' occurred when I was about five years old. The incident also prompted the mood of my own *Song of the Road*. At that time, my maternal uncle served in the Canadian army as a radar expert. He was — interestingly, given my own occupation — a communication expert. He was posted in Sri Lanka, then part of India. When he came back home to Canada, I spent some time with his family. Uncle

*Published in *Ray at Work: Images by Nemai Ghosh*, Dept. of Mass Comm. & Videography, St. Xavier's College, Kolkata, 2005, pp. 37-51.

used to talk to us about the Indians he had known. He did not speak of India, but of Indians. He spoke with such love that I must have been filled with it. I used to wonder who these extraordinary people might be. Uncle showed us photographs, not of landscapes, but of faces — a face being the landscape of the heart. In his emotionally-laden baggage, he had also brought back from India the skins of a tiger and of a boa. These added to the mysterious character of the 'Indians'. Surprisingly, at a conscious level, I soon completely forgot that loving introduction to India. I remembered Uncle's talk over twenty years later, when I had already come to India, and I was trying to answer the question often put to me: how is it that you came to India? Only now do I know the answer: 'I loved the Indian people.'

I eventually came to India for the first time in 1961. I was 26. About two years before that, I had become interested in Mahatma Gandhi and in Rabindranath Tagore. Especially, the latter. At that time I had no intention, not even a thought, of going to India. I learnt yoga from Swami Vishnudevananda, a (Keralite) monk of the Sivananda Ashram in Rishikesh who had settled in Canada. I also read Mircea Eliade's book on yoga. It revealed to me fascinating aspects of Indian philosophy and spirituality. I had already started to write — in French, my mother tongue — and I wrote an article entitled, 'Dialogue with Tagore' (1959). In that article, I imagined a dialogue between Tagore, on a visit to London, with a local student. In the course of the dialogue, I have Tagore say that people in the West derive joy from controlling life, whereas people in India derive joy from living. I already felt that Westerners had little time to live and to enjoy life at a deep level.

From then on, there grew in me an urge to come over to India, to dialogue with her people, and learn from them whatever I might discover that I did not know, especially about God. In return, of course, I was keen to share whatever my own tradition had given me. But my 'road' was one of discovery, not of colonization, religious or political. I had joined the Society of Jesus at 21. I already had, therefore, five years of religious life when I volunteered to come to India, and my superiors decided I should join the Jesuits of Kolkata.

THE JOURNEY BEGINS IN EARNEST

My *Song of the Road* had been mostly in the mood of love. An extraordinary event would add a new emotion to it, that of wonder. Here is what happened. In September 1961, I left for India. I proceeded from Montreal to New York. I spent one night there before boarding a boat *en route* to India. While glancing at the newspaper I found that an Indian film, in fact a trilogy, was being shown in an art theatre on Fifth Avenue, near Times Square. I had heard about the trilogy, for, it had been screened at the 1961 Montreal Film Festival. But I could not attend the film show. In view of my imminent departure for India, I had asked my superior permission to go and see the film. But my superior felt I would have every opportunity to see it in India. Instead of allowing me to go to see the film, he sent two other young Fathers to see it. So, in New York, when I found that the trilogy was being shown, I went to the cinema. And there opened in front of me *Pather Panchali, The Song of the Road*, Satyajit Ray's masterpiece, my doorway to India. I saw the entire *Apu* Trilogy in one sitting. It had a tremendous impact on me.

I was somewhat prepared to appreciate Ray's three films because I had been a member of a film society ever since I was 16. My first film, as a cineclub member, had been *The Battleship Potemkin.* The film had greatly disturbed me. Perhaps the very idea of a revolution was itself disturbing. For, I was brought up in a different cultural atmosphere. It took me years to understand that, according to Eisenstein's avowed intention, the film had ploughed deeply in my psyche in a particular class orientation.

Pather Panchali had as deep an impact on me. But the impact was not disturbing: it was fulfilling. Durga and Apu shared with me their sense of wonder at the world. Under Ray's masterly touch I was made to see the way a young Indian sees. Similarly, I was made to deeply appreciate the relationships binding people to each other. Above all, it was the humaneness of the characters that literally enchanted me. The great Nargis, who opined that *Pather Panchali* should not be shown abroad because it would give a wrong impression of India to foreigners, was greatly off the mark as far as I was concerned.

The black and white print of the films was sparkling in a way I had rarely seen before, even as a member of a cineclub. The very quality of the image itself cast a spell on me. Of course, I did not know cinematographer Subrata Mitra at the time. I was to know him later.[1]

There were mostly Indians in the small hall. I was fascinated by the elegance of the sari-clad women. But I was amazed. I felt I had never seen a garment so impractical and yet so well designed to enhance the human body. But then, I thought, is clothing primarily for use or for enhancement of the human person? Is the body, and the person, just functional? The environment of the film show was itself a cultural initiation for me.

The impact of *Pather Panchali* on me continued during the screening of the two other films. But the entire trilogy was too much for me to fully absorb it in one screening. Nonetheless, *Aparajito* and *Apur Sansar* brought the hero further ahead on the road. Until he was Apu. No more the charming, immature boy (*abodh*, in Bibhutibhushan's word), but the mature man, well prepared for the long stretch of road yet ahead of him.

THE JOURNEY: ARRIVING IN THE WORLD OF APU — BENGAL

While, on the one hand, I felt comfortable in the screen world of Apu, and while I was in harmony with its moods of love and wonder, during the few weeks of the journey to India, I was asking myself: 'Who am I?' If there was in me any of the arrogance of some newcomers in India with their keen desire to help the 'poor', I think it was largely tuned down. My admiration for Apu and his world was unbounded, and I was wondering how I might relate with the real world of Apu from which the film was created. Yet, when I met the Apus, Durgas,

Sarbajayas, Harihars, Pishimas of real Bengal, I just passed effortlessly from the screen world to the real world. I discovered that part of that world was tolerance and openness. My uncle had filled my mind with love for the Indians. Satyajit Ray instilled in me a love of, a confidence in, an admiration for the people of Bengal.

During the months after I saw *Pather Panchali,* as I mused over Ray's *The Song of the Road,* keeping its 'tune', so to say, in my mind, some points struck me. For instance, Apu learns to grow self-sufficient. He loses his sister, his auntie, his mother, and his wife — all females. In time, of course, he also loses his father. I slowly discovered that although the Bengali society is patriarchal, the place of the woman is central. That is reflected in the Trilogy. For all his qualities, Harihar is somewhat inefficient as head of the family. The strong character is Sarbajaya, the mother. And that predominant role of the woman is seen again and again in Ray's other films. For instance, in *Charulata.* But this characteristic is not peculiar to Ray. The same predominance of women can be seen in Hindi films as well. For instance, *Mother India.* In that film, not only is the husband inefficient, but he is literally dispensed with — he disappears from the film, not without first having had his two arms cut-off, a symbol of castration. So much for the patriarchal figure![2]

Ray himself lost his father when he was hardly three years old. He did not consciously experience losing his father, he experienced not having one. Perhaps the deaths of the women in *Pather Panchali* were particularly significant to him. But this consideration brings in the biographical aspect of the Ray films, a subject I will touch upon further on in this chapter.

What I liked so much in *Pather Panchali,* what I found
vas the sheer joy of being, of living, of pulsating in
the world, for instance, when Durga just enjoys
ng on her, even though with devastating effects.
enjoyed seeing people in communion with one
the wonder experienced in front of the world,
nd Durga are eating homemade — clandestinely

— pickles, or listening to the sound emitted by telephone lines, or watching a train passing by.

There is a similar scene of a man in awe at the passage of a train in a prairie in the film *Mother and Son* of Alexander Sokurow, 1997. Homage to Ray? I was not able to find out. The train has a different significance in the two films. Yet, in both the films, the train is present visually and aurally, that is, not only its own sound, but the sound it emits, like a call, is heard. In both the films, the hero 'hears' the 'call' of the train before he sees the train. I shall again discuss the creative use of sound in Ray's film. For now, I would like to emphasize that the train in *Pather Panchali* is a rich symbol of life's journey. The train comes from outside one's little territory, and it goes beyond. Apu, indeed, will soon feel an irresistible urge to journey beyond the confine of his little world. Thus, the world of Apu will be opening up and expanding. We shall see in what direction. But the train is also a symbol of modernity: it is propelled by technological power. At this stage of his life, Apu is fascinated by modern technology —telephone and train. Later on in his journey, he will learn to sing another tune about modernity.

JOURNEYING ALONG WITH MANIKDA

It is only in 1970 that I dared to meet Satyajit Ray. My first visit to him was like a second departure on my journey. My *Song of the Road* was enriched by new melodies in many a new mood. Indeed, I found, the world of Apu was the world of Satyajit Ray. And in Ray, Apu kept going on *the road*. Or was it Ray who kept going on in and through the character of Apu?

And then came the *agantuk*. I saw clearly where Apu — and myself with him — was heading, namely, the cave of the heart. While most people, especially the moderns, see the
of life as a thrust forward, towards the future, in A
world, the fulfilment is in depth. In the heart. Pr
Apu became Manomohan Mitra — the enchanti
of *Agantuk*. The same 'wanderlust', the same irresis
to travel; but not travel aimlessly, travel inward.

the forty years that separate Apu and Mitra, one can see that the look of Apu has become more mature and more critical. For all his fascination for modernity, Apu Mitra (if I may call him that way) sees its blatant flaws. These are clearly spelt out in *Aguntuk*: (1) civilization has degenerated to the point when at the touch of a button one can destroy an entire city, and remain undisturbed; (2) modernity deals with human persons as if they were individuals as defined by a 'passport'; (3) the sap of culture and civilization is to be found neither in the West nor in the East (after World War I, Tagore hoped it might be in the East) but in the cave of the human heart.

Apu's journey begins in *Pather Panchali,* it ends in *Agantuk.* That is again symbolized, discreetly, by the train. In *Pather Panchali* the train leaves Nischindipur, it is heard passing by in *Gana Shatru* [3] and in *Sakha Prosakha*. In *Agantuk,* Apu Mitra is seen in the train, and the train itself is finally seen arriving in Kolkata. But that is not the final destination of Apu's train. For, Manomohan goes by train from Kolkata to Shantiniketan. The final destination of the train is Shantiniketan. The full significance of *Pather Panchali* is evident only in *Agantuk.*

In *Pather Panchali,* after Durga's death, Apu discovers the necklace that Durga had been accused of having stolen. He thus has the proof of her theft. He accepts Durga's human weakness and he forgives her in a magnanimous gesture. He simply throws the stolen necklace into the nearby pond, the silent memory of the family life. In *Agantuk,* Apu Mitra discovers the full humaneness of his niece, and he acknowledges her as his niece when he sees her joining a group of Santalis in a dance. The 'song of the road' is in harmony with tribal music, a collective expression of shared human life. The Bengali *jalsaghar* reverberates at once harmoniously to a tribal song or to a classical *khayal.* Here you have the bond that binds life together. Had not Ray said: 'I find myself trying, through my films, to trace the underlying pattern that binds this life together.'[4]

There is yet another aspect to Apu's early experience, his wonder at the mystery of life. In *Agantuk,* Apu Mitra takes time off to initiate his grand nephew and his young friends to the mystery of the heavenly bodies. Thus, what was first a sense of wonder in Apu becomes in Mitra a perception of the whole. A more explicitly philosophical perception of the world.

SATYAJIT RAY AND THE CRITICS

I have also mentioned that the superb quality of the film as I first saw it was part of its charm on me. There are other technical aspects of the film that would deserve to be mentioned here — photography, editing, acting, music. Of course, these technical qualities are a surprise in a cineaste's first film, but the depth of the film's significance is no less of a surprise. When *Pather Panchali* was first shown in Cannes, Ray was unknown, and the film did not attract many viewers. But film personality André Bazin alerted his colleagues and eventually the film was given a special award for its humane quality. I do not say that I do not take the technical achievement of the film seriously. To an extent the technical quality is taken for granted. And what matters in a film like *Pather Panchali* is its significance. And significance unfolds in a social context. Less than ten years after India achieved her independence, here was a film that affirmed the beauty of the life of Bengali peasants, without arrogance, but with self-confidence.

Unfortunately, while Ray's first trilogy was gradually well-received at home, the same cannot be said of his last three films,[5] films I like to call 'the Heart Trilogy', not only because they obviously allude to Ray's heart ailment, but they lead us to the 'heart of the matter'[6] to, indeed, the 'cave of the heart'.

Even then, local critics did not show much interest in what Ray was saying.[7] They trivialized his message and misled the public. Yet, by the time he produced the Heart Trilogy, Ray had established himself as the continuator of Tagore, starting off where the Kabi Guru had stopped and moving ahead. If Apu displayed a way of life in *Pather Panchali*, in *Agantuk,* Apu Mitra delivered a cine-speech on civilization, a speech reminiscent of Tagore's 'Crisis in Civilization'. Several critics have noted the almost harsh tone of Ray's criticism of 'civilization', but they seem to have failed to perceive that in the Heart Trilogy, in spite of everything that might hinder Apu Mitra's life fulfilment, Apu — and in him Ray — does not lose faith in man. In that, Ray was truly the continuator of Tagore.[8]

See, in *Sakha Prosakha*, the bond between the ailing father and his mentally disturbed son. Experience the peace that is his. Similar things can be said of the end of *Gana Shatru* and of *Agantuk*. The more acute Ray's perception of corruption is, the greater his faith in the resources of man, if only man reconnects with the human heart. The statement of Anila in *Agantuk* is significant in this respect: she will address the 'agantuk' with the title 'uncle' if the impulse to do so comes from her heart.

SATYAJIT RAY AND THE INDIAN TRADITION OF PERFORMING ARTS

I have discussed (in Chapter 4) the pace of cutting, often found slow, especially in the *Apu* trilogy. There were even people who said that if Ray were to re-cut the film twenty years after it was released, he would cut it faster. I am not sure of that. First of all, the pace of the film matches the pace of life in Apu's rural village. It would be possible to cut the series of close-ups faster, and you would still have the same meaning. But only superficially. The overall meaning would be different. You would have another film. For in art, if you change the form, you change the work itself. In my way of seeing it, the film is made, consciously or not — that is not the point here — on the principle of enjoyment of an emotion. You need time for that.

When I saw it for the first time — and every time afterwards — I did not find the film slow, precisely because I enjoyed what I saw. And here is the crux of the matter — the 'heart' of the matter? Those who find the film slow, obviously, find enjoyment not in the mood of the film so much as in its unfolding story. And thus these viewers have in mind an Aristotelian principle where the structure of a dramatic performance is the foremost element. In that case, every frame of a film must contribute to that structure. But if you approach the film with a desire to enjoy its mood or *rasa*, then as long as the mood is sustained, you enjoy the film, the longer the better, the more enjoyable. And the pitfall of film criticism in India is that often films are assessed according to Aristotelian rules, disregarding Bharat Muni's *Natya Shastra*. On the other hand, the Indian public generally enjoys films for their *rasa*, not for any catharsis of emotion the films might offer by a rigid dramatic structure and precise character delineation. And here you have it: some enjoy controlling life, the others enjoy living.

SATYAJIT RAY AND HIS FILMS: AN AUTOBIOGRAPHY?

I come to another question I raised earlier in this chapter: how much of the *Apu* trilogy reflects Satyajit Ray's life experience? Any artwork reflects it's maker's life experience. But the artwork can never be taken to be an exact reflection of its maker. For, there is a chasm between the two. For instance, if a novel starts in the first person, 'That morning, when I went out, . . .' we may not assume that the 'I' is that of the writer. Otherwise, it would be impossible to write freely. Moreover, the imagination would have no space for creative activity. Nonetheless, there may be elements in a novel or in a film that are reflections of events that happened to the author. For instance, in *Aparajito*, Sarbajaya gives a slap to Apu. Critics have remarked that no Bengali mother would hit her son thus. The answer of Ray was that his mother had once slapped him. We could not know this fact from the film itself. Only Ray or a witness of his life could tell us. Hence, it is not possible to see in a film a documentary on its maker.

Nonetheless, a particular artist inhabits a particular mental world. And the artist shares that world with others through his/her artwork. A study of Ray's films, for instance, reveals his mental world. In that sense, we speak of the cinema of Satyajit Ray. In that cinema we find attitudes, opinions, a sense of values that may or may not be Ray's. If they should happen to be, Ray would not be committed to them for the rest of his life. He is not bound by the mental world he has shared with the viewer of his films. He remains free. And, again, he remains greater than the mental world he shares with the viewers of his film. Only a biography of Ray could reveal the extent to which he is committed to the mental world depicted by his films.

On the other hand, the artwork is always more significant than what the artist has wanted to express. And the author has no authority to determine and limit the meaning of his/her film. The only thing he/she can affirm is what he/she means, not what the film means. But for artists, to say what they mean is redundant because they say what they mean in their very artworks. The artwork is their medium. Inevitably, because of its polysemy and of its semiosis, that is, the ongoing process by which meaning is established, involving an interaction among the signs of a an artwork, the artwork means more than what the author intended it to mean.

One has to clarify one's goal: to know Ray through a study of his works? Or to study Ray's films in the light of his life and milieu? No doubt, the two endeavours cannot be totally separated. It is a question of emphasis. In the present chapter, I am more concerned with the films than with their maker.

THE JOURNEY ENDS — THE CAVE OF THE HEART

The cave of the heart is where humans commune and are bound together. When, in *Sakha Prosakha*, Prabodh and family take leave of the ailing Ananda Majumdar, they do not really commune at the level of the heart. But Prashanta does. And that is symbolized by the joining of hands, a gesture displayed by Ray already in *Gana Shatru*. Here it is further emphasized by the fact that Ananda and Prashanta have joined hands tightly on Ananda's heart.

That gesture, I found out, was very significant to Satyajit Ray. One day, I had gone to visit him at the nursing home where he was under intensive care. First, I wished to have a word with his son, Sandip, to know if I could enter Mr. Ray's room. But I was told that Mr. Ray was sleeping holding Sandip's hand on his chest. Any movement of Sandip would awake Mr. Ray. So, that day I could not see him.

The joining of hands not yet achieved in the concluding scene of *Charulata*, is, in *Agantuk*, an embrace of each other by Prabir and Anila in full reconciliation. There ends the journey.

The return to the 'tribal' and more drastically to the bison of the Altamira Cave is not a nostalgic journey to the past. The impulse to draw from life — drawing, in the sense of receiving from life and of making drawings of life — is there, in one's own heart. The skill of the Altamira caveman, and the bond with the world experienced by the tribals, are also there in one's heart. In a word, the tribal, the caveman, are in me. Striving to find ever-new expressions in and through me. But for that to happen, I need to undergo that journey away from the biases of 'modernity' and *en route* towards an ever-fuller experience of life with the eyes of reason and the ears of the heart. That is, precisely, what we see happening in Apu's life journey, from Nischindipur to Shantiniketan. From boyhood to maturity, to ever-fuller life until is reached the cave of the heart.

And life is what Ray was after. He wrote:

> For a popular medium, the first kind of inspiration should derive from life and have its roots in it. . . . The Indian filmmaker must turn to life, to reality.[9]

NOTES

1. It was much later that I had the privilege of meeting Subrata Mitra personally. In 1975, he had accepted my request to be camera person-cum-teacher on a small team producing an educational film, *Vigyan ki Parhai,* for the Satellite Instructional Television Experiment (SITE). I could see by myself that Mitra was a thorough professional as well as an extraordinary teacher.
2. It is striking that although Nargis felt justified in objecting to Ray's film, where a deep material poverty is depicted, she seemed unaware of the spiritual poverty she herself depicted in *Mother India*. In that film, she is the mother who takes a gun and shoots her own son dead just because she stands by self-imposed moral rules.
3. Once, perhaps, in the entire film, when Dr. Gupta decides to go and hand in his article to the editor of the newspaper.

4. From the commentary written and spoken by Satyajit Ray for BD. Garga's two-reeler *Creative Artists of India: Satyajit Ray* (1963). Quoted in *Montage*, nos. 5/6, July 1966. See 'Why I Make Films.'
5. I have discussed the Heart Trilogy in my book *Communication Cinema Development,* From Morosity to Hope. New Delhi, Manohar Publishers & Distributors 1998, Chapters 34, 35, 36, pp. 174-91.
6. I was happy when I heard Dr. B.M. Deb in a lecture on Satyajit Ray, he delivered at the S.N. Bose National Centre for Basic Sciences, Kolkata, on 19 January 2005. He began with these words, 'Satyajit Ray went to the heart of the matter.'
7. Andrew Robinson, *Satyajit Ray: The Inner Eye: The Biography of a Master Filmmaker,* Oxford University Press, 2004, xii, see pp. 339-64.
8. In his documentary film, *Rabindranath Tagore,* Ray had quoted Tagore saying: 'I shall not commit the grievous sin of losing faith in man.'
9. Satyajit Ray, *Our Films, Their Films,* Orient Longman Ltd., 1976, p. 127.

References

The following references do not constitute a bibliography on Satyajit Ray. They are a list of the sources quoted in the essays in the present book.

Abelson, H., and Sussman, G. (in *The Structure and Interpretation of Computer Programmes*) quoted by Benjamin Geer, in his 'The Engineering Approach to Social Processes.' http://www.open-organizations.org/view/Main/Engineering Approach?skin=print

Bateson, Gregory, *Steps to an Ecology of Mind*, New York, Ballantine, 1972.

Brecht, Bertolt, *Écrits sur le cinéma,* éd. de l'Arche, 1970.

Browne, Nick, 'The Spectator in the Text', *Film Quarterly*, Winter 1975/1976, pp. 26-38.

Caldwell, John Thornton, ed., *Electronic Media and Technoculture*, Rutgers University Press, 2000, viii.

Caldwell, John Thornton, *Televisuality, Style, Crisis, and Authority in American Television*, Rutgers University Press, New Brunswick, New Jersey, 1995, xiv.

Chakravarty, Indranil, *The Transcript*, New Media Pedagogy: The Offline Meet., Rachna Sansad, Mumbai, 17 June 2005. http://groups.google.co.in/group/e-XploreCOSMOS

Corrigan, R.W., 'The Drama of Anton Chekhov', in *Modern Drama:* Essays in Criticism, ed. T. Bogard and W.I. Oliver, New York, Oxford University Press, 1965.

Das, Santi, ed., *Satyajit Ray: An Intimate Master,* Allied Publishers, 1998, xvii. The book contains essays by Gaston Roberge: 'Satyajit Ray: True-to-Life Image Maker', which is a compilation from 'For Love of Satyajit Ray', 'The World of Apu', 'True-to-Life Image Maker', 'Ray's Faith in the Youth', pp. 62-78. The book also reproduces essays on: 'Sakha Prashakha', pp. 152-4, and 'Agantuk', pp. 155-9.

Dasgupta, Chidananda, 'Classicism', in *Satyajit Ray Issue*, 1980, Kakinada Film Circle, Andhra Pradesh.

Dasgupta, Chidananda, *The Cinema of Satyajit Ray*, New Delhi, National Book Trust, 2001.

Das Mollick, Subha, 'The Thrid Revolution', pp. 87-97, in Rajiv Mehrotra, ed., *The Open Frame Reader.*

Dey, Ajoy Kumar, 'Film Society Scene in West Bengal', in West Bengal Film Centre, 1985, pp. 30-2.

Fisher, William, 'Entretien avec Satyajit Ray' in *Cahiers du Cinéma*, no 417, March 1989.

Freire, Paulo, *Pedagogy of Hope: Reliving Pedagogy of the Oppressed*, New York, Continuum, 1996.

Ghosh, Nemai, *Ray at Work: Images by Nemai Ghosh,* Dept. of Mass Comm. and Videograpy, St. Xavier's College, Kolkata, 2005, pp. 37-51.

Gopalakrishnan, Adoor, 'In the Beginning There was *Pather Panchali*', in Santi Das, ed., *Satyajit Ray: An Intimate Master,* Allied Publishers, 1998, pp. 57-8.

Happé, B., *Basic Motion Picture Technology*, Focal Press, 1971.

Haque, Usman, 'Hardspace, Softspace and the Possibilities of Open Source Architecture' (2000) in NicePaper no. 2, 2004, pp. 4-5.

Kael, Pauline, *I Lost It At The Movies*, Boston/Toronto, Atlantic Monthly Press Book, 1954/65, ix.

Kauffmann, Stanley, *A World on Film: Criticism and Comment*, New York, Harper & Row Publishers, 1966, p. x.

Kracauer, Siegfried, *Theory of Film: The Redemption of Reality*, Oxford University Press, 1960, p. xix.

Lessig, Lawrence, 'The People Own Ideas!' in *The Technology Review,* June 2005.

Mehrotra, Rajiv, ed., *The Open Frame Reader: Unreeling the Documentary Film*, Public Service Broadcasting Trust (India), Rupa & Co in association with PSBT, 2006.

Micciollo, Henri, *Satyajit Ray*, Editions l'Age d'Homme Lausanne, 1981.

Montagu, I., *Film World*, Penguin Books, c. 1964 p. 16.

People's Communication Charter, see http://www.pccharter.net/

Prasad, M. Madhava, 'The State in/of Cinema', in Chatterjee, Partha, ed., *Wages of Freedom: Fifty Years of the Indian Nation-State*, OUP, 1998, pp. 123-46.

Ramonet, Ignacio, *La Tyrannie de la Communication,* Paris, 1999, Éditions Galilée.

Ray, Satyajit, *Our Films, Their Films*, Orient Longman Ltd., 1976.

———, 'Why I make films', From the commentary written and spoken by Satyajit Ray for B. D. Garga's two-reeler, *Creative Artists of of India: Satyajit Ray* (1963), Quoted in *Montage*, nos. 5/6, July 1966.

Reisz, K. et al., *The Technique of Film Editing*, The Focal Press, 1968.

Roberge, Gaston, *Chitra Bani*, a book on film appreciation, foreword by Satyajit Ray, essay on Indian Cinema by Kironmoy Raha. analysis of *Bobby* by Gaston Roberge, Ramesh Sharma and Kobita Sarkar. Calcutta, *Chitrabani*, 1974, xi.

———, *Communication Cinema Development: From Morosity to Hope*, New Delhi, Manohar, 1998, 217 pages. [National Award (special mention) at the 46th International Film Festival of India in 1999]

———, *Cyberbani: Being a Human in the New Media Environment*, Anand, Gujarat Sahitya Prakash, 2005.

———, *Films for an Ecology of Mind: Essays on Realism in the Cinema*, Calcutta, Firma KLM Private Limited, 1978.

———, *Mass Communication and Man: Elements of Social Communication and Film Appreciation for Indian High Schools* (provisional edition), Calcutta, 1971.

———, *The Ways of Film Studies: Film Theory and the Interpretation of Film*, With an Essay on Freud by Dr Somnath Zutshi, Delhi, Ajanta Publications, 1992. xi.

Robinson, Andrew, *Satyajit Ray: The Inner Eye*, London, Andre Deutsch Ltd, 1989. Revised edition: *Satyajit Ray : The Inner Eye: The Biography of a Master Filmmaker*, Oxford University Press, 2004.

Sanchez Vazquez, Adolfo, *Art and Society: Essays in Marxist Aesthetics*, New York and London, Monthly Review Press, 1973.

Sen, Amartya, *The Argumentative Indian: Writings on Indian History, Culture and Identity*, Penguin Books, 2005.

Seton, Marie, *Portrait of a Director: Satyajit Ray*, Delhi, Vikas Publications, 1971.

Smallman, K., *Creative Film Making*, London, 1969.

Sobchack, Vivian: 'The Scene of the Screen: Envisioning Cinematic and Electronic Presence', in John Thornton Caldwell, ed., *Electronic Media and Technoculture*, Rutgers University Press, 2000, VIII, see pp. 137-55.

Tesson, Charles, 'Le bruit du monde', In *Cahiers du Cinéma*, no. 422, July-August 1989, pp. 20-5.

Tesson, Charles, *Satyajit Ray* (Series - *Cahiers du Cinéma* Collection 'Auteurs' Paris, Cahiers du cinéma, 1992.

Tsivian, Yuri, http://www.cinemetrics.lv/cintsi.php

Walter, E., *The Technique of the Film Cutting Room*, The Focal Press, 1969.

Web site on Satyajit Ray: http://www.satyajitray.org/films/Aranyerdinratri.htm 8/17/05

Filmography

SATYAJIT RAY (1921-1992)

Films: Bengali/English/French

1955

1. Pather Panchali/The Song of the Little Road/La Complainte du Sentier

1956

2. Aparajito/The Unvainquished/L'invaincu

1958

3. Parash Pathar/The Philosopher's Stone/La Pierre Philosophale
4. Jalsaghar/The Music Room/Le Salon de Musique

1959

5. Apur Sansar/The World of Apu/Le Monde d'Apu

1960

6. Devi/The Goddess/La Déesse

1961

7. Teen Kanya/Three Daughters/Les Trois Filles
8. Rabindranath Tagore

1962

9. Kanchenjungha

10. Abhijan/The Expedition/L'expédition

1963

11. Mahanagar/The Big City/La Grande Cité

1964

12. Charulata
13. Two/Deux

1965

14. Kapurush-o-Mahapurush/The Coward and The Holy Man/Le Lâche et le Saint

1966

15. Nayak/The Hero/Le Héros

1967

16. Chiriakhana/The Zoo/La Ménagerie

1968

17. Goopy Gyne Bagha Byne/The Adventures of Goopy and Bagha/Les Aventures de Goopy (le Chanteur) et de Bagha (le Joueur de Tambour)

1969

18. Aranyer Din Ratri/Days and Nights in the Forest/Des Jours et des Nuits dans la Forêt

1970

19. Pratidwandi/The Adversary/L'adversaire

1971

20. Seemabaddha/Company Limited/Enfermé dans des Limites
21. Sikkim

1972

22. The Inner Eye/L'oeil Intérieur

1973

23. Asani Sanket/Distant Thunder/Tonnerres Lointains

1974

24. Sonar Kella/The Golden Fortress/La Forteresse D'or

1975

25. Jana Aranya/The Middle Man/L'intermédiaire (La Jungle Humaine)

1976

26. Bala

1977

27. Shatranj Ke Khilari/The Chess Players/Les Joueurs d'échecs

1978

28. Joi Baba Felunath/The Elephant God/Vive Le Seigneur Félu (Le Dieu Éléphant)

1980

29. Hirak Rajar Deshe/The Kingdom of Diamonds/Le Royaume des Diamants (Au Pays du Roi Hirak)
30. Pikoo

1981

31. Sadgati/Deliverance/La Délivrance

1984

32. Ghare Baire/The Home and the World/La Maison et le Monde

1987

33. Sukumar Ray

1989

34. Gana Shatru/An Enemy of the People/Un Ennemi du Peuple

1990

35. Shakha Prosakha/The Tree and the Twigs/Branches et Brindilles

1991

36. Agantuk/The Stranger/L'étranger

Index